AF657629

Essays on Rural Development

Essays on Rural Development

P. R. Dubhashi

Kaveri Books
New Delhi - 110 002

© Padmakar Ramchandra Dubhashi (1930-)

First Published in 1996
Second Impression 2025
ISBN: 978-81-7479-008-8

All rights reserved including the right to translate or to reproduce this book or part thereof in any form and through any means except for brief quotations in articles or critical reviews.

Published by
Kaveri Books
4832/24, Ansari Road
New Delhi-110002 (India)
Tel: 011-23288140
E-mail : info@kaveribooks.com
kaveribooks@gmail.com
Website: www.kaveribooks.com

Typeset at
Delta Book World, New Delhi - 110 002.

PRINTED IN INDIA

Dedicated to the revered memory of Mahtma Gandhi and Vinoba Bhave who considered rural development as the key to India's Progress

Contents

Introduction

A large part of my administrative career spanning over thirty five years was associated with rural development — at the field level when I served as Project Executive Officer, District Deputy Commissioner, Director Tungabhadra Project, Divisional Commissioner, Belgaum and Administrator, Malaprabha and Ghataprabha Projects; and at the policy making level when I served as Director of Youth and Deputy Development Commissioner and later as Secretary Development Cooperation and Panchayati Raj in Karnataka Secretariat and Deputy Secretary, Director, Joint Secretary and Additional Secretary in the Union Government in the Ministry of Agriculture, Community Development and Cooperation. I was also a trainer in Rural Development in my capacity of Director of the National Institute of Community Development, Mussoorie. During all these years, I spent considerable time reading and reflecting on various facets of rural development and putting my thoughts and ideas in writing. I thought some of these writings passed on thought and experience should be brought together.

The publication brings together 32 of my papers on various aspects of rural development. They are divided into six parts viz. (1) Dimensions of Development; (2) Approaches to Rural Development; (3) Policy and Planning; (4) Organisation and Administration; (5) Sectors of Rural Development; and (6) Case Studies of Rural Development.

The first paper in the first part gives a comprehensive overview of "development"— the theme of the second half of the twentieth century. Development is not synonymous with economic development. It has political and social dimensions as well. Development is more than mere economic growth. Development brings about structural transformation. It is a complex process and requires a critical combination of various factors and processes which cannot be brought about by the forces of demand and supply in the market but require to be stimulated by conscious effort of the State apparatus. But as the second paper points out, the developing countries should not blindly follow the western model of development. The development in the Western countries was based on the market mechanism, capital intensive and energy intensive production, acquisitive materialism and exploitation of nature. This development model has led to irrational squandering of natural resources, fouling of environment, inequality, debasement of humanity and low quality of life. The developing countries should reject this Western model and adopt an alternative model of development which would be sustainable, preserve and promote native skills, use the traditional extended family to strengthen social life, fulfil basic human needs, empower the poor, decentralise production and consumption, use labour intensive appropriate technology and build up harmonious relationship between people and their natural environment. This should be people centred development focused on people and their capacity to address to their needs rather than centralised bureaucratic structures.

These two basic papers on models of development provide the context and the framework in which the rest of the papers in this compilation should be considered.

The second part of the book contains a series of papers on the problems of rural development and the various approaches for dealing with them. Rural development has a place of priority in the concerns of the developing countries since bulk of the population of these countries lives in the rural areas. However rural development bristles with problems and difficulties. The rural scene is characterised by a vicious circle of poverty caused by low income, backward technology, illiteracy and illhealth, and superstitous and fatalistic outlook. To deal with such a situation, the strategy of rural development has to be multifaceted, multisectoral and multipronged. Agriculture has to be modernised. Results of research have to go from lab to land. Inputs have to be delivered at the door of the farmer. Non–farm occupational opportunities have to be expanded and diversified, "public consumption" facilities viz. potable drinking water, education, health facilities, road and transport facilities have to be made available. Since rural communities are scattered over areas, the arrangements for rural development have to be decentralised and participative in character. Planning for rural development has to be a combination of centralised direction and decentralised organisation and implementation, comprehensive planning with intensive effort in important sectors, and special attention to the disadvantaged sections of the rural community. Administrative agencies should be linked with a vast network or rural institutions like local government institutions, cooperatives, rural banks, farmers' associations, youth and women clubs etc. Personnel with requisite knowledge and skill, suitably trained and with proper attitudes should be selected to undertake the tasks of rural development.

The next paper in this section deals with a variety of programmes of rural development introduced in India after Independence—National Extension Service, community development, panchayatiraj, cooperatives, programmes for supply of a variety of agricultural inputs provision of public consumption facilities, provision of house sites, applied nutrition programme, rural industries programmes, rural banking facilities and special poverty alleviation programmes for the small farmers, marginal farmers and the landless and rural works programmes.

The next series of three papers make a critical analysis of the integrated rural development programme in terms of concept and implementation. The programme envisaged subsidies and loans for small and marginal farmers, training for rural youth, and rural employment programme. The implementation of the programme has however suffered from a number of inadequacies - the share of the poor was not adequate; the programmes were not linked and integrated with general development programme; trainees under Trysem programme lacked confidence and lacked finance to use their training; widespread leakage and corruption was complained about; there was implementation gap. The paper suggests remedies to get over these inadequacies - strategetic management with focus on objectives, formulation and implementation of technically sound and economically viable projects, participative management, integration of budgetary and bank financing and institution building.

The antipoverty programmes introduced in the seventies were aimed at the raising poor families above the poverty line. But the job of converting families below the poverty line - the families of marginal farmers and landless labour - was entrusted to the whittled down machinery of block development without realising that to convert even a single poor family into a selfreliant viable family on a permanent or enduring basis was a Herculean task and could not be accomplished through a simple act of giving a loan or a subsidy to that family. The poor family has to be given a sense of confidence to undertake a productive activity which could be a source of selfreliant living and that activity has to be supported by linking it up to a larger productive enterprise which can support the poor family in terms of supply of input, marketing of output and technical expertise. A new extension machinery is needed consisting of technical specialists, development workers, cooperative organizers, bankers and financiers, teachers and welfare workers. What are required are group or cluster approach, collective enterprise and back-up support of a bigger organisation like a cooperative dairy.

The next two papers deal with communication in rural development. Development of people must begin with development of their awareness - of their surroundings and opportunities. This is above all a human process. People have to be reached and that is the task of communication or adult education. Development programme must go hand in hand with community education. Unfortunately we lay greater emphasis on the hardware of physical programmes and financial expenditure and neglected social or community education. Actually the communicator must work hand in hand with the development worker. Today we have available the powerful modern means of communication viz the radio or more so the television. But these do not do away with the continued relevance of the older means of communication for rural development viz visits to villages, distribution of publicity material like posters, exhibitions and melas, training programmes and mobilisation of rural institutions. Mass media of communication are no substitute for intensive rural development work.

The third part consists of papers on agricultural policy and planning. The paper on agricultural policy contests the popular view that agriculture should be treated as industry. Agriculture has its own peculiar characteristics. Agricultural operations are seasonal in character, they are dispersed and carried on by millions of small families, the goods they produce are perishable in character and pose special problems of storage and transport and agricultural policy must take into account these special problems. The policy, inter alia, must lay emphasis on dry land and drought prone area problems, extension of the green revolution techniques to areas and crops left out so far, and cooperative marketing, processing and export. The paper on agricultural planning, policy and administration makes a comprehensive review of developments since Independence - covering technological, institutional and economic aspects. The paper on agricultural marketing outlines the steps to be taken to strengthen and diversify cooperative marketing particularly in the context of our new approach to export promotion. The paper on Agricultural Census gives a brief history of its introduction, indicates the content of the operations and draws attention to the phenomenon of increasing accentuation of the inequality of land ownership and rapid increase in the category of marginal farmers. This points out to the need of more radical land reforms and policies for redirection of inputs and agricultural credit to an increasing number of small and marginal farmers.

The fourth part contains papers on organisation and administration of rural development. The first paper in the part draws attention to the accumulated experience in the field of rural development and the variety of institutional arrangements - extension agency of the department of agriculture, agricultural universities and research institutions, farmers clubs and youth clubs - all for the function of agricultural extension; government depots, private agencies and cooperatives for delivery of inputs; agricultural banks, commercial banks and non-institutional agencies for supply of credit; marketing cooperatives, commodity boards, regulated markets, warehousing arrangements, price support operations and co-operative and other agroprocessing enterprises to provide incentive for agriculture; land reforms, abolition of intermediaties, protection to tenants, ceiling on holdings and land tribunals for ushering in a more just system of land structure; and local development administration, elected local government institutions and autonomous and voluntary organisation for general promotion of rural development activities. Efficacy of each of these institutional arrangements needs to be critically analysed - specially from the point of access to and participation of the poor. Institutional building is crucial for rural development.

In this context two aspects emerge as of critical importance - decentralisation of arrangements so that access is not a problem and participation. The poor will not participate unless they see the benefits of participation. The earlier approach of "Shramdan" or customary obligation for maintenance of irrigation works failed because the poor saw it as a means of their exploitation. The farmers under major irrigation works did not construct field channels because they thought it was the work of Government. Marginal farmers and landless labourers did not participate in the programmes meant for them because the benefits were grabbed by the well to do sections. People were indifferent to Panchayati Raj institutions and did not participate in their working because they saw them more as arena of politics than as instruments of service to them. Panchayati Raj institutions failed to grow as institutions of vibrant direct democracies and so did cooperatives as economic democracies. Nor did rural people participate in the formulation of local development plans at village, block and district levels. Planning has continued to be from above and not from below. Grass root planning has not come into effect so far. The issue of decentralisation is closely connected with local participation. Decentralisation means transfer of planning and decision making to agencies at local level-governmental or non-governmental. Decentralisation is an instrument of generating people's participation. In India decentralisation was attempted through the establishment of local machinery of development administration, establishment of Panchayati Raj institutions and block and district planning. However, decentralised institutions still suffer from several weaknesses and look to centralised agencies for direction and initiative. The paper "New Thrusts in Decentralisation" deals with the subject of decentralisation in a broader prospective bringing out its politico administrative as well as economic implications and connotations. It deals with the working of our federal system and need for a better balance between the States and the Centre as equal and coordinate members of federal polity. It advocates the inclusion of Panchayati Raj institutions as the third tier of our federal polity - a task recently accomplished by the 73rd amendment of the Indian Constitution. In the context of economic decentralisation, it deals with the process of liberalisation of economy and promotion of managerial auto- nomy of public enterprises. The paper begins with reference to decentralisation in China and erstwhile USSR and analyses our recent attempts towards decentralisation in that context. The paper "Power to the People" sets out conditions for the success of the Panchayati Raj institutions as Constitutional entities under the 73rd amendment of the Constitution. Decentralisation has been a concern of several developing countries and they have tried to give a practical experience to the concept.

In the final paper in this part, attempts towards decentralisation made by several Asian neighbours are briefly analysed - the concept of district budgets and district Minister in Sri Lanka, gramsarkar in Bangladesh, red book system in Malaysia, bottom level development planning in Thailand, commercial autonomy in State owned and collective units in China, and deconcentration for regional development in Indonesia and Philippines. The paper concludes by saying that the advantages of decentralisation cannot be reached without strong and capable local government institutions with adequate resources and trained personnel.

The fifth part of the collection is concerned with some of the principal sectors of rural development viz. command area development, drought and development, rural energy, rural industry and growth centres.

After the attainment of Independence a number of mighty irrigation projects have been constructed and vast irrigation potential created in hitherto parched areas but there has been considerable delay between the creation of irrigation potential and its utilisation. The irrigation projects have been constructed at considerable cost and a country as poor as India cannot afford anything but the quickest utilisation of the irrigation potential created by the river valley projects. There are many reasons why command area development does not automatically take place after the construction of reservoir. A package of measures is necessary to bring this about - construction of water conveyance system, localisation of cropping pattern, efficient water management and equitable water distribution, landlevelling, imparting irrigation skills and entrepreneurship to farmers used to dry farming and subsistence agriculture, arrangement for supply of inputs, post harvest facilities, promotion of auxiliary occupations like dairy and fishery - these are some of the components of a comprehensive programme of command area development.

If irrigated areas under command area projects constitute fortunate areas of prosperity, the drought prone areas are unfortunate areas of depression. Drought leave behind a trail of denudation of underground water resources, malnutrition, indebtedness and impoverishment. It takes several years for areas the areas afflicted by a severe drought to come back to normality. India has been fortunate to have seven successive years of good rains. But we cannot forget that recurrent droughts have been a part of the climatology of our country. Larger parts of the country have suffered from droughts and a long term strategy rather then crisis management is the right way of tackling the drought problem of the country. This is what the paper "Drought and Development" does in a comprehensive manner. "Coping with Seasonality and Drought" provides illustration to make the point about the need for a long term strategy of sustainable development.

Energy provides the fuel for the engine of development. The rural energy scene in India is grim. Compared with the energy consumption in developed countries, energy consumption in India is very low. In rural areas it is much lower. It is, therefore, necessary to augment availability of energy in rural areas. It is with this end in view that the integrated rural energy programme was started during the Sixth Five Years Plan and continued thereafter. A paper describes this programme which aims at an optimum mix of different source of traditional, non-traditional and renewable energy resources for meeting the energy needs for subsistence and production activities in rural areas over a planning horizon upto the year 2000 A.D.

The lopsided structure of the rural economy demands the revival of rural industries - traditional industries and handicrafts as well as agro industries. If we succeed in dotting rural areas with agroprocessing enterprises, we would have taken big strides in the total transformation of the rural economy. While endorsing the recommendation of the National Commission on Backward Areas on village and cottage industries, the paper recommends the cooperative approach which the Commission has not thought fit to recommend.

The last paper in the part relates to the development of growth of centres as a strategy of development. The Indian economy has been characterised by apoplexy at the centre and anaemia at the periphery. In Maharashtra, for example, development was concentrated on Bombay metropolitan areas and urban and industrial area around Pune, Nasik and Aurangabad and over years great disparities developed between these areas and rest of the rural hinterland. The economic scene has been characterised by duality and disparity. Deliberate action is, therefore, required to move away from "sectoral planning" to "spatial planning". It is necessary to adopt regional approach to development. Taking this into account, attempt was made for the first time in the Seventh Five Year Plan to reorient development planning by identifying agro-climatic regions and prepare region specific schemes and programmes. Growth centres should be planned in relation to such development. Agglomeration of common facilities at such growth centres may greatly support the dispersed process of development. Rather than treating rural and urban development as separate water tight compartments we should think of a new model of "rurbanisation".

The last and sixth part of this compilation comprises a number of case studies. The first case study is of the village Ralegansiddhi in Ahmednagar district made famous by the pioneering work of Annasaheb Hazare who turned a dacoit infested drought prone village community steeped in poverty and bad habits of drinking into a progressive and productive village community of virtuous citizens growing a variety of vegetables and fruits and even exporting them to the Middle East. The main strategy was to store water through watershed planning, conserve it and use for growing a variety of crops. The village has now become a model for similar development in villages in drought prone areas. What is required is imaginative leadership. The second case study is that of Saemaul Undong, the South Korean experiment of rural development, based on my personal visit and observations. Deligence, selfhelp and cooperation are the watchwards of this movement. The programme instilled a new spirit to dispel lethargy and poverty in which the rural society in Korea had sunk through centuries. The programmes elevated the quality of rural life and resuscitated the rural communities. The third case study is my attempt at development planning at the village level. Substance of the national plan does not consist of some grandiose projects with huge investment but in innumerable little projects that had to be implemented in rural areas. But such village development plans are seldom prepared. The paper contains a first hand account of my personal attempt to produce an all round development plan for Manoli village lying in the command area of Malaprabha project. The last paper is based on case studies collected by professor Norman Uphoff for rural development and promotion of local organisation in South Asia i.e. in India, Bangladesh, Pakistan and Sri Lanka. The general conclusion arising out of the case studies is not favourable to the role of the rural local organisations in promoting agricultural and rural development. However, they have not been given a fair trial. If they are given reasonable chance, they can make a significant contribution to rural development.

Part - I

DIMENSIONS OF DEVELOPMENT

1

Development : An Overview

The second half of the twentieth century has seen the increasing preoccupation of social scientists and policy makers with 'development'. The United Nations announced the sixties as the first and the seventies as the second decade of development (United Nations 1962). This concern with development was the direct result of the fact that in the fifties an increasing number of countries in Asia and Africa, hitherto under colonial domination, attained independence and as free countries dedicated themselves to development. They looked upon their 'political freedom' as a means of 'economic freedom' and economic freedom was expected to follow a successful programme of economic development.

Dimensions of Development

The experience of recent years has, however, brought home the fact that 'development' cannot be considered synonymous with economic development as it has political and social dimensions as well.

Political development could be assessed in terms of the stabilisation and consolidation of participatory political institutions. Where such development takes place, the political authority is responsive to the people; and conversely people have faith in the political authority and indeed have opportunities to participate in the political process. The example of Iran has shown that spectacular economic progress can come to an abrupt halt due to political explosions thus reducing the glittering trappings of apparent success.

Social development may be conceived in terms of progressive social integration. Where society is fragmented into different warring groups or sectoral cleavages, where there is social discrimination against minority groups, where one section of society dominates another; or where one social group has privileges while another has social disabilities, development cannot take place in a smooth and harmonious manner. Social homogenisation is integral to development. Without it there cannot be unity and social solidarity and without them no society can develop. That is why it has to be affirmed that development is not only economic but also social and political development. Without one of the three, the other two cannot survive. It is an illusion that an authoritarian political or social system can accelerate economic development. Indeed, it is a contradiction in terms to talk of economic development through authoritarian political and social systems.

It is this realisation which has also altered the concept of economic development itself. Even economists have increasingly realised that economic development is not purely an economic phenomenon. There are non-economic factors as well which need to be taken note of in understanding the process of economic development.

Economic Development in the West

Ever since the beginning of the fifties, economists and social thinkers have tried to define and unravel the process of economic development. Development economics and development planning have emerged as distinct branches of economic and social sciences. Does this mean that there was no thinking on development in the past?

The process of development in the countries under colonial rule started in the second half of the twentieth century. In the Western countries however, it started with the advent of the industrial revolution and Britain was the first country to become the 'workshop of the world'.

The industrial revolution came to Britain between 1760 and 1820 and transformed it from a feudal agricultural economy into a capitalistic industrial economy. Historians have ascribed many causes to the revolution. They included agricultural, commercial and transport revolutions which preceded and accompanied the industrial revolution. Also, a series of new technological inventions like the water frame, spinning jenny and steam engine made possible the replacement of the human motive force with a mechanical motive force. The establishment of the factory system was an innovation in economic organisation which was part of the industrial revolution. These events in Britain were soon followed by a similar industrial revolution in other European countries like France, Germany and the new world of the United States of America. By the turn of the century, it took place in the remaining European countries. Japan, after the Meji restoration in 1868, also embarked upon the path of modern industrial development.

Soon countries like Sweden, Germany, the United States of America, and Japan overtook Britain.

The early years of industrial capitalism in most of these countries were characterised by a *laissez faire* economy. Development was not the conscious goal and objective of the State but the result of the efforts of private entrepreneurs in pursuit of self-interest. The *laissez faire* philosophy was embodied in the maxim that 'that government is the best which governs the least,' where the State should confine itself to the sovereign functions of law and order, currency and coinage and national defence. The theoretical inspiration for the philosopny of *laissez faire* was provided by Adam Smith (1937) who wrote the first scientific treatise on economic science, namely, *Inquiry into the Wealth of Nations.* He spoke of the 'invisible hand of Providence' in the market which transformed the fruits of private entrepreneurs in pursuit of self-interest into the production and supply of goods and services needed by the society. He pointed out that the butcher, the brewer and the baker produced and supplied meat, wine and bread, not to serve society but were in fact seeking a means of livelihood for themselves. The philosophy of Adam Smith's economics was reinforced by the jurisprudence of J. Bentham who maintained that 'the greatest good of the greatest number' can be realised by widening the area of freedom to individual citizens.

From *laissez faire* to State Intervention

However, as industrial capitalism gave rise to a number of problems, the *laissez faire* philosophy was modified in favour of a series of justifiable cases of State intervention. Thus the rise of monopolies and oligopolies provided the justification for entire monopoly legislation and its enforcement. The inequalities made a case for progressive taxation and other measures for the redistribution of income and wealth and eventually for ushering in the Welfare State or the Social Service State. The occurrence of business cycles and particularly the Great Depression of 1929 made a case for a compensatory fiscal policy and public investment for which theoretical validity was provided by Keynesian economics. Pigou discussed the issue of social costs and benefits and justified intervention by the state to reduce social costs and increase social benefit. John Kenneth Galbraith carried this further and constrasted private opulence with social squalor. State intervention was thus aimed at optimising the use of resources and maximising the satisfaction of the consumers.

Malthusian Theory—Population and Production

These writings drawing up a case for the intervention of the State in the market mechanism did not, however, deal with problems of development *per se*. Amongst the political economists, it was Malthus who drew attention to the basic problem of development, namely, the balance between the growth of population and the growth of production. Malthus pointed out that while production grew in arithmetic proportions, the population grew in geometric proportions, thus creating an increasing imbalance between population and production which could only be set right by natural solutions like pestilence, famine and disease unless successful population control measures could be introduced.

Widening the market and increasing production at a rate faster than that of population were the two basic ideas of classical economists in relation to development. In more recent times, Schumpeter (1955) introduced a concept to explain the process of development. He pointed out that development takes place through innovations. While the normal entrepreneurs carry on day to day production, it is only a few who can play the role of innovators through the introduction of new products or through technological or organisational changes. Each innovation provides the thrust to development which gets assimilated through a gradual process of diffusion.

All these theories of classical and neo-classical economists or even modern economists did not amount to any comprehensive theory of development. On the other hand Marx, starting from the basic concept of Ricardian economics provided a theory of the historical evolution of the process of development, explained through the logic of dialectical materialism of thesis, antithesis and synthesis. He pointed out that beginning with primitive communism, the economy passed through the stages of feudalism, capitalism and socialism. Though he predicted the decline of the capitalistic system, he appreciated that the achievements of capitalism were more magnificent than Egyptian pyramids, Roman aqueducts and Gothic cathedrals. However, capitalism based on the exploitation of the working classes was bound to collapse and give rise to socialism which would provide a just economic system based on the principles of 'from each according to his means and to each according to his needs'.

When in the early fifties new thinking began on development, Rostow (1960) came forth with his analysis of the stages of growth which was published by the *London Economist* under the title 'New Non-Communis

Manifesto.' Rostow provided a theory of historical development in terms of five stages—traditional economy, the transition, the take off, the self-sustained growth, culminating in high mass consumption economy.

The historical theory of development, however, did not unravel the factors behind development. To be sure, Rostow did talk of the leading sector and the lagging sector but the point still remained as to what led to the forward thrust of the leading sector.

Harrod-Domar Equation

A more cogent formulation of the theory of development was therefore required to explain the causes of development. A simple version of this was provided by what has come to be known as the Harrod-Domar equation which laid down that $g = \frac{I}{c}$ where g is the rate growth, I is the amount of investment and **c** is the capital-output ratio. Harrod-Domar stipulated that **c** being stable at any point of time for an economy, growth depended upon investment and investment depended upon savings. Following this analysis, W. Arthur Lewis in his book *Theory of Economic Growth* pointed out that the rate of savings in underdeveloped countries was as low as 5 per cent and it has to be raised at least to the level of 12 to 15 per cent. This alone would ensure a growth rate of about 4 to 5 per cent on the assumption of the capital-output ratio being three. Thus in this analysis capital formation provided the keynote of economic development.

Experience has, however, shown that investment by itself cannot trigger off development if the productivity of investment is low. Investment will yield low returns if the capital is used ineffectively, if for example, the productive capacity is underutilised or if the complementary factors of production—particularly the human resources—are not properly developed or if the technology is not sufficiently productive.

Role of Technology

Historical studies by S. Kuznets (1959) have shown that technology has as much to contribute to development as capital. Indeed, without technological progress, capital would not have been productive. The developing countries are fortunate in that, they have at their disposal a considerable amount of accumulated technology of the industrial age of the already developed countries. All that they have to do is to absorb that technology into their productive system. Japan, for example, developed through the quick acquisition of Western technology. In the early years of development in Japan, their technicians and managers were sent in large numbers to the United States of America and Germany where they visited enterprises and industrial establishments, took photographs and notes and reproduced the plants and machines in their own country. In the beginning, the products of Japanese industry were looked upon as of low quality. However, the Japanese proved to be outstanding not only in absorbing Western technology but improving upon it and adapting it to their own conditions. The results have been spectacular. The Japanese have been able to beat the Western countries at their own game and excel in them with respect to technology and industry by developing a productive system which can produce superior goods at a lower cost. Cars and electronic goods made in Japan have been able to capture markets in America and Europe. Can the Japanese path be followed by other developing countries? To the extent that it is possible, the developing countries can certainly take a leaf out of the Japanese book.

However, the question that remains is whether the developing countries should go in for the most up-to-date or sophisticated technology. It has been rightly pointed out that in absorbing the technology of the Western countries or even of the USSR and other East European countries, developing countries should not needlessly saddle themselves with obsolete technology. At the same time in the name of modern technology, they should not absorb a capital intensive technology since they (certainly India) are abundantly endowed with human resources which need to be fully harnessed. In many cases labour intensive technology would be more 'appropriate' than capital intensive technology. This was the principal thrust of the book *Small is Beautiful* !, by Schumacher (1976), who himself drew inspiration from Mahatma Gandhi in making out a case for labour intensive technology. Much of this labour intensive technology may have to be developed indigenously as it may not be possible to borrow it from Western technological development which is geared more and more to automation. It has been pointed out that in the field of agriculture, the bias of Western technology has been in favour of large scale farms and that such a technology is not suitable to the small and marginal farmers in India. The agricultural technology should be such as to cater to the requirements of marginal farmers who are forced to be agricultural workers in their spare time.

Role of Manpower

The idea of labour intensive technology brings out the importance of the productive utilisation of idle manpower resources in India. Here again it was Mahatma Gandhi who wrote at length on the use of the spinning wheel and of cottage industries for removing unemployment and underemployment in rural and urban areas. This concept of mobilisation of idle manpower resources in developing countries also received attention from the economists of developed countries and one of the earliest books by Ragnar Nurkse (1960) was concerned with capital formation through the utilisation unemployed and underemployed manpower resources. He pointed out that underdeveloped countries may be short of capital resources but they have abundant manpower resources, which if put to productive use (even the unskilled manpower), can produce capital assets such as earthen dams, rural roads and social services. It has been pointed out that in the early years of development. China was able to improve its agricultural production mainly by the mobilisation of rural labour. Even in India the earthen dams like Nagarjunasagar dam were constructed by mobilising the labour resources of the country . This idea is also embodied in programmes like the Food for Work Programme or the currently operating National Scheme for Rural Employment. In their book on poverty, Dandekar and Rath (1971) had suggested that the work programmes providing employment to the unskilled manpower of the country is perhaps one of the most important ways of raising people above the poverty line. It was Marx who said that capital is congealed labour. Following his dictum the underdeveloped countries can transform their idle labour into capital assets.

But this does not mean that the drudgery of unskilled labour is the only fate of underdeveloped peoples. Their skills can be improved and with simple machines can be put to more productive use. Also, development, in the ultimate analysis, means human development. It implies improving the capability of the population and one of the best ways of achieving this is to make them literate. Literacy seems to be the minimum precondition for development. Without near total literacy, no nation can make the transition from underdevelopment to development. From that point of view the fact that literacy in India is as low as 52.11 per cent according to the 1991 census is certainly a very disturbing fact. Even the neighbouring countries of Asia have a much higher rate of literacy. India's development plans have , therefore, to be geared towards achieving 100 per cent literacy at the earliest. This should be followed by programmes for the development of skills such as training for rural youth in self-employment. Also their education system should be geared more and more to the dissemination of technological skills rather than traditional courses in the general arts. Thus education through building up our human resources can make a significant contribution to development.

The importance of human resources can be emphasised by once again taking the example of Japan. Japan lacks natural resources like petroleum or coal or even agricultural land. Only 1/10th of Japanese land is cultivable; and yet with a hard working, disciplined and skilled population, Japan has been able to import raw material from all over the world and convert it into finished products for which they have been able to get a market through aggressive salesmanship all over the world.

Above all, the change in human resources must mean a change in the attitudes to work and life. Many Western authors have pointed out that the other worldly and fatalistic attitudes of Hindus that leaves everything to karma or fate, rather than self reliance or the efforts of human beings, has been the major obstruction to development and progress in India. This, however, does not mean that Hindu religion and philosophy are antithetical to development as was insisted upon by Gunnar Myrdal in his *Asian Drama* (1968). It is not correct to say that Hindu religion is responsible for making India a 'soft state'. It has to be recognised that Bhagwad Gita, the holy scripture of the Hindus, gives the call to human beings to awake, arise and to do their duty rather than give up in the face of danger. This philosophy can provide a great source of inspiration to the development effort in our country.

Some Western economists had developed a theory of the backward sloping supply curve of labour as typical of the attitude of workers in the underdeveloped countries. The theory states that Indians have limited ambitions and are satisfied with minimum conveniences of life and therefore with a low level of income. If offered higher wages they tend to work less rather than work more. It is doubtful that such a theory can be uniformly applied to all Indians. Experience has shown that given incentives, Indian farmers can produce more and that it is not correct to assume that they are unresponsive to incentives.

A similar theory has also been propounded, through with much different implications, by John Galbraith. While dealing with the problem of poverty in underdeveloped countries, he has pointed out that poverty perpetuates because poor people have come to terms with it (1979). They know through experience that they cannot afford to take risks even small risks, and therefore they are reluctant to respond to any change. This attitude also explains the unwillingness of the marginal farmers to readily accept the hybrid seeds and other green revolution innovations. While the unwillingness of the poor to undertake risks can be understood, it is not necessary to assume that the poor in underdeveloped countries will remain poor for all time to come. Given an organised social effort, the poor can get over their accommodation to poverty. Thus what development requires, is a combination of capital formation, appropriate technology, and a motivated and trained population. These have to be galvanised in an organised social effort.

Development : More than Mere Growth

The concept of development is rightly distinguished from that of mere growth. The term 'growth' connotes only an increment to the gross national product. On the other hand, development connotes a qualitative and structural change. The structure of an underdeveloped country is characterised by a 'dual economy' and a 'dual society'. While there are manifestations of development in a few metropolitan centres in the shape of modern industrial and commercial establishments, the bulk of the country, the vast hinterland of rural areas, is underdeveloped in every sense of the term. Life there could be described, if not as nasty, brutish and short, certainly as short, poor and isolated. Thus metropolitan centres are only enclaves in vast areas of darkness and backwardness. As against this, a developed country is characterised by the homogeneous development of social and economic life in all parts of the country. The standard of living and social amenities in the developed countries are the same in the urban areas as in the countryside. In the underdeveloped countries economic and social dualism is also accompanied by institutional dualism. Institutions like banks, technological and training institutions necessary for development and modernity, are confined only to metropolitan centres and do not exist in rural areas.

Development and Structural Change

Development brings about structural transformation. Colin Clark has divided the structure of the economy into primary secondary and tertiary sectors. The primary sector is concerned with economic activities directly connected with natural resources such as agriculture, animal husbandry and mining. The secondary sector is concerned with the transformation of the products of the primary sector into manufactured commodities. The tertiary sector is concerned with all those activities which are required to make the products of the primary and secondary sectors available to the final consumer, and connected with the activities of trade, transport, marketing and retail consumer distribution. In a typical underdeveloped country, 90 per cent of the population is engaged in the primary sector, especially in agriculture carried on at a low level of technology and productivity. On the other hand, a developed country has a large secondary and tertiary sector. The economy benefits a great deal from value added to the products of the primary sector. In a developed country like the United

States of America only 3 to 4 per cent of the population is engaged in agriculture. Yet, due to the improvement in technology and productivity, American agriculture is able to provide foodgrains in large quantities to other countries of the world. Similarly, in Sweden, barely 5 per cent of the population is engaged in the primary sector, On the other hand nearly 75 per cent of the Indian population is still engaged in agriculture despite more than forty years of planning. Development, therefore, requires diversification of the economy in the shape of larger secondary and tertiary sectors.

However, a reduction in the proportion of people engaged in the primary sector does not by itself bring about development. Nor can this be brought about in an artificial manner. What structural transformation does imply is that an agricultural revolution must be followed by the industrial revolution. However, there could be no industrial revolution without the agricultural revolution which is its conditional precedent. An increase in the productivity of agriculture provides raw material as well as surplus manpower for economic activity in the secondary and tertiary sectors. Thus the path of development is an agricultural revolution followed by an industrial revolution, and the expanding production and productivity of the industrial and agricultural sectors may then require a large tertiary sector.

The Circle of Poverty and the Circle of Progress

The state of underdevelopment is often described as the consequence of a vicious circle of poverty. The vicious circle in which an underdeveloped country is caught consists of low income, low savings, low investment, low rate of growth and therefore a low level of income. Similarly, the low level of income and low standard of living implies low education, low level of health and therefore low productive capacity and low income. Gunnar Myrdal (1958) in his Cairo lectures talked of the law of cumulative causation. Just as a series of positive factors like higher level of investment, higher technology, higher education and training leads to further development—a kind of a 'virtuous circle of progress'—there is conversely a 'vicious circle of poverty'—low income, low savings, low productivity, low development and therefore low income. Progress and development require that the underdeveloped countries should break through this vicious circle. This requires 'a critical minimum effort'. Without such an effort, it is not possible to overcome the various constraints from which the economy and society of a poor country suffer.

Balanced and Unbalanced Development

Such a critical minimum effort might well require 'a big thrust' in some directions so that direct and secondary consequences of that big thrust would spread throughout the economy. Such a big thrust might either be in the shape of intensive agriculture, export drive or industrialisation, and this alone can introduce dynamic change. Anything else would just get lost in the vicious circle of poverty or caught in the low level equilibrium trap. A big thrust would have forward and backward effects and would also stimulate complementary investment. A joint investment with a number of backward and forward linkages and benefits of external economies can trigger off development,while anaemic efforts towards development might well prove futile (Rosenstein-Rodan 1964).

A similar idea has been expressed by Hirschman (1960) in terms of balanced and unbalanced development. The so-called balanced development with resources spread over the entire field of economic development might not be effective. On the other hand, a big thrust even though appearing to give rise to unbalanced development to start with, would in fact create opportunities of investment in complementary fields of activities and would eventually stimulate wide ranging economic development.

Another structural transformation that has to take place is that between the urban and the rural population. Development leads to greater urbanisation. England which was the first country to be the workshop of the world is urbanised to the extent that 75 per cent of the population lives in urban areas. This process is going on in other countries as well. In South Korea within a period of two decades- between 1960 and 1980- the ratio 75:25 of rural-urban population has been reversed. In India 10 per cent of the population lived in urban areas at the beginning of the century but this has grown to nearly 25 per cent.

However, this transformation has to be the result of economic development and cannot by itself create development. Development does not simply mean reducing rural population and adding to urban congestion. In the developed countries what led to urbanisation was the urban pull —the pull created by increasing employment opportunities in the wake of industrialisation. On the other hand, in many developing countries unbanisation is the consequence of the push factor created due to the pressure of population on land. There is growing unemployment, underemployment and disguised unemployment in the rural areas. It is these unemployed landless people who in desperation throng to the cities to eke out a livelihood. Unfortunately, these employment opportunities are not available even in the cities and this gives rise to a large number of unemployed people living on the pavements or in the shanties, doing almost anything in the so-called unorganised sector, and this may well include petty crime. Urbanisation of this sort is the very negation of development. Thus, even though development brings in its wake structural transformation, we have to make a distinction between real development and the mere migration of population out of agricultural and rural areas.

Development, the Role of the State and Planning

Development is then a complex process and it requires a critical combination of various factors to be brought about. Rather than leaving the onset of such a process to the operation of the forces of demand and supply in the market, many developing countries have felt that development could be stimulated and promoted through conscious efforts under the auspices of the State. The example of socialist countries has shown how the State initiative can help in the transformation of the economy and in the promotion of industrialisation. Moreover, the State could introduce development through well chalked out plans.

Though the concept of planning has been widely accepted today and indeed has been adopted in countries with different types of economic systems, several leading economists like Ludwig von Mises and Frederick von Hayek had questioned the very basic premise about planning. They felt that innumerable decisions regarding production and the working of the economic system which are taken by innumerable producers and consumers in the economic system could never be taken by a few individuals who assume responsibility for planning. There is the problem of an information gap. Moreover, suppression of decisions of individual producers and consumers by a few planners in the surest way to serfdom. However, such views which totally reject planning as a method of management of an economic system are nowadays less frequently expressed. On the other hand , it is pointed out that in this scientific age society must consciously arrange its economic future in such a way that the social goals are attained. The discussion, therefore, is centred not around whether the plan should be there or not but rather as to how planning for development should be attempted.

Methodology of Development Planning

A development plan begins by stipulating the rate of growth of the economy , with regard to the fiscal and physical resources available. Once the growth rate is stipulated, the planners decide upon the level of investment required for achieving the growth rate and the allocation of investments between the various sectors of the economy. This is followed by detailed sectoral plans—principal sectors being agriculture and allied activities, industry and allied activities, the infrastructure and the tertiary sector.

Sectoral Development in Agriculture

The importance of the agricultural sector for development is well recognised. Agriculture provides the raw material for industry. Above all, it provides foodstuff required for maintaining the working population and indeed for the very survival of the nation. An agricultural development plan includes allocations for related non-agricultural sectors, such as production of fertilisers or the development of irrigation and power projects. Agriculture is a vast system with several sub-systems which include agricultural research and extension supply of inputs like fertilisers, seed, insecticides and pesticides as well as water, organisation of agricultural production itself and the marketing and processing of agricultural produce. Agricultural development requires the creation of a network of institutions at various levels including cooperative institutions for the delivery of agricultural inputs and credit. Cooperative structures have to be built from the bottom upwards in the shape of primary agricultural cooperatives at the village level, district cooperative central banks and the state cooperative banks. These in turn have to be supported by apex institutions like the Reserve Bank or the National Bank for Agricultural Development. A network of storage facilities for both inputs and outputs are also equally important. The agricultural development plan has to take into account not only investment but institutional and technological developments and proper economic policies. These economic policies are required to provide minimum remunerative prices for agriculture.

Industry

In the field of industry as well, the development plan must include facilities like industrial estate and credit through financial institutions like the finance corporations and industry development banks. The extension and organisational guidance have to be provided through institutions like district industrial centres. Special programmes might be required for industrial development in backward areas and the promotion of small and cottage industries. Special training institutions might also be required for training industrial workers and skilled and semi-skilled professional people.

The infrastructural development plan should include irrigation and power projects, transport and communication and educational and health facilities. The allocation to these various sectors becomes an important issue of plan priorities, and it has to be resolved by taking into account the contribution of various sectors and projects to the desired rate of growth of the economy (For a lucid description of Planning see my book Grammar of Planning : Concepts and Applications. — Published by Indian Institute of Public Administration, New Delhi).

National plans would have to be followed by and related to state plans and the district development plans. Decentralisation of the planning process is considered essential to get the benefit of local resources and local knowledge.

The success of planning depends on its effective implementation. A great deal of attention has, therefore, to be given to the efficient management of not only the development programmes as a whole,but of the public sector enterprises as well. Large amounts of resources are invested in the public sector but if they do not yield necessary dividends, they could well be a drag on the development plan. The efficient management of public enterprises requires a proper balance between managerial autonomy and public accountability.

Management in development has many dimensions. Apart from being oriented to public services, it is also necessary to evoke popular participation and cooperation without which several development programmes would not succeed.

Development and Inflation

If the development plans do succeed in augmenting the stream of goods and services, they would not give rise to inflation. It is sometimes stated that inflation is an inevitable concomitant of the development plan. It is true that development projects do not immediately yield results, but if they are completed on time, and do yield the goods and services expected, development would not be accompanied by inflation. Successful development has to be anti-inflationary in character.

The pace of development must keep ahead of the increasing growth of population or else development may well prove a Sisyphean effort. Measures for population control should be a part of development strategy.

New Dimensions of Development

Successful development planning should lead to an increase in the gross national product, higher per capita standard of living, fuller employment, reduction in poverty and improvement in the quality of life. These may appear to be multiple objectives of development but they are related to each other and often flow from each other. Development only in terms of increase in the GNP is no longer considered acceptable since what matters is the composition of the GNP. Does it consist of luxury goods consumed only by the rich or of goods of mass consumption ? Do the masses have the requisite purchasing power so that their essential needs can be translated into effective demand ? Masses would have the requisite purchasing power only if they have opportunities for gainful employment. Hence, full or near full employment must go along with development and equitable distribution of the fruits of development. The latter may require that priority be given to minimum social consumption, redirection of the productive system, banking resources, ownership of assets and entitlements in favour of the poor. What it implies then is a direct assault on poverty rather than reliance on 'the trickle down effect'. Finally, the development must not be at the cost of the nations's life supporting system consisting of soil,water, forests and other natural resources. Environmental protection is thus a new dimension of development which cannot be overlooked.

India's Approach to Development

India embarked on the process of planned economic development in 1951. The National Planning Commission headed by Prime Minister Jawaharlal Nehru was set up to comprehensively assess the natural and manpower resources of the country and to prepare plans for the mobilisation of these resources of economic development aimed at raising the standard of living of masses of people. Jawaharlal Nehru was committed to planning ever since 1927 when he visited the Soviet Union and saw how planning brought about economic transformation in that country. Even before Independence, he was appointed by the Indian National Congress as the Chairman, National Planning Committee which produced valuable development plans for different sectors of the economy. However, after Independence, when Nehru broached the idea of planning, he was opposed by his Finance Minister, John Mathai who raised many objections. As a result of this difference of opinion, John Mathai resigned. It was not that Nehru alone was amongst the public men who accepted the idea of a planned approach to economic development. As far back as 1934, Sir M. Visvesurariah, the engineer-statesman advocated planning for India's economic development. Even private businessmen had produced a Bombay plan before Independence. The adoption of planning as the instrument of development was thus a logical culmination of ideas that had gathered momentum in the years before Independence.

India has now completed more than four decades of planning. Except for the three annual plans during the years 1966 to 1969 , which came to be described as plan holiday, India has been preparing five-year plans with a long term perspective. Within the framework of the five-year plans, annual plans are also prepared and are integrated with the budgetary process. Every five-year plan has a mid-term appraisal.

Indian plans are comprehensive in the sense that they cover both public and private investment and also all sectors of the economy. Second, the Indian approach to planning has been described as that of democratic planning as distinguished from totalitarian planning as in the erstwhile Soviet Union. It gives an important place to popular participation. While it envisages that the public sector would be in charge of the commanding heights of the economy , it gives considerable scope to private enterprises as well as the cooperative sector which is expected to provide a sense of value and direction to the economy. Third, India's approach to planning is for balanced development, in the sense that all sectors including agriculture,industry, infrastructure, as well as the service sector have been accorded their own place. The second Five-Year Plan followed the Mahalanobis model and put greater stress on heavy industry. However, the importance of agriculture and rural development was always recognised and the plan strategy was based on interdependent and mutually enforcing growth of different sectors of the economy.

Fourth, India's approach to planning is aimed at the establishment of the socialist pattern of society. In other words, equitable distribution of income and provision of full employment opportunities have been the objectives along with that of increasing the rate of growth of the gross national product. Lately the objective has been defined in terms of the anti poverty approach. Planning for development has not always succeeded in reconciling the different goals. The Indian approach to planning for development aims at evolving the 'third way' — steering clear of unbridled capitalism on one side and unmitigated totalitarianism on the other side.

Finally, India's approach to development has tried to combine the economic, technological, human and institutional aspects of development. Within the field of technology the concept of 'intermediate technology' has also found its place. India's plans for development assume that science and technology provide the basis for development. The Central Ministry for

Science and Technology has been established which has enunciated a science policy. One of the aspects of the Indian approach to development is that of a self reliant economy and society. In order to have self-reliance in the field of science and technology, India has introduced a chain of scientific laboratories. However, so rapid has been the technological advancement in some of the developed countries, that India has also found it necessary to import high technology in various fields of development. At the same time attention has been paid to the improvement and upgradation of the more traditional technology adopted by village and cottage industries and handicrafts.

India's approach to planning is therefore eclectic in every sense of the term. It tries to reconcile planning with democracy, increased production with equitable distribution, establishment of large industry with promotion of cottage industries, introduction of high technology with upgradation of traditional technology and upholding human values with the pursuit of material advancement.

REFERENCES

Anderson, Robert S. 1982. *Science, Politics and the Agricultural Revolution in Asia - Rural Poverty for Growth*, Boulder, Colorado: Westview Press, p. 468.

Dandekar, V.M. and Nilkantha Rath. 1971. *Poverty in India*, Pune: Gokhale Institute of Politics and Economics.

Domar, Evsey D. 1960. *Essays in the Theory of Economic Growth*, New York: Oxford University Press.

Dubhashi, P.R. 1983. Grammar of Planning: Concepts and Applications, New Delhi: Indian Institute of Public Administration.

Galbraith, John Kenneth, 1979. *The Nature of Mass Poverty*, Cambridge: Harvard University Press.

Hirschman, Albert O. 1960. *The Strategy of Economic Development*, New Haven: Yale University Press.

Knowles, L.C.A. 1953. *The Industrial and Commercial Revolution in Great Britain During the Nineteenth Century*, 4th ed.. London: Routledge and Kegan Paul, p. 4161.

Kuznets, Simon. 1959. *Six Lectures on Economic Growth*, Glencoe: Free Press.

Lewis, W.Arthur. 1955. *Theory of Economic Growth*, Homewood: Irwin.

Myrdal, Gunnar. 1958. *Economic theory and Underdeveloped Regions*, Bombay: Vora & Co.

Myrdal, Gunnar. 1968. *Asian Drama: An Inquiry into the Poverty of Nations*, London: Lane.

Nurkse, Ragnar. 1960. *Problems of Capital Formation in Underdeveloped Countries*, New York: Oxford University Press.

Rosenstein-Rodan, P.N. ed. 1964. *Capital Formation and Economic Development*, London: Allen & Unwin.

Rostow, W.W. 1960. *The Stages of Economic Growth : A Non-communist Manifesto*, Londor Cambridge University Press.

Schumacher, E.F. ed. 1976. *Small is Beautiful : A Study of Economics as if People Mattered*, Londo Blond & Briggs.

Schumpeter, J.A. 1955. *The Theory of Economic Development : An Inquiry Into Profits, Capita Credit, Interest and the Business Cycle*, Cambridge : Harvard University Press.

Smith, Adam. 1937. *The Wealth of Nations*, edited by Edwin Cannan, N.Y. : Modern Library. Firs published in 1776.

United Nations. 1962. *The Developing Countries in the World*, Economic and Social Affair Department of World Economic Survey, p. 120.

2

An Alternative Model of Development : People Centered Development

The under-developed countries of Asia and Africa where most of humanity lives emerged to freedom in the second half of the 20th century. The first objective of the leaders of these countries was to fulfil the aspirations of the masses of people living in these countries to have a better, richer and fuller life. This aspiration could only be fulfilled through a sustained process of development. Hence, the attention of the policy-makers and thinkers was revetted on the subject of 'development' in all aspects. The United Nations declared the sixty's as the first development decade, the seventy's as the second and the eighty's as the third.

In the fifty's the concept of development was mainly concerned with increase in the gross national product and investment was considered to be the engine of development. Development was considered to be synonynous with economic development, westernisation and modernisation. It was taken for granted that development must faithfully immitate the already successful model of the West. In Soviet Union and Japan, thanks to industrialisation and urbanisation millions of people were moved out of agriculture into mass production. It was taken for granted that all the countries of Asia and Africa had to do was to follow the footsteps of the Western countries (recently known as the countries of the 'North'). The model to be followed was already there and the countries of Asia and Africa had to be a carbon copy of the Western model.

Western Models of Development Not Suitable

In the light of the experience of the last three decades, a realisation has dawned that these formulations of development are no longer valid and the Western model of development cannot be blindly copied in the countries of Asia and Africa. There are many other aspects of development than those in terms of economic growth alone.

The development in the Western countries was based on the application of the scientific methods, industrialisation through organisation, division of labour and machine, reliance on the market mechanism governed by acquisitiveness and materialism of the economic man, individual responsibility for his own destiny, work ethic and man seeking the control over nature. However, this model of development has led to the weakening of the sense of the community, increased sense of alienation and purposelessness, increased occurance of violent crime, personal distortions, mental illness and social disruption, dominance of acquisitive behaviour at the cost of quality of life and environmental degradation. In addition, persistent inflation, chronic unemployment and approaching limits of non-renewable resources like petroleum, gas and fresh water have made the Western model of development non-tenable. The planet cannot support a mass consumption society. An economic order where non-industrialised countries achieve an economic affluence comparable with that of the highly industrialised countries may not be sustainable. Ever increasing consumption of goods and armament sales are bound to be disastrous. Development has only led to irrational squandering of natural resources, fouling of environment, technological displacement of labour, debasement of humanity and low quality of life.

Kenneth Boulding makes a distinction of the *cow-boy economy* and the *spaceman* economy. The cow-boy economy is associated with reckless and exploitative use of natural resources. In such an economy, consumption is regarded as a good thing in itself and the limited resources are over exploited to provide it . The spaceman economy, on the other hand, is concerned with conservation of resources, not production or consumption perse. Our pre-occupation with production and consumption to the exclusion of conservation is most undesirable. It leads to waste in the shape of planned obsolescence, competitive advertising and poor quality of consumer goods. It has led to the deterioration of the quality of environment and pollution of the atmosphere. Price mechanism has failed to make people pay for the losses in the shape of degradation of environment caused by the productive process.

Alvin Tofflin has talked of the third wave. The first wave being the invention of agriculture ten thousand years age and the second wave touched off by the Industrial Revolution. The second wave of industrialisation was dependent on the hidd n subsidies and cheap energy and cheap raw materials. The third wave is ushered in by the information and communication technology.

What we have seen over the last two centuries are new technologies, intensification of production, and depletion of resources. Development and modernisation have produced a horrendous run-down of resources and pollution of the biosphere. At the same time, we are adding "millions" to the world population every year.

Inappropriateness of the Market Mechanism

As a result of the excessive reliance on the market mechanism, unemployment and inequality have become and most typical characteristics of the recent experience of LDCs. Development has trickled up, rather than down.

Hence for the LDCs, the appropriateness of the market mechanism needs to be called into question. The conventional policies based on the assumption of the equilibrating market mechanism instead of spreading development may actually increase the back-washing effects. The price mechanism is supposed to be a device for economic development by promoting adjustments in response to price signals and introducing gradual marginal changes. Everybody benefits from the process since the benefits of growth trickle down. However, development often generates systematic biases that increase inequality. The technological change imported by the LDC from the developed countries give increasing importance to economics of scale, capital intensity and inflexibility in production processes making it difficult for substituting plentiful factor of production namely labour for the scarce one namely capital. The importation of modern technology pre-empts the market of the indigeneous firms that operate with intermediate scale and technology. The multinational corporations have monopoly of enterprise, marketing and management and enjoy monopoly on a global scale. They impede the growth of local concerns. In that market, prices and costs are systematically distorted in favour of the wealthy. They have distinct advantages in anticipating prices. The cost of collecting milk from small farmer is prohibitive as also distribution of fertiliser, seeds and other modern inputs to them. There is a systematic distortion of market price against the poor and in favour of the rich. The institution of the market sucks people into it and imbibes biases favourable to the experienced and the rich and unfavourable to inexperienced and the poor. The strong consume the weak. The market induced break-up of the extended family, leads to the disintegration of the institution which can play unique role to bring about efficiency and development with a minimum of inequality. The extended family is an institution that provides for complementarity, conservation and credit without dependence on money. It promotes maximum cooperation and is an epitomy of a successful team. These are the factors which explain a basic characteristic of recent development experience of growth with every greater inequality. There is pervasiveness and multiplicity of market imperfections in the LDCs. Only a frontal attack on them and the distortions that they create can remove the source of disequilibrating impulses and systematic biases. While the orthodox paradigm condones intervention as an attempt to correct market imperfection in order to allow market forces to operate freely, the disequilibrium paradigm advocates intervention in order to offset the systematic biases attributable to the operation of the market in the early stages of development. One of such measures is to bolster the policy of financial institutions to deliver financial services to small but hard to reach potential client. The viability of non-market activities and influential aspects of traditional institutions such as the extended family need to be assured. Social security systems should be brought to the non-commercial sector. Traditional modes of self-reliance should be encouraged by removing artificial incentive by participation in the markets.

Alternative Model — People Centred Development

Attention is now focussed on the new dimensions of development ignored in the earlier writings. First, economic development and increase in production have no meaning unless they lead to elimination of poverty. Second, production would be self-defeating if it leads to destruction rather than preservation of the productive capacity of the environment. Thirdly, development is for the people and unless it leads to increased participation of people in the development process, development can be meaningless. In particular, development must involve a strategy focussed on increasing the access of the small farmer and the self-employed to land, water, crop and other facilities that would alone lead to increase in their productivity and fulfilment of their most basic needs. Thus "people centred development" emerges as an alternative to "production centred development."

Corporations Should Respect Macro Decisions of Society

In the alternative model, it is important that corporate goals of large economic organisations should include social responsibility and non-profit corporations and voluntary associations should play a more significant part. Operative goals of big corporations should become more congruent with those of the overall society. The result of micro-decision by individual corporations should not result in unsatisfactory macro decisions for the society.

Appropriate Technology

The new strategy for the poor should lay emphasis on rural development, fulfilment of basic human needs, food self sufficiency, labour intensive decentralised production and appropriate technology. Many of the newly developed countries can go directly from the first wave to the third wave. Decentralised energy creation through bio-gas plant rather than vast supply of electricity, use of solar energy, new grain varieties which can give yields even on non-irrigated lands, wind power wheels, ocean farming, green manure from underutilised plant life, genetics to revolutionalise the world food supply, new composite material, stronger and lighter than aluminium, plastic mortar, and micro-electronic technology — all lend themselves to decentralisation of production. Satellite communication system and computer chip, thanks to plummeting cost of communication, can substitute many transport functions. Industries can help in this process. There can be radical new synthesis of Gandhi with satellites. In this third wave, production and consumption should be combined. Many industrial technologies were a disaster when transferred to a poor country. What are required are labour intensive appropriate technologies suitable for decentralised small scale enterprises. Such technology should also free the poor from unremunerative unproductive work and excessively expensive systems. A single flush of a modern toilet facility requires 19 litres of water. An improved traditional toilet would be more suitable. The capital outlay required for hundred standpipes which can benefit a large number of poor families is equivalent to the annual cost for one foreign consultant.

Self-reliance of the Poor and their Native Skills

The key to the survival of the millions in the underdeveloped countries is part-time employment plus imaginative new policies aimed at making their presumption i.e. production and consumption more productive. For example, the poor can build their own houses, the government providing land and relaxation of the building code. Education can be combined with work.

Native Skill

As rural people migrate to cities, they lose their folk culture and folk songs and their native skills and everything that goes up to make richness and complexity in a culture built on generations. Conscious efforts should be made to preserve them.

New Sources of Energy

There has to be a harmonious relationship between the people and their natural environment. Human society receives its input from the earth, atmosphere and water. The available supply of fossilware would be a mere matter of centuries particularly at a present rate of growth. As regards nuclear energy, fissionable material is still presently scarce. Of course, through fusion much larger source of energy would be available but it has to be economic. We have not gone very far with the technology of solar energy. A biological revolution such as methyne producing algae could provide a solution.

Constructive Use of Environment

Human productivity in the ultimate analysis can only be sustained over time by partnership with nature. Human action must harmonise with the ecosystem. Arrogant rationality has led man to create arbitrary human systems which do not fit with the vast natural system of which we are a part. We must use the environment constructively instead of destructively.

Garret Hardin has talked of the "tragedy of commons". Herdsman share the commons but each herdsman increases his herd. Each looks to his own best interest, believing in the freedom of the commons. But this can only bring ruin to all. As a result of independent rational free enterprisers we are "fouling our own nest", putting radioactive chemicals into water, noxious and dangerous fumes into air and distracting by unpleasant advertising signs. We must impose coercive laws or taxing devices which makes it cheaper for the polluter to treat his pollutions than discharge them untreated. The individual exploiting a common should be restrained for the general good. Billions of dollars are spent to create supersonic transport which disturbs 50,000 people for every one person who is whisked from coast to coast three hours faster.

Rapid growth of trawler fleets has seriously threatened small-scale fisherman's employment opportunities, apart from inflicting damage on vulnerable resources through non-selective capturing anything that comes in the paths of their nests. Restrictions have to be placed on the number of trawlers though it might reduce economic efficiency measured by conventional profitability criteria. Loan programmes for promoting trawler fishery would create problems rather than solving them. There should be collective management of the commons according to rules prescribed by the local community. Several well intentioned developmental efforts have been beneficial only to the few. We should rather have programmes which promote creative abilities of the poor.

Famines allow those who occupy positions of influence and wealth further to widen the gap between themselves and those in a dependent situation. For example, once a natural calamity triggers expectations of a food shortage, the landowners begin to divert food supplies into storage and wait for the prices to rise — thus turning adversity into their opportunity. Drop in production also reduces the demand for the labour of the landless — the only resources they possess. Wage rates fall and the wage labourers find themselves at the mercy of those who can offer work or have cash to offer. The landless pawn their goods to money-lenders and they are never able to get their goods back because of crippling interest. Inspite of this, the borrower is in a subservient position vis-a-vis the lender. He is in a position of utter helplessness. Relief operations always arrive from the intermediary and the local elite. A large part of the relief is siphoned of by influential local people. For example, wheat is used by the landlords to feed labourers whom they hire for their own work. Altogether a new longterm strategy is needed to deal with the consequences of drought and famine. It should be in terms of a number of simultaneous measures for sustainable development.

Poverty Alleviation

The most pressing problem of the under developed countries is that of poverty of low income households. The over-riding goal of very low income household is to produce or earn enough to eat. Access to land for subsistance production partially insulates the household from rising food costs, providing an important form of food security. But the food needs are not inadequately met. Even the landowner's family has to take the most demeaning jobs despite low pay. There is a regular indebtedness. The workers' ignorance and their lack of organisation enables the landlords to undercut the minimum wage rate. Rapid loss of forests by the commercial contractors leads to forest destruction and affects the supply of cooking fuel to the small farmers. Coastal waters have been overexploited threatening the livelihoods sustaining fisherman. The plantation agriculture ties up substantial land assets in the hands of a few. Thus, income distribution remains as it is and does not trickle down to the poor. So, unless the vicious circle is broken, increasing number of people are displaced and make their way to large cities. The action that is required is slower population growth, balanced equitable development, specific attention to the needs of the landless to improve their survival strategies and sound management of environment. Impact rather than administrative expediency should be the guiding principle of intervention.

Market Accentuates Poverty

The poor - between one-quarter and one-fifth of the people of the world - are overwhelmingly poor landless labourers or marginal farmers who must supplement their income by wage labour. The disparity between the urban and the rural standards is much greater in poorer countries. It persists mainly because less than 20 per cent of the investment for development has gone to the agricultural sector, though over 65 per cent of the people and over 80 per cent of the really poor in the LDCs depend for their living on agriculture. The proportion of skilled people who support development going to rural areas is very low. Prices of industrial production have gone up relative to farm production. Education facilities encourage bright villagers to train citizens in urban jobs. Though the impact of input of investment is higher for agriculture than elsewhere, public policy and private market power have combined to push domestic savings and foreign aid in non-agricultural uses. Concentration on urban development and neglect on agriculture have pushed resources away from activities where they can help growth and benefit the poor. The rich farmers are favoured by the organised biases, policies in the shape of cheap loans and fertiliser subsidies. It is, therefore, necessary to transform the mass rural sector through major resources inputs prior to substantial industrialisation. The correct strategy would be to concentrate on high-yielding mass rural development supported by ancilliary industry.

The view that economy can grow rapidly and employment eliminated as a function of increased investment is fallacious because if in the process of investment there is capital intensive technological modernisation, creation of employment opportunities in the modern sector would be accompanied by the destruction of employment opportunities in the primitive sector and this would lead to increase in the rate of unemployment and underemployment as in Latin America. The income generated by additional investments in the modern sector mainly enlarges the incomes of the higher income groups. The demand for skilled human resources grows rapidly while the demand for unskilled manpower falls leading to stagnation or decline in the wages of unskilled labour. This accentuates unequal distribution of income. The capital investment activities leads to obsolescence of existing products and premature replacement of installed capacity.

The relationship between the developed and developing countries is one of dominance and dependence. In the developed countries, the developed structures prevail while backward and marginal activities are exceptional. In the underdeveloped countries, large segments of population have absolutely low levels of living while there is a growing gap between the rich and the poor. The magnitude of the high income sector is a function of the economic magnitude of the high productive activities and its political capacity to obtain a large share of the income generated by that sector. It is also a function and the capacity of that group to extract the part of the income generated in the low productivity activities through the maintenance of an institutional structure in the factory and goods markets and in the income transfer mechanisms which restricts the access of large sectors of population to sources of reasonable and stable income.

People Centred Development

The production-centered development has favoured command system form of organisation. People-centered development favours self-organising system geared to community goal setting and problem solving processes and to innovative and adaptive action. People-centered development focusses on people and their capacity to address their needs.

Programmes of cooperative and community development were implemented through conventional and bureaucratic structures with reliance on centralised bureaucratic organisations and inadequate investment for building the community with problems-solving capacity. But what is required is the appropriate community oriented management system as in the case of cooperative dairy development in India and Grameen bank activities as in Bangladesh which are examples of community based family services. A blueprint approach is inadequate response to the rural development problems. Rural development has to be a learning process.

Participatory Development

Effective development planning must be participatory. The proper role of the professional planner is to provide others with information, instruction, motivation and resources that can increase the effectiveness with which they plan for themselves.

In conventional production centered development model the needs of production system assume precedence over the needs of the people. People lucky enough to participate in the development enterprises find their lives dominated by large impersonal bureaucracy who exert inordinate control over their lives, including the access to sources of livelihood and limit their opportunities for creative individual initiative. The conventional development has been dehumanising and environmentally unsustainable. This has led to serious search for alternatives.

The new people-centered approach focusses on people, on improving directly the lives of the poor in the Third World countries. The poor rural households have considerable resourcefullness. They can fashion the economy composed of household production units. While the modern sector is a primary source of conventional economic growth, the traditional sector is the primary source of livelihood for most poor households. The new approach requires reoriented institutional capabilities. The poor are the creative individuals sustaining themselves under difficult circumstances and measures must be taken to relieve them of their constraints. Production-centered development concentrates on industry over agriculture, concentrated investment rather than dispersed investment, exploitation of natural resources rather than their conservation. It encourages large production units which are energy in efficient, lack adaptability and are prone to serious disruption. It externalises social and environmental causes. In people centered analysis, the people and the environment are the primary variables. Education, health care, nutrition of the poor are the social indicators of progress.

Local Self-reliance and Self-sufficiency

Every development process must be able to meet the basic needs of its people. Development must be organised on a territorial basis. The question of production and distribution should be jointly solved. The resource base for development of productive forces in every area must be continuously expanded. Masses must be involved in development. There should be less reliance on outside aid and there should be a conspicuous process of social learning. Social power is an inexhaustible resource whose potential capacity increases with use. Within territorially integrated communities, everyone must have an equal chance of gaining access to the use of common resources. Development should aim at diversifying the territorial economy; making development of physical resources consistent with the principles of conservation; promoting self-finance and social learning. Such development efforts should come from within. The sequence of development will be as follows: increased agricultural productivity, industrial diversification in decentralised locations, increased occupation of labour, increased demand for wage goods, increased demand for machinery and simple transport equipment, technological and product innovations, enhanced capacity for export of domestic manufactures abroad. Continuously upgrading of agricultural production, manufacture of tools for farming, agricultural processing, self built-housing, appropriate institutions at district and regional levels - these are the components of such planning. The role of the state is protective, developmental, facilitative, regulatory and redistributary.

Decentralising Decision Making by Empowering People

Public policy should strengthen the role of the family, the voluntary association, the neighbourhood, and the small working group.

The paralysis of the parliaments, the ineptitudiness of giant governmental bureaucracies, the wild swings of political attention, and the general crisis of industrialism have made the system incapable of taking quick competent decisions. Demands fall into decision-makers from a wide range. The political decision-making machinery was never designed to cope up with such a high level of diversity. There is mismatch between decisional technology and decisional environment leading to countless self-cancelling decisions. Executive policy-makers are over-loaded. The government is doing too much. Government bureaucracies are not adaptive. The government are pumping uniform services for an increasingly non-uniform population leading to a gap between what people need and what they would get from government. Programme designed in the Nation's capital are not tailored for local needs. At some points the decision load is greater than the system can handle. The decisions load should be reduced by sharing it with more people, allowing more decisions to be made down below or at the periphery instead of concentrating them at the already stressed and mal-functioning centre. We must have democratic alternatives to obsolete structures before they fall by their own weight.

Public policy should utilise radiating structures for realisation of social purposes and for expanding government services without direct government operations. People should be empowered to do things. The management mindset of the megastructure is biased towards the unitary solution. The goal of public policy should be a pluralistic policy. The main purpose of involving poor in their own development is to strengthen their initiative and critical abilities. The process of responsible participation should constitute a primary concern in all development process. The solidification of the centralised power leads to corruption as a way of life and legitimizes bureaucracy's claim to be its own watchdog. Development must be complimented by the evolution of representative political institutions conducive to stability. Only broad-based local effort, hard work and initiative can sustain the prosperity of the nation. Political development must provide the essential underpinnings of social trust on the basis which alone majority of the people can take risks. What is required is enduring local foundation rather than flashy national monuments. Political maturity should take root throughout the nation. There should be society based on wide trust and there has to be a stable political order based on strong participatory structures.

There has to be a local activisim and network of participative community. Network composes of selfreliant autonomous participants. In a network, person is more highly valued than the paper. Networks are bound up with relationships, links, actions and communications, and shared values.

The central concerns of people-centered development are human growth and well being, equity and sustainability. It emphasises quality of life. It emphasis human values in decision-making and social earning concepts and methods. Its approach is territorial rather than functional. It uses the framework of human ecology in analysis of production and performance. It makes people the very foundation of the development process. People centered development implies decentralisation of decision-making processes. The decision-making by the people injects richness.

Basic to people centered development are : (1) creation of enabling settings which encourage people's effort to meet their needs; (2) development of organisational structures and processes that function according to the principles of self-organising systems; and (3) development of territorially organised production-consumption systems based on principles of local ownership and control. It requires reorientation of the purposes, structures and operations of government bureaucracies. It requires informal network structures. Bureaucratic value system should not be the major instruments of development action. People centered development requires orientation of development bureaucracy so that they become organisations that appreciate and enchance the humanity of both their members and the citizens they serve. Villagers are not clients. They have to contribute to their development as creative citizens. The logic of local-self reliance requires self-sustaining human ecological systems. The role of units such as local governments is central in the coordination of local development policy. There should be emphasis on local community control and management of resources.

Part - II

APPROACHES TO RURAL DEVELOPMENT

3

Problems and Planning of Rural Development in Developing Countries

The developing countries of Asia and Africa are predominantly rural in character. Their goal is rapid economic development for raising the level of living of their people. And in seeking rapid economic development they often look to the past experience of the developed countries.

The history of the developed countries brings out the fact that urbanisation has been the concomitant of development. England, the first country to undergo the process of development beginning from the industrial revolution during 1760 and 1820, is also the most urbanised country with 75% of the people staying in urban areas.

But what is the implication of this concomitance of urbanisation and economic development? Does it mean that the developing countries can develop simply by transfer of population from rural areas to urban areas? Or by according higher priority to urbanisation to the neglect of rural development?

Economic development has to be an evolutionary process. Urbanisation if it has to result in economic well being rather than growth of slums, shanty towns and urban unemployment must be accompanied by the development of secondary and tertiary sectors. Industrial diversification and organisation of variety of services should provide expanding scope for productive employment to skilled population. All this must be a process of evolution and cannot be a product of a hot-house growth.

Nor can the developing countries neglect rural development. If the bulk of the population lives in rural areas, the developing countries must concentrate on rural development. Moreover agriculture and allied occupations in which bulk of the rural population are engaged are vital to economic development because they are the source of food-stuff to feed the growing population and raw material for expanding industry. Besides industry cannot sustain without market and in a predominantly rural country, the rural population must be reasonably prosperous to provide the requisite purchasing power for absorbing the products of modern industry. The developing countries, therefore, have rightly provided a place of priority to rural development in their schemes and plans of socio-economic development.

II

Rural development, however, is not an easy task. It bristles with problems and difficulties. In most developing countries, the standard of living in rural areas is very low. There is a pressure of population on land. The agricultural technology is primitive. Facilities like irrigation, electrification, transport, communication which are all necessary infra-structure for development, are not adequate. Health and educational facilities are lacking. Even potable drinking water is not always available. Non-farm occupations are not well-developed. While new industrial enterprises do not come up in sufficient numbers in rural areas, traditional industries stagnate. Institutions like banking and marketing are very small in number.

Low level of living is the cumulative effect of all these inadequacies. These are made worse by traditional attitudes and institutions. The rural people are often superstitious and fatalistic in outlook and lack the urge to change and innovate. There are many social taboos. Custom is king. The traditional social structure is feudalistic and rigid in character. The status of an individual is often based on ascription rather than achievement. Often, gerontocracy prevails.

A leading thinker of a developing country described rural areas as a den of ignorance and a sink of narrow mindedness and localism.

The situation is often described as that of a vicious circle of poverty in rural areas since the level of income is low, savings are low, and investment is low. Since the rate of capital formation is low, the rate of growth is stagnant and so, there is less income. Also, since the level of education is low, the standard of management is low, which is turn, leads to low rate of development.

To initiate rural development, therefore, it becomes necessary to break the vicious circle of poverty, to initiate change and innovation and to trigger off the process of development. But it is not always clear as to where a nation should begin in tackling the problems of rural development.

Most developing countries have found on experience that the strategy of rural development has to be multifacetted, multi-sectoral and multi-processed in character.

In the first instance, agriculture has to be modernised. The standard of agricultural productivity has to be raised. Thousands and millions former families have to be introduced to modern methods of agriculture. This itself is a complicated task. In the first instance it has to begin with agricultural research which should identify the causes of low productivity and come out with a package of ideas of technology and practices to raise productivity. Often, introduction of high yielding varieties of seeds sometimes called "miracle seeds" has triggered off the process of increasing agricultural productivity.

But research cannot be confined to the research centres. The results of research must go from lab to land. There has to be, therefore, the conveyer-belt for dissemination of the fruits of research to thousands of individual holdings. This is a task of adaptive research and agriculture extension. But such machinery of agricultural extension was lacking in most developing countries and hence sustained efforts are needed to set up such a machinery of agriculture extension. Persons have to be trained in extension to man the organisational machinery of extension in rural areas before it could be entrusted with the responsibility of the net-work of extension to take the technology from lab to land.

Research and extension, however are not enough. They need the underpinning of various inputs-water, seeds, fertilizer, pesticides, implements and credit.

Water is the most important input since uncertain rainfall not only provides a set back to agricultural production bu often leads to drought and famine. Dependable supply of water, therefore, has to be assured through major, medium and minor irrigation projects. In most developing countries, water resources, both surface and ground, have not been tapped. As a result surface water flows down the river into the sea while underground water remains un-utilised. The exploitation of these water resources requires considerable investment in the shape of reservoirs, water conveyance systems, tanks, wells, etc.

But where storage of water is not enough, farmers have to be educated in optimum utilisation of water and this again is a task of agriculture extension and training.

Just as water would not be available for the asking so would not be the seeds. The improved varieties of seeds have to be grown under supervised conditions, tested, certified and then made available to the farming community taking care that the seed is not adulterated in the process.

Another important input are the fertilizers. Use of chemical fertilizers is a part of modern agriculture. But the consumption of fertilizers depends on their availability. The developing countries do not have fertilizer factories to begin with. They have to be set up but they require huge investment. They also require technical manpower of high level. The developing countries which do not have these will have to depend on imports of chemical fertilizers. Even when fertilizers are available, their distribution and use requires a lot of organisation and extension.

What has been stated about fertilizers also applies to pesticides and insecticides.

For the supply of all these inputs, namely, seeds, fertilizers, pesticides and insecticides, the whole net-work of storages is required in rural areas This has to be accessible to the farming community.

Often, the agriculturists do not have the resources to buy fertilizers anc other inputs nor to adopt modern agricultural practices. They, therefore require credit. In the developing countries, rural credit institutions were no available and the farmers were mainly dependent on the money-lenders who often charged usurious rates of interest. Agriculture credit institutions therefore, need to be set up in rural areas.

The farmer would adopt improved agricultural practices and spenc resources to buy inputs to raise the standard of cultivation only if he coul be guaranteed the fruits of his labour. This, however, does not obtain. Thi is because very often, the agrarian structure in the developing countries i retrograde in character. The cultivator is not always the owner of the lanc He works for his master who is a feudal land-lord. The land-lord systen often results in exploitation. While the absentee-landlord takes the fruits c cultivation on the ground of his ownership of land, he does not contribut to it. Often, there is a system of share-cropping in which a large portion c the produce is taken away by the landlord and the cultivator is left wit pittance hardly adequate to make his both ends meet. Agrarian reform therefore, is often a pre-condition for modernisation of agriculture.

If retrograde agrarian structure is one source of exploitation an deterrence to incentive and higher agricultural productivity, deficier agricultural marketing system is another. Typically, prices of agricultur commodities crash at harvest time, when bulk of the produce is cornered b the money-lender - trader to whom the farmer is indebted. The middle-ma then harvests a huge profit by raising the prices in the lean season. He profi largely at the cost of the producer and the consumer. A very small fractio of the consumer rupee reaches the producer. A big price spread between th producer and the consumer is typical in most developing countries. Wh incentive can the farmer have when bumper production brings him onl reduced income due to crash in prices? Orderly marketing has, therefore, a extremely important place in any agenda of rural development. It includes storage facilities, cooperative marketing, regulated marketing, appropriate buffer stock and price-support policies etc.

Agriculture in the narrow sense of the word, namely, crop husbandry, has to be supplemented by animal husbandry including dairy, poultry, fishery, piggery horticulture, sericulture, tree crops, bee-keeping etc. This is called "mixed farming". Each of the supplementary occupations, however, has its own problems. For example, dairy development would require improved breed of cattle, arrangement for feeding and for marketing and processing. Horticulture development requires improved plant material and credit resources so that the farmer can wait till the tree crop starts yielding. Similarly, fishery development depends on the availability of fish seed, facility for their multiplication and later marketing of fish.

Thus, agricultural development and development of mixed farming requires a whole net-work of a variety of organisations for extension, supply of inputs, storage, marketing and processing.

Development connotes diversification of occupations. Often, possibilities of non-farm occupations arise out of farming itself. Industrial enterprises are required for the supply of inputs like fertilizers and modern implements. Industrial enterprises are also needed for processing of agricultural produce. A large number of agro-processing enterprises can trigger off a chain process of economic development.

Just as there is a nexus between the primary and secondary sectors, there is also a nexus between the primary and tertiary sectors. A number of institutions in the field of marketing, credit, banking, insurance and distributive trade, supply of producers' and consumers' goods follow in the wake of developing and diversifying agriculture.

Apart from industrial enterprises connected with agriculture, such as sugar factories, spinning mills, cotton ginning and pressing units, oil extraction units, rice mills, floor mills, fruit processing units, etc., there is the other field of traditional industries like handloom, weaving, shoe making, tailoring, etc. and handicrafts like jewellary and sandalwood products which can also provide productive employment provided facilities are available for improvement in technology, organisation for purchases of inputs and marketing.

Apart from expansion, diversification and enrichment of occupational opportunities, rural development also requires facilities to raise the general level of the people through what is called "public consumption" in the shape of education, health, roads and transport. The level of literacy and standard of health in rural areas is often very low. Hence institutions of primary and secondary education and rural dispensaries have to be set up. Many people in rural areas cannot avail of factors making for change because they have no access to them. They do not have an approach road to the main market. They do not have any means of transport since neither the bus nor the railway is accessible to them. Rural people, therefore, require these basic facilities before they could hope for development.

III

In the previous paragraphs I have briefly sketched the problems and programmes of rural development. The solution to these problems requires administrative planning because without such planning, no development can take place. It cannot be left to the vicissitudes of market forces. It requires conscious planning. But what kind of administrative planning is called for?

This planning cannot entirely be centralised since the human habitations in rural areas are widely dispersed. Rural communities are scattered over in vast areas and this makes centralised planning difficult. The machinery of planning for rural development has, therefore, to be decentralised in character.

Hand in hand with decentralisation is the principle of participation of the local communities in the programme of rural development. This ensures that rural development programmes deal with the *real* problems of the rural people rather than those perceived by the planner in his air-conditioned office in the administrative capital situated for away from the rural communities. It also enables the local resources to supplement resources from the Central budget.

The idea of community development was mooted as a part of the decentralised approach to rural development. Community development requires rural communities to be encouraged to identify their felt problems and needs and to work out solutions for solving these problems and provide for those needs. The Governmental machinery of extension and community development, in such an approach is of the nature of aid to the self-help of the rural communities. Community development approach of ten led to the establishment of rural local Government institutions as agencies of rural development. However, the community development effort was not found by itself to be sufficient since many activities necessary for rural development such as the construction of the system of irrigation, of health and education, of transport and of agricultural research and extension, of marketing and agro-processing was seen to be dependent on centralised initiative, investment and direction.

In the light of experience, it has now been realised that the best approach to rural development is the optimum combination of planning from below and planning from above. It is not easy to lay down any definite criterion for such an optimum combination nor to indicate how it can be brought about. One way would be to work out at the Centre, broad schemes with budgetary allocations and leave the local Government institutions and the local communities to implement them with local flexibility within the broad framework of the scheme. Another would be to earmark some definite resources for local development and place them at the disposal of the local Government institutions. A third way would be for Central Govt. to work out regional and local comprehensive development plans in consultation with the local people.

Administrative planning for rural development is often confronted with a dilemma. Is it better to concentrate on some significant sectors or undertake integrated and comprehensive development? The advantage of integrated development is that it establishes links between [illegible] and sectors of rural development. On the other hand, sucn comprehensive development plans often lead to the dilution of resources without significant results in any sector. Attempt then is made to concentrate on certain sectors like agriculture or dairy or fishery according to the potentialities of the area.

A third aspect of planning for rural development is whether the entire population needs to be covered or special attention should be given to the weaker sections of the community like the small farmers or marginal farmers, agricultural labourers, etc. Thus, the approach to development is oriented to target groups rather than to rural development generally. The target group approach becomes more and more imperative when it is realised that very often public investment to bring about general rural development is cornered by the richer sections of the rural community leaving a large majority of the rural population high and dry. In recent years, it has been realised more and more that general rural development programmes have not benefitted the bulk of the rural community and efforts are made to introduce schemes which would direct resources more and more for the benefit of the disadvantaged sections of the rural community.

There is also the question of the priority given to rural development in national plans. It often happens that the urban sector is more vociferous and articulate and gets a disproportionate share in the cake of plan resources. The planner will then have to make a conscious effort to see that this does not happen.

Thus, administrative planning for rural development requires combination of central direction with decentralise organisation and implementation, comprehensive planning with intensive effort in important sectors and special attention to the disadvantaged sections of the rural community.

Administrative system in developing countries often suffers from apoplexy at the Centre and anemia at the periphery. Administrative officers and personnel are cencentrated in the capital cities. This would not do for rural development where administration has often to go to the people. Increase in the number and strength of field agencies must, therefore, follow in the wake of rural development.

However, tasks of rural development cannot be done by the field agencies of administrative departments alone. They need to be linked with a vast network of rural institutions including local Government institutions, cooperatives, rural banks, farmers' associations, youth and women clubs etc. In fact to promote, sustain and support such institutions becomes the principal task of the field agencies.

Both the field agencies and the rural institutions need to be manned by competent people - educated, well trained with requisite qualifications and skills. But these are often attracted by the lures of the city life. Also rural development is not considered as a prestigious branch of administration though in a developing country it should occupy a high place in the scale of preference. Special incentives are, therefore, necessary to attract competent personnel to the field of rural development. Such personnel need to be properly trained not only to impart requisite knowledge and skill but to develop proper attitudes. Man-power planning should thus form an integral part of the plan for rural development.

4

Approaches to Integrated Rural Development in India

Introduction

Most of India has been and even now continues to be rural, and most of the rural economy has been agriculture based and hence rural development mainly connotes development of agriculture, including development of subsidiary occupations like dairy, poultry, fishery, etc. Besides, it also includes development of rural industries and work-programmes providing employment opportunities to those who do not get them in their normal occupations.

Many approaches to rural development have been adopted ever since the country embarked upon planned programmes of economic development in 1951.

National Extension Service and Community Development

One of the first programmes was that of the National Extension Service and Community Development. Started in 1952, the programme went on for nearly two decades broadly covering the entire rural India through community development blocks. Each block attempted to bring about multipurpose rural development through the help of an extension and development agency consisting of a block development officer, extension officers, i.e. subject-matter specialists in different areas of rural development and the village-level workers. As a result of this programme, a number of rural facilities were provided and a certain degree of development conscience was also created among rural folks.

Panchayati Raj

Following the recommendations of a report of a committee on plan projects, it was felt that community development would not have adequate popular support unless an institutional basis was provided through three-tier rural local government institutions, known as the Panchayati raj. Subsequently, Panchayati raj institutions came into existence in one form or another in all states. A basic defect of the community development approach was that it thought of the community as a whole without realizing that it was broken up into various social and economic stratifications. Consequently, while some attention was paid and programmes were devised for weaker sections, including the tribal communities, the community development approach by and large degenerated into a somewhat stereotyped, undifferentiated and diluted programme of rural development. It was alleged that both community development programmes and Panchayati raj institutions catered to the demands of the dominant class and caste groups. In spite of all this criticism, the positive contributions of the community development programme - providing certain basic minimum common facilities, special assistance for the members of the scheduled castes, and creating consciousness - should not be overlooked.

The community development programme as such has now been more or less given up and what we have are a number of special programmes.

Cooperatives

Another important instrument of rural development has been the cooperative movement. The blueprint of the cooperative development programme as an integral part of rural development was provided by the famous Rural Credit Survey Committee Report. It looked upon cooperation as an alliance of the weak against the dominance of the strong elements, i.e. the landlord-trader-money lender group supported by the banking and trading institutions in the city and metropolitan centres. The blueprint of the constructive programme of rural development recommended by the Committee was known as the scheme for integrated rural credit. The scheme was for integrated rural credit in the sense that agricultural production was to be linked to agricultural finance, and recovery of agricultural loans was to be linked to cooperative marketing and processing. These were essential elements of the crop-loan scheme which was also a scheme for supervising credit. One of the features of the crop-loan scheme was that credit was to be given to credit-worthy purposes rather than credit-worthy persons; it was production rather than security oriented. In other words, credit was to be linked with the standing crop rather than to land security.

For encouraging cooperative marketing and processing, the Committee recommended the establishment of a special organization at the national level. This was the genesis of the National Cooperative Development Corporation.

While the credit institutions referred to above were to provide short-term and medium-term credit, for long-term credit there was a system of land mortgage banks now known as Land Development Banks. In the past they provided finance only for redemption of credit. With the establishment of the Agricultural Refinance Corporation in 1963, they were geared more and more to providing long-term finance for purposes like digging irrigation wells, land reclamation, horticulture, mechanization, etc. With acceptance of the principle of repaying capacity as the proper security, it has been possible to provide long-term finance as short-and medium-term finance to tenants also.

The programme of providing agricultural finance and development of agricultural marketing and processing has impressive results to its credit. But the question is: To what extent has it benefited the weaker sections of rural community. As in the case of community development, it is pointed out, the cooperative development also has gone to the richer and middle peasants rather than to small farmers and tenants. Deliberate attempts had therefore to be made to see that there was a large enrolment of the smaller farmers and those belonging to scheduled castes in the cooperatives, and that they got a fair measure of the services of these societies. The programme of agricultural marketing, processing and supply through cooperatives continues to suffer from many managerial shortcomings and the development is not as integrated as was expected by the authors of the crop-loan scheme.

Other Agricultural Development Programmes

Some programmes of agricultural development existed outside the pale of community development and cooperation. They were essentially programmes of a technical nature, like supply of improved seeds, improvement of agronomical practices, development of green manure and compost, popularization of chemical fertilisers etc. They were all of a general scope and not particularly developed for the smaller farmer or weaker sections. An important landmark in programmes of agricultural development was the intensive agricultural district programme. This was introduced following the recommendations of the Ford Foundation team on India's food crisis. Under the programme the most promising districts in the country were selected for the application of a package of services and practices to increase agricultural production through concentrated effort. This approach tended to concentrate on the bigger farmer and neglect the small.

Then followed what came to be known as the new strategy of agricultural development based on the introduction of hybrid seeds. This strategy proved particularly successful and ushered in what came to be known as the green revolution. The strategy relied on miracle seeds to be combined with increased dosage of chemical fertilizers and water. The implementation of the new strategy, particularly in states like Punjab, had one promising feature. It showed that the new techniques were indifferent to the size of holdings. They could be employed as much by the small holder as by the large. In other words, the so-called economic holding can be very small provided agriculture is intensive enough.

For the landless, cooperative farming and rural industries have been tried. The landless are settled on cooperative farms which were expected to develop joint farming, subsidiary occupations and common facilities and common living. Unfortunately, as pointed out by the Gadgil Committee, these have become successful only in that rare combination of circumstances where all favourable factors have tended to converge — factors like good leadership, enlightened membership, and understanding administration.

Rural Industries Programmes

As regards the programmes of rural industries, they cannot be said to have been a spectacular success. The most important rural industry, weaving, is organized through industrial cooperatives. Half of them are dormant and the whole movement is more or less in the doldrums.

Recent Programmes

There has recently been a radicalization of the rural development programmes. Its impact on rural development has been three-fold. First, in the field of provision of public consumption facilities; second, in modification of the production programmes; and third, in provision of massive employment programmes. As regards the first, the common consumption facilities which have been given priority are provision of drinking water facilities, and provision of rural house sites. It is a matter of disappointment that even after several five-year plans, a number of villages are without potable water and even where drinking water wells are available, the lot of scheduled castes is particularly difficult.

Under a massive programme it had been decided to provide a house site for every landless person by August, 1973. The programme has made considerable headway. But the problem still is how to provide houses. Some states have introduced massive programmes of rural housing.

The applied nutrition programme also made an attempt to provide nutritious food, particularly to the vulnerable, i.e. children and expectant mothers. Programmes have also been launched to provide comprehensive rural communication so that no village is left without a connecting road. The rural health centre facilities are being strengthened.

SFDA and MFLA

A reorientation of the production system is sought to be achieved through selected programmes like the small farmer development agency and through marginal farmer labour agencies. From the economic point of view the special feature of this new approach is to provide a proper economic base to the operations of the small farmers and the marginal farmers helping them to take up subsidiary occupations, like dairy with agriculture, and by providing organized common facilities, like marketing. From the administrative point of view, the special feature of the programme is to concentrate and identify the small and marginal farmer and provide him with special assistance to make him viable. The principal instruments for this still are the cooperatives.

Bank Nationalization Measure

Another radical measure was the nationalization of the banks and the re-direction of their resources to agriculture. What the nationalized banks have accomplished in this field is of considerable significance. But their success in helping the small farmer is not yet an accomplished task.

Work programme

The most important component of the radical programme is the programme of employment on works in rural areas. The study of poverty in India by Dandekar and Rath showed that the poor have been left outside the mainstream of economic development. According to them this problem cannot be solved without putting into the hands of the poor the needed purchasing power by providing guaranteed employment on works. Works programmes have been taken up under many schemes, like crash schemes for rural employment, droughtprone affected areas programme (DPAP), World Food Programme, Food for Work Programme, pilot programme for intensive rural employment, etc. The World Bank has also come forward to assist the pilot programmes in providing full rural employment.

The scope of the DPAP has been widened to include a number of productive programmes like minor irrigation, diary, horticulture, sericulture, pisciculture etc.

Integrated Rural Development Projects for development on the basis of a comprehensive inventory of local resources have also been established.

5

Integrated Rural Development Programmes: Suggestions for Improving Implementation

The programme of "Integrated Rural Development" has been described as the single largest programme for providing direct assistance to the poorest amongst the poor in our society. It was expected to cover 15 million families in all the five thousand and odd Blocks of the country during the sixth five-year plan. It was targetted that during the seventh Five Year Plan, 20 million families would be assisted of which 10 million would be new households and 10 million old beneficiaries who had been unable to cross the poverty line and required a second dose of assistance. On an average, 3000 families in a Block were to be provided assistance during this plan period. A sum of Rs. 1500 crores had also been provided as outlay for this programme. Banks had been called upon to provide another Rs. 3,000.00 crores by way of loans to selected beneficiaries. The programme gave special priorities to the Scheduled Castes and Scheduled Tribes. At least 30% of the families assisted were to be drawn from them. Also at least 30% of the subsidies and loans were earmarked for these beneficiaries. Under the programme, the poorest amongst the poor families were to be identified and helped in a phased manner to acquire income generating assets or acquire new skills and upgrade the present ones to take up skilful employment. The other programmes, like National Rural Employment Programme, drought prone area programme, desert development programme, trysem and development of women and children in rural areas were considered to be complementary to the integrated rural development programme.

All these programmes aimed at alleviation of rural poverty. This had become the major objective of planning in our country. In the earlier Plans, emphasis was on economic development in terms of increasing gross national gross product. The most important economic development was, of course, agricultural development since this constituted the main occupation in the rural areas. The new agricultural strategy initiated in the year 1967 ushered in the green revolution in some parts of the country. However, the very success of the green revolution made it necessary to consider whether the benefit of the green revolution had spread even to those people in the rural areas who were at the low end of poverty. It was realised that the old "trickle down strategy" could not be adequate for alleviation of rural poverty and a direct assault had to be made on poverty. The Integrated Rural Development Programmes and other complementary programmes were the results of this realisation.

In order to understand properly the strategy of integrated rural development and the complementary programme, it is necessary to comprehend the nature of poverty in the rural areas. All these families whose annual earning is less than Rs. 3,500 are defined as belonging to the rural poor eligible for assistance under IRDP. The figure was later raised to Rs. 4800 per annum. The members of these families have monthly per capital consumption of less than Rs. 55. It is estimated that according to this criterion, more than 50% of the rural people are below the poverty line.*

Most of the rural poor consist of small and marginal farmers and the landless labourers. According to the agricultural census in 1975-76, out of the 81 million land holding 58 millions consisted of small and marginal farmers. They constituted 72% of the agricultural holdings, though the land owned by them was only about 23%. On the other hand, the top 3% of the agricultural holdings belonged to the large land holders owning above ten hectors. They owned 30% of the land. The ownership of land is thus extremely unequal. The plight of the marginal farmers holding less than one hectare is particularly very difficult.

Equally difficult also is the condition of the agricultural labourers. In a Seminar on "Administration of Minimum Wages", the Minister for Labour, in his address, drew attention to the conditions of the rural labourers. According to the 1981 census, there were over 55 million agricultural workers, in the country representing about 25% of the total workers. About 25% of the rural house-holds were agricultural labour house-holds deriving major portion of of the total income from wages for labour in agricultural occupation. Nearly 50% of these labour house-holds had no land. The others had some, but the size of their holding was very small. The average size of the land cultivated by the labour-house-holds stood at 1.11 acres. About 50% of the rural house-holds were having cultivated land of less than one

* Currently, the poverty line is fixed at Rs. 11,000 per annum.

acre. Overwhelmingly majority of the house-holds were cultivating land less than half an acre.

With such a large number of small holdings as well as large number of agricultural workers as farm servants, the incidence of unemployment, under-employment and disguised un-employment is very large . 5 to 6% of the rural farmers are fully unemployed. Many others are engaged in work but do not earn enough to pull themselves above the poverty line. Most of the agricultural workers could get employment for less than 200 days per annum, and the employment is only for few hours and it is at a level much below their productive and earning capacity.

What should be the strategy for dealing with the poverty arising out of extremely inadequate land holding and absence of employment opportunities? It was expected that the new technology would help the small and marginal farmers as well as medium and large farmers. It was pointed out that the now technology based on the use of miracle seeds i.e. hybrid and high-yielding varieties was land augmenting and labour intensive in nature and would raise production and productivity of small and marginal holdings as also the medium and large holdings. It was, however, realised that to derive benefits from hybrid seeds, it is necessary to have more intensive use of fertilizers and water as also use of pesticides and insecticides, since the new varieties may be more prone to posts and disease. Thus, while in theory the new technology is neutral to scale, in order to take advantage of the technology, the small and marginal farmers have to have adequate access to the inputs and credit required to buy the inputs and these are not always available. It is necessary to re-organise delivery and credit system to make inputs available to small and marginal farmers.

What about the land-less? They have only two ways to improve their lot. One would be productive occupations in what are called activities subsidiary to agriculture, viz. dairy, poultry, fishery, goat and pig rearing, sericulture etc. The other would be employment in works programmes.

Yet another way of improving the plight of the rural poor would be enforcement of the minimum agricultural wage. A rural labour enquiry revealed that hardly 2% of the workers were aware of the fact that the Government had prescribed minimum wages. This was due to wide-spread illiteracy and lack of organization.

Another major approach to help the poor is through land reforms which would throw up surplus land for distribution amongst the rural poor. Because of the various ways of avoiding the land reform legislation, sufficient agricultural land has not been thrown up for distribution amongst the landless.

It was under these circumstances that the alleviation of the rural poverty required:

(i) programmes like Integrated Rural Development Programme to provide loans and subsidies to the poor people to acquire productive assets.

(ii) training for rural youths for self employment at the rate of 40 youths per block in the country to upgrade the traditional skill and productive capacity of rural youth belonging to families below the poverty line and

(iii) the national rural employment programme to generate 3 to 4 hundred million man days per year.*

The implementation of these programmes have been entrusted to district rural development agencies.

How far have been these programme succeeded in alleviating poverty? This is the question that needs to be answered.

A government evaluation in 1989 showed that only 28% of IRDP beneficiaries had been able to cross the poverty line which was then fixed at Rs. 6400 a year despite the fact that Rs. 21,432 cr. were given as bank credit and Government subsidy to 447 lakh families since the inception of the IRDP in 1979. A more critical analysis of these programmes has shown that the implementation of these programmes suffers from the following major inadequacies:

(i) The share of the poorest of the poor in selected beneficiaries is not adequate.

(ii) The peoples' representatives are not involved for implementation of the programmes.

(iii) These programmes are not integrated with the general development programmes.

(iv) The works implemented through the N.R.E.P. are often not co-ordinated with requirements of the families identified for assistance under I.R.D.P.

(v) An evaluation of the trysem has shown lack of confidence amongst the trainees and lack of finance for them to settle down in their occupation.

(vi) Also there are complaints of widespread leakage due to corruption as a result of the emergence of a system of brokerage in the

---

* This programme was supplemented by the totally Centrally Financed Rural Landless Employment Guarantee Programme introduced in 1983 and the Jawahar Rozgar Yojana launched in the last year of the Seventh Five Year Plan with a total allocation of Rs. 2600 cr to generate 931 million man days of employment.

implementation of these schemes. Most of the illiterate poor are found to require a class of intermediaries for gaining access to the bureaucracies and bankers who administer the programmes of subsidies.

(vii) There is absence of linkage - horizontal or vertical - which contributes to inadequacies. Coordination between agencies is lacking. It is necessary to provide linkages between various programmes.

The Ministry of Rural Development had laid down detailed guidelines for the implementation of these programmes. In these, it was clearly pointed out that block plans should be prepared for integrated rural development and they should be integrated with the development programmes of other departments. Also indicated were detailed steps to be taken for provision of prospective plan inventory of local resources, review of on-going programmes, formulation of sectoral programmes and projects and credit plans, selection of clustors, survey of house-holds and preparation of credit plans to reflect the family plans. However, inspite of these detailed instructions to have block level plans the deficiencies mentioned above have been noticed.

How to overcome these deficiencies? Obviously there is an "implementation gap" which needs to be overcome.

In order to bridge this implementation gap, I would suggest the following techniques of management in the implementation of the Integrated Rural Development Programme and other programmes.

Strategy Managements

Here the focus would be on the objective of the programme and the entire strategy of organisation, procedure, method and working of personnel should aim at reaching the goal which is not just fulfilling the targets of loan and subsidy distribution, but rather bringing the rural poor above the poverty line.

Project Management

Here the emphasis would be on the assistance given to individual families being an integral part of technically sound and economically viable projects. Unless the individual beneficiaries are made productive participants in a well-conceived project, the goal would not be reached. For example, a beneficiary of a loan for purchase of a cow or a buffallo must not be an isolated individual, but be a member of a dairy cooperative. Similarly, labour construction co-operative of the land-less may undertake work on various projects.

Participatory Managements

Unless the people are aware of the programmes and are also the participants in the implementation, the programme would not succeed. There has to be, therefore, re-orientation of the development bureaucracy itself, who should have the skill to elicit the participation of the people in these programmes. To the development workers, I can command the credo of the movement of rural reconstruction which says:

> " Go to the people, live amongst the people, learn from the people, plan with the people, work with the people, start with what the people know, build on what the people have, teach by showing, learn by doing, not a show-case but a pattern, not odds and ends but a system, not piecemeal but integrated project, not relief but release".

Fiscal and Budgetary Management

The idea behind the Integrated Rural Development Programmes and the other programmes is that the two streams of fund - one from the Bank and the other from Government Agencies - should be combined. This would require a technique of fiscal and budgetary co-ordination of resources into a meaningful plan.

Institution Building

This programme would not succeed without sound functioning of institutions like primary co-operatives, land development banks, agricultural branches of Commercial Banks and regional rural banks, technical training institutions, and administrative agencies. Without sound institutional buildings, the programmes would not succeed.

Co-ordinations

Co-ordination is required between various agencies, schemes, functions through integrated development plans.

The introduction of these techniques of management in the implementation of the Integrated Rural Development Programmes would enable us to get over the shortcomings that have been noticed in the process of implementation.

6

Problems of Extension and Finance for Anti-Poverty Programmes

Administrative Extension

The approach to agricultural and rural development in India since we embarked upon the planned process of economic development in 1951 seems to have moved between two extremes. On one hand was the concentration on those who were likely to respond most and whose example was expected to provide leadership to the rest. On the other hand, was preferential treatment to those who needed and help most i.e. under-privileged including the small and marginal farmers, landless and the rural artisans.

We began in 1951 with the establishment of a network of agricultural extension but soon under the compulsive requirements of the immediate and significant increase in food production and following the report of the Ford Foundation team on Food Crisis in India, the approach of *general extension* was abondoned in favour of intensive *agricultural district programmes* and to the new agricultural strategy based essentially on a technocratic approach. In the new context, the village level workers were expected to devote 80% of their time for agriculture. Moreover, they were expected to concentrate on progressive farmers who were to act as multipliers of change.

The same approach has been further strengthened under what is called 'T & V' system of agricultural extension which has been established under the World Bank Project over a large part of the country.

With concentration on agriculture and progressive farmers, the set-up of block development administration was dismantled. The Block Development Officer was left as a captain without a team.

When in the beginning of the seventies the anti poverty programmes were introduced, it had to be entrusted to the whittled down machinery of block development administration reinforced marginally by the staff of small farmers development agencies or marginal farmers and agricultural labour agencies which were later merged in district rural development administration.

This machinery seems to be inadequate to deal with extremely difficult problem of converting families below the poverty line into viable self reliant families. It does not seem to be adequately realised that to convert even a single poor family into a self reliant viable family is a Herculean task. It cannot be accomplished through the simple act of giving a loan or a subsidy to that family and expecting that a single loan or subsidy by itself would convert the poor family into a self reliant family on a permanent and endurable basis.

In fact the implication of extension services needed to convert a poor family into a self reliant family has been little understood or analysed. The task has to begin with the lifting of a hopelessly desperate poor family with not even a square meal a day into a psychology of confidence, to induce it to take up a productive activity which can provide a source of self reliant living, support the productive activity by linking it up with a larger productive enterprise which can provide the poor family support in terms of inputs, technical expertise, and marketing of output. This is an indispensable support needed by a poor family whether in the field of agriculture, dairy, fishery, sericulture, poultry or any other small industry.

What is, therefore, needed is to evolve *a new extension* machinery which will be a mixed task force consisting of technical specialists in the field of agriculture or allied activities, development workers, cooperative organisers, bankers, financiers, teachers and social welfare workers.

Finance for Anti Poverty Programmes

At present the finance is available in the shape of loans and subsidies or wages under programmes like integrated rural development and national rural employment programmes. More important is to ensure that the finance available under these schemes does reach the poor without leakages and further this finance so made available does have the necessary impact. It has been found that in the absence of adequate organisation, there have been leakages and intermediaries have taken away a large chunk of assistance meant for the poorer classes. What is required, therefore, is an honest administration and close supervision as well as some grass root organisation of the poor themselves and greater consciousness on their part. Also are needed the various inter-linkages which will ensure that productive effort of a single poor family is linked to a large and more organised effort which will take care of supply of inputs , technical supervision and marketing of output. Without such organised projects in which the poor are participants, it will be futile to expect a single poor family to make a permanent transition from deprivation to self reliance. In the programmes as now conceived, the approach is to give assistance to individuals families rather than making them partners into a higher and well organised project. The organisation can be provided by various functional cooperatives including labour construction cooperatives. Unfortunately these organisational and functional linkages which alone can give opportunities to the poor to participate in gainful production are not sufficiently taken care of.

What is required is, therefore, on the one side an extension services oriented to the poor and on the other side projects for productive organisation in which the poor are partners. Then alone will finance available under anti poverty programme enable a poor family to make a *permanent transition* across the poverty line towards the stage of self reliance.

7

Integrated Rural Development Programme: The Need for a New Approach

The Integrated Rural Development Programme was introduced as a major attempt to alleviate rural poverty. It sought to realise this objective by enabling the rural poor to acquire productive assets, from the assistance extended in the shape of loan and subsidy.

The programme has been criticised for its failure to achieve this objective. Very small fraction of the beneficiaries it has been pointed out, have been able to cross the poverty line. In the light of such appraisal, it was felt that such of the beneficiaries who could not cross the poverty line could be given a second loan. The programme was, therefore, modified during the 7th Five Year Plan to allow second loan to be given to those already assisted with the first loan.

It is not certain that even with the second loan the goal of crossing the poverty line would be accomplished. Let it be remembered that the goal is not just raising the income of the beneficiaries above threshold level; it is also to make it possible for the beneficiaries to remain there. It has to be a permanent shift above the poverty line eliminating the possibility of a lapse back to a position below the poverty line. The philosophy behind the programme is that the productive asset acquired under it would create a stream of income, year after year, which will raise and maintain the family above the poverty line. The poverty line for the 7th Five Year Plan has been defined at Rs. 6400 per family of 5 persons. Families below this level are categorized as poor, very poor, very very poor and destitutes.

The evaluation studies of the working of this scheme have shown that it would be unrealistic to assume that just because a loan has been given to a family to acquire a productive asset, it will necessarily go or remain above the poverty line. There are many snags. There are possibilities of leakages which have been pointed in several evaluation studies. The leakages may take many forms. The entire quantity of loan or subsidy may not reach the family or even if a productive asset is purported to have been acquired with the help of the loan in reality it might not be so, and as has been sarcastically pointed out, "the same buffalo may be going round".

But even if the question of leakages is kept aside there may still be other snags. For example the beneficiary assisted to obtain a buffalo may not be able to sell milk at a remunerative price, or the buffalo may die of some illness. Hence the need for a back-up support, in this case, in the shape of marketing, veterinary service and cattle insurance. Would an individual beneficiary be able to arrange or obtain such a back up support? If an individual family by itself is not able to do so then surely what is required is a *group approach.*

Manual of instructions and guidelines regarding IRDP do mention concepts like "group approach", "cluster approach", "project approach" or the "area development approach". But these concepts are not fully developed or explained to the field workers and the individual family orientation of the scheme continues. If it is beyond the capacity of individual family, by itself, to raise it above the poverty line, no doubt assisted by a loan or subsidy, then the individual approach of the scheme must surely be considered as it is a fatal flaw. Unless the individual approach of the scheme is replaced by a group approach the scheme is unlikely to meet its objective of raising the poor above the poverty line.

What do we mean by group approach? Assisting a group of beneficiaries with a loan and a subsidy to obtain assets does not constituted a group approach. What the group approach really requires are: (a) a collective or common enterprise in which each individual would participate and (b) an organisation to support such a common enterprise. Thus individual families given loans for obtaining buffaloes or milch cows become participants in a collective enterprise only when they are linked to a common dairy where the milk is regularly delivered. But to run a dairy there is need for an organisation. The organisation may be private, public or co-operative. A private dairy may no doubt provide marketing facility but there would be dichotomy between the poor who sell the milk and the capitalist owner of the dairy who buys milk, and with the unequal bargaining capacity of the two parties to the transaction, its terms are likely to tilt the benefit in favour of the capitalist dairy owner rather than the poor who deliver the milk. A public organisation like a Government dairy would not inherently have such a conflict of interest, but would provide little sense of participation to the poor. On the other hand, a co-operative dairy which is owned by members consisting of the poor families who are assisted under IRDP to obtain milch animals would not only provide the support of an organisation but would also give a sense of participation. Cooperative effort and organisation should, therefore, be an essential part of IRDP scheme. It has been rightly stated that co-operative is "the shield of the weak". If IRDP is a programme for the weak, then it should be in the nature of things that the programme organises the beneficiaries on cooperative lines.

The cluster approach also really falls in the pattern of group approach. There may be ten beneficiaries in a single village who may not constitute a viable group for the organisation of a cooperative dairy but such groups of ten in a cluster of villages can constitute a viable base for organisation of a cooperative dairy.

This also ties up with the project approach. The project is for a dairy, the organisation for the project is provided by a cooperative. A cluster of villages constitute the field of work for the cooperative dairy and groups of villagers in the cluster of villages constitute the membership base of the cooperative dairy.

Thus it is that the group, the cluster and the project approaches all become vital links in a chain of organisation which can provide collective strength and stability to individual families which are enabled not only to cross the poverty line but to remain there for all time to come. An area development approach is the culmination of the group approach, cluster approach and the project approach. A plan for an area may consist of a number of projects, such as dairy development, organisation of rural transport, fishery development, horticulture development, basket making, garment making etc.

IRDP will achieve its objective only if it provides this kind of collective orientation which is outlined above.

8

Communication and Rural Development - I

Development is above all a human process and not just a mechanical or technological change. Development does not mean the construction of physical structures however imposing, installation of machines however complicated or adoption of latest technology however sophisticated. In the ultimate analysis, it is the development of people. Indeed, structures, machines and technology would not serve their purpose if the human beings are under-developed and hence are handicapped in utilising these as a means of development.

Development of the people implies development of the awareness of their surroundings, understanding of their problems, identification by them of opportunities available for a better life and a capacity to work out what needs to be done and formulate programmes to solve problems and fulfil their needs, goals and aspirations. If development of the people has to be accomplished in the manner indicated above, what is required is education of an entire people for a better living. This is of paramount importance not only in the so-called developing countries but also in the developed countries. No where did I realise more strikingly than in the course of my sojourn to one of the most developed countries of the West, namely, Sweden, which has more comprehensive programme of adult education. In the course of my visits to "Breve Scolan" the school of adult education in Sweden – I realised that what Sweden is doing is a continuous process of education and re-education of its adult population in order to update their knowledge, skill and outlook which would make them fit into a continuously changing and dynamic socio-economic and technological environment. When we are in the midst of knowledge explosion all around us, a nation cannot keep pace with the changing world unless its entire population is brought uptodate through a comprehensive programme of adult education.

No where is the need for this is more imperative than in the field of rural development. That is why when the programme of community development was initiated in 1953, high priority was given to social education amongst men, women and youth and to agricultural extension as a basis of community action in the field of not only agriculture but all other aspects of rural life. Taking into account the importance of agricultural extension and social education, all development workers in the community development blocks including village level extension officers were educated in the techniques of extension and community work. Extension was a part of the two years course for village level workers, as well as shorter duration courses for other extension officers. Extension education institutions and social education training centres were specially established for the purpose. The underlying idea was that development programmes must go hand-in-hand with community education if the development programmes were to succeed. In recognition of the important role of social education, every Block Development Office had an Information Centre where through Charts, Models and Graphs the rural people visiting the Block Office were educated in new techniques and ways of living.

In more recent years in the field of rural development more emphasis has come to be placed on the hardware of physical programmes and financial expenditure as compared with the education of the community. The communicator must work hand-in-hand with the development worker. The development worker knows what needs to be communicated, but perhaps not how. The Communicator is an expert in how to communicate, but does not know what. The techniques and programmes to be communicated form part of what is called 'development' and is the stock in trade of the development work. What is, therefore, required is a communication between the communicator and the development worker before both could be effective.

Development is a micro-process whereas mass media of communication involve certain amount of centralisation. What is required, therefore, is, decentralisation and localisation of the media of mass communication, whether radio or television. So varied are the socio-economic and agro-climatic conditions that centrally conceived and designed programmes are bound to be irrelevant unless they are completely transformed to meet the local situation. We have to look upon communication policy as an integral part of the development policy. For every development programme there has to be a communication component. It is only when communication and development come near to each other that both have a chance of success.

9

Communication and Rural Development—II

Implications and Rationale of Integrated Rural Development

Integrated rural development implies development of all sectors of the rural economy and all sections of the rural society.

The rationale of development of all sectors of the rural economy is that they are inextricably inter-linked with each other. Thus, agriculture is linked with allied activities like dairy, poultry, fishery and piggery, sericulture, sheep-farming, forestry etc. and with rural industry. Agriculture itself covers a vast field and has various aspects. Development of irrigation, rural electrification, plant protection, distribution of improved seeds, fertilizers and pesticides, agricultural extension, agricultural credit and investment, agricultural storage, marketing and processing, transport for movement of agricultural commodities, health, education and sanitation in rural areas, are so many aspects which are inter-linked with each other. Integrated rural development connotes suitable programmes in all these fields.

The rationale for development covering all sections of the rural society is that if modernisation of agriculture and increasing agricultural productivity and prosperity is confined to the larger land-holders, then small and marginal farmers and agricultural labourers will not be the beneficiaries of the green revolution and would provide a potential for a red revolution. It would lead to social tension and conflict. That is why special programmes like small farmers development agency (SFDA), marginal farmers and agricultural labour agencies (MFAL), drought, prone areas programmes (DPAP), rural works programme (RWP) and Antyodaya programmes have been designed to deal with the less privileged sections of the rural society.

Comprehensive Programme of Rural Communication Needed for Integrated Rural Development

A comprehensive programme of rural communication is required to deal with rural programmes covering all sectors of the rural economy and all sections of the rural society. The content, means and methods and techniques and agencies of such rural communication programme need to be discussed.

The rural development programmes in India have been going on since 1952 when the National Extension Service and Community Development Programmes were initiated. They were followed by various specialised programmes of rural development like IADP, DPAP, SFDA, MFAL, IRD, etc. For reaching these programmes to the remotest corners of this vast country, a number of techniques were employed with different degrees of success. They could be listed as follows:-

(1) Visits to villages, organisation of demonstrations on farms, village meetings and seminars.

(2) Distribution of publicity material like posters and leaflets.

(3) Use of mass media of communication like radio and television; special mention may be made of the radio rural forum as also Instructional Television Experiment.

(4) Training programmes for farmers and rural leaders including village women and youth at the training centres.

(5) Exhibitions in the villages at rural training institutions and agricultural universities.

(6) Mobilisation of rural institutions like Mahila Mandals, Yuvak Mandals, Cooperative Institutions and Panchayati Raj Institutions.

These different methods and techniques of rural communication can be employed singly or together. Thus, at the village meetings, demonstrations, posters and exhibitions could be organised. Leaflets can be used as training material at the training courses given by the training institutions. The youth organisation can provide radio rural forum or a listening group.

The techniques also may be used in a sequence of communication. Thus, a village meeting or a demonstration could be used to pick up potential leaders. They can then by brought together for a training programme and then may be followed up in the villages through village visits, counselling and organisation of radio listening groups or television viewers groups.

The Agents of Communication

In the beginning, the communication with the rural people has to be made by the village workers. They may be either multi-purpose workers or single purpose workers like the agricultural demonstrators or the health or family planning workers. They have to be supported and surprised by the supervisory personnel at the Block and District level. The effectiveness and impact of communication, however, depends ultimately on the quality of the field or village personnel. They are the agents of change and hence also the agents of communication. They have, therefore, to be trained in the art and techniques of communication. The extension training in the country has been mainly organised with a view to impart skills in communication.

It has to be remembered that the radio, television or the printed word may reach the better-off farmers but not the small farmers, marginal farmers and agricultural labourers. Programmes of the SFDA, MFAL, IDP or Works Programme have to reach the illiterate people and people without access to the mass media. New institutions like commercial banks and the regional rural banks have introduced special assistance for these havenots under the Differential Interest Scheme. If these new programmes have to reach the havenots, reliance cannot simply be placed on the radio, television or distribution of printed liberature. Village visits and even door-to-door visits are required by the rural workers. Hence the importance of intensive work in rural areas by the field workers; mass media of communication or libraries are still not a substitute for intensive rural development work in the developing countries.

Part - III

POLICY AND PLANNING

10

Agricultural Policy: Industry Status not Feasible

The government of India constituted a high-powered committee on agricultural policy and programmes. The committee was required to examine the desirability and feasibility of according the status of industry to agriculture. While setting up the committee the government had observed that though there had been an Industrial Policy Resolution, there was no similar agricultural policy resolution. The agricultural policy resolution was placed before the Parliament for its consideration and approval.

Let it be stated at the outset that there cannot be an agricultural policy resolution analogous to the industrial policy resolution. The industrial policy resolutions of 1948 and 1956 were essentially concerned with the demarcation of industrial activity between the public and the private sectors. The question of such demarcation does not arise in respect of agriculture which is wholly in the private sector. The public activity extends only to infrastructural support in the shape of research and extension, supply of input and institutional credit, crop insurance and marketing and processing.

Nor is it easy to see any point in according the status of industry to agriculture except to large plantations of tea, coffee and spices which already partake of the nature of industry. For the rest, agriculture differs so vastly from industry and has so many peculiarities that it is these which need to be taken into account in formulating a policy so as to deal with special problems of agriculture. Surely those who are anxious to accord the status of industry to agriculture do not want them to be overlooked.

The special problems of agriculture which arise out of its peculiar nature are well known. There would have been no need to recapitulate them but for the fact that some insist that agriculture should be treated as industry. Firstly, agriculture is exposed to the vagaries of nature. Substantial addition to irrigation has no doubt given Indian agriculture a measure of security. But this has not entirely overcome its vulnerability. Secondly, agricultural operations are seasonal in nature unlike industrial operations which are carried out repetitively throughout the year. Though modern technology has made some dent on the season-bound nature of agriculture, by and large agriculture cannot succeed without adhering to seasonal requirements whether of tillage or supply of inputs especially water.

This creates special problems of storage and marketing. Agricultural produce has to be carried over time and space. In today's market economy these require special institutional arrangements. From the point of view of the agriculturist, a particularly disagreeable feature of agricultural marketing is the wide spread between the producer's price and the consumer's price. Prices of agricultural produce crash after the harvest and rise during the lean period.

Thirdly unlike modern industry with productive activity concentrated in the factories, agricultural activity is carried out by millions of farmers in small holdings scattered all over the country.

These are some of the special features and problems of agriculture which distinguish it from industry. The agricultural policy has to address itself to these special problems of agriculture.

Agricultural policy in independent India has evolved over the years in a haphazard manner. For the first twenty years the focus was on building up the institutional and administrative infrastructure in the rural areas. In 1952, a beginning was made with the process of setting up, in a phased manner, a network of agricultural extension and community development agencies throughout the length and breadth of the country. Then in 195 and later to encourage people's participation in development programme and three tier structure of Panchayati raj institutions was set up at distric block and village levels. To provide agricultural credit and input lik fertilisers and facilitate marketing of agricultural produce, cooperativ credit, marketing and processing institutions were established from villag to national levels. To put an end to the exploitative land tenure structure an provide incentive to the tillers, land reform measures were introduced They contained provisions to eliminate absentee zamindari, to provid security of tenure and fairness of rent to the tenant, to make tiller the owne and to impose ceilings. They were implemented with different degree c success in different parts of the country.

The availability of the hybrid varieties of wheat, thanks to Nob

Laureate Norman Borlough, and the Taichung. Tainan varieties of rice, thanks to the IRRI, made possible the 'Green Revolution' in Punjab, Haryana and Western U. P. The new policy supported by the institutional structure created in the fifties led to rapid increase in food (especially wheat) production.

The new technology was described as neutral to the size of holding. Yet it was found that only the well to do farmers could muster the additional resources needed for hybrid seeds and the needed inputs like fertilisers, pesticides and water. A large proportion of small and the marginal farmers remained unaffected.

Hence in the seventies programmes like IRDP which focussed on subsidiary occupations were introduced for them and the employment programme for the landless to enable them to cross the poverty line. However it was observed that leakage and absence of forward and backward linkage and backup support prevented commensurate return from substantial funds spent on these schemes.

It is against this background that the government should aim at evolving a comprehensive and integrated agricultural policy which takes into account the institutional technological as well as economic aspects, the production aspects as well as the distributional. The main elements of this policy should consist of the following:

(1) Extension of the green revolution to areas and crops left out so far - specially the eastern states and crops like oil seeds, pulses and minor millets; and to small and marginal farmer who should be organised on a group and communitarian basis to enable them to avail of the new technology.

(2) Optimum return from irrigation - Despite command area development programme, there is still a gap between creation of irrigation potential and its utilisation. Moreover, extravagant use of water in the absence of proper arrangements for regulated consumption and enforcement of crop localisation plan has led to water logging and returns from irrigation. Techniques like Warabandi, organisations like Pani Panchayats, and fiscal measured like proper water rates should be universally introduced for optimum use of irrigation facilities.

(3) Dry land and drought prone areas have not received adequate attention so far due to excessive preoccupation with irrigation in the past. Extensive programmes for soil and water conservation, horticulture and afforestation should be undertaken in these areas on the lines of programmes undertaken with popular effort in Ralegan Ralegansiddhi village in Ahmednagar district in Maharashtra.

(4) Cooperative marketing is the weakest link in the cooperative system requiring costly state intervention as in the case of marketing of onions. Absence of adequate fruit processing facilities leads to almost 25 per cent of fruit going to waste. A big effort is needed for marketing of individual crops on cooperative lines. The way is shown by successful cooperative marketing and processing of milk in Gujarat.

If we compare our productivity of crop per acre compared with that in some other countries, it is obvious that we have a long way to go and our scientists, technologists, extension workers and agricultural administrators cannot rest on past laurels. It is good to remember that while China produces 391 million tonnes of food on 110 million hectares of land, we produce, despite the success of the Green Revolution, 180 million tonnes of food on 140 million hectares of land.

11

Agricultural Policy, Planning and Administration

Agriculture has always been accorded an important place in Indian planning. This is easy to understand because Indian economy has been predominantly agricultural. It was so when we embarked on planning in 1951 and even now it continues to be so. 75 per cent of the population has been and continues to be engaged in agriculture. However, the share of agriculture in the gross national product, over the plan period has gone down from about 70 to 40 per cent.

The importance of agriculture in the Indian economy stems from the fact that it provides food for the survival of the population and raw material for industrial growth. Also increasing production of food and other agricultural crops would enable the economy to reduce imports and to stimulate exports. The goal of Indian planning has, therefore, been food self-sufficiency and even generation of surplus for export. This was not possible in the early years of planning and India had to depend on PL 480 for the import of American foodgrains and had literally to live from ship to mouth. In more recent years, thanks to the green revolution in Punjab and Haryana, dependence on imports has been less but in drought years, some imports have become unavoidable.

It one has to assess the importance of agriculture in our planning, one way to do it is to take note of the allocation for agriculture in the Five-Year Plans. The table below gives the position over the successive Five-Year Plans.

The agricultural development policies and programmes formulated since the inception of planning could be considered under the following three heads:

Public Sector Outlay for Agricultural Sector

	First Plan (1951-56)	Second Plan (1956-61)	Third Plan (1961-66)	Fourth Plan (1969-74)	Fifth Plan (1974-79)	Sixth Plan (1980-85)	Seventh Plan (1986-90)	Annual Plan (1990-91)	Eighth Plan (1992-97)
Agricultural Sector	238	275	591	2059	3356	6440	10524	3803	12618
All Sectors	2347	4800	8099	15902	39322	97500	180000	64717	247865

Source: Eighth Five Year Plan Document.

(1) Technocratic Support

(2) Social Mobilisation

(3) Economic Incentives

Technocratic Support

Since agricultural productivity in India has been very low because of its primitive technology and since after the mid-sixties, it became obvious that additional land could no longer be brought under cultivation, it became most important to concentrate on raising productivity through technological advancement. The various elements of the technological approach were the following:

(1) Developing technological breakthrough in agricultural research stations and laboratories.

(2) Extending the findings of research to individual family farms.

(3) Supplying agricultural inputs and services to the farmers and providing investment resources.

For the performance of these technological tasks, it became necessary to refashion agricultural administrative system in the country.

Research

In the field of research, Indian Council of Agricultural Research was constituted into an autonomous organisation headed by the Director General and a large number of research institutions working in different fields of agriculture were brought under its auspices and a coordinated programme of agricultural research was undertaken on a nationwide basis. At the state level, a number of agricultural universities were established all over the country. Each of the agricultural universities was also expected to set up an extension wing.

Extension

From 1952 onwards, the National Extension Service was established throughout the country. It consisted of village level workers each in charge of about ten villages supported by agricultural extension officers at the block level and the subject matter specialists at the district and higher levels.

Agricultural extension was a new concept in Indian administration. As the process of agricultural development gathered momentum, it was realised that agricultural extension needs to be intensified. Therefore on the basis of the recommendations of the Ford Foundation Team on "Indian Food Crisis and how to deal with it" (1959), a number of intensive agricultural districts and intensive agricultural areas were established all over the country. In these selected districts agricultural extension was intensified and technical personnel strengthened.

In the early years agricultural extension was combined with community development and was an integral part of block administration. In later years as the technological approach was emphasised to a greater extent, village level workers who were originally multi-purpose workers were asked following the recommendation of Ram Subhag Singh Committee Report on Agriculture to devote 80 pr cent of their time for agriculture. Many agricultural officers were appointed as Block Development Officers and an attempt was made to set up agricultural administration as a single line of command and obedience.

In more later years T & V approach was adopted in agricultural extension. While this has worked well in some areas, in other areas complaints have been made that T & V system is isolated from other important elements of development and agricultural administration. This point needs to be examined in the light of experience.

Supply of Inputs

Intensive technological approach was embodied in the 'new strategy of agriculture' adopted in 1967. It was possible to introduce the new strategy because of developments of hybrid and high yielding variety of seeds - Maxican variety of wheat, Taichung, Tainan, IR 8 and IR 20 varieties of rice, CHS varieties of Jawar, Varalakshmi long staple cotton, Ganga maize, Spanish groundnuts.

Chemical Fertilisers: Chemical fertiliser consumption in Indian agriculture in early years after independence was a fev' thousand tons. Today it is well above 13 million tons.

The supply of these new varieties of seeds and chemical fertilisers requires establishment of an extensive delivery system.

Hybrid & HYV Seeds: For the production and supply of seeds, it was contemplated that while breeder and foundation seeds would be produced on the state farms, their multiplication in the shape of certified seeds will be taken up by private seed farms. There was a further question of supply of certified seeds to the large number of farmers. Here the co-operative network of marketing societies and credit societies was pressed into use. The same organisation was also required for the supply of fertilisers as well as improved implements. At the national level, National Cooperative Development Corporation established in 1962 provided an intensive support to the cooperative system for constructing godowns and handling increasing volume of fertiliser business.

To supplement the co-operative system, agro-industry corporations were also established.

The delivery system consisting of various institutional agencies should be considered to be an integral part of agricultural administration. A number of agencies here come into picture - co-operative agencies at the village, tehsil, state and national levels, agro-industry corporations and their branch offices as well as the departments of agriculture and co-operation. One of the important factors in efficiency of agriculture administration in the country is the co-ordinated and integrated functioning of the various departments, corporations and co-operatives at different levels. Both vertical and horizontal co-ordination is very necessary.

Irrigation: Hybrid seeds and chemical fertilisers could be effective only with the necessary supply of water. Irrigation is, therefore, an extremely important part of agricultural development - minor, medium and major irrigation, surface and ground irrigation. A large number of major irrigation projects across important rivers were constructed which made sizeable addition to irrigation potential. However, it was soon realised that it was one thing to create irrigation potential but quite another to use irrigation potential for increased agricultural production. The latter requires a series of activities like water conveyance, land levelling, localisation of crops on the basis of soil survey, drainage, agricultural extension and other infrastructure facilities. A decision was therefore taken to establish systematically command area development projects and authorities. This is yet another new aspect of agricultural administration. To what extent have the command area development authorities fulfilled their purpose, needs to be discussed.

So far as the ground water irrigation is concerned, it depends on the enterprise of individual farmers, supported by financial assistance. Here the Land Development Banks were developed as the machinery of extending loans to individual farmers for digging wells and fitting them with pumps. The Agricultural Refinance Corporation (later National Bank for Agriculture & Rural Development) in turn assisted by the International Development Association of the World Bank was instrumental in providing loans to farmers for the purpose.

Energisation of wells and lift irrigation projects required a large programme of rural electrification. For supporting this was established Rural Electrification Corporation.

Irrigation development requires close coordination between administrators, engineers, agricultural officers and co-operative departments and institutions.

Credit : Agricultural credit has to provide support for agricultural development. The Co-operative Land Development Banks provide long-term finance for agricultural investment. Short-term and medium-term finance for seeds, fertilisers, impliments and manure is provided by a whole network of primary credit societies supported by district co-operative central banks and the State Co-operative Banks, Reserve Bank of India and now NABARD provide support from the top.

Since it was felt that in spite of efforts of the co-operative institutions, there would nevertheless be an agriculture credit gap, the commercial banks after nationalisation were expected to provide agricultural finance in a big way to supplement the co-operative credit. These banks opened rural agricultural branches. A new type of banking system came with the establishment of the gramin banks or the regional rural banks. The banks were expected to coordinate with each other through district credit plans and the institution of the lead bank.

Thus the picture of agricultural administration today is extremely complex and requires full participation and coordinated operation of a large number of different types of institutions and agencies. Sometime coordination between them is missing. Hence the importance of integrated plans for agricultural development at block, district and state levels.

Social Mobilisation

From the very beginning of the planning, there has been a distinction between technocratic approach and social mobilisation approach. The community development concept gave a great deal of importance to social mobilisation. The co-operatives were also agencies of mobilisation. To enhance social mobilisation Panchayati Raj institutions were established in 1959 onwards on the recommendations of Balwant Rai Mehta Study Team. The three-tier Panchayati Raj institutions were expected to evoke popular enthusiasm in programmes of agricultural development. It was particularly expected that these rural institutions would provide opportunities to the disadvantaged sections of the rural community. This did not always happen and the co-operative and Panchayati Raj institutions were accused of being dominated by larger farmers. A deliberate reorientation was, therefore, sought to be given to the co-operative institutions in favour of small and marginal farmers and even the landless. Guidelines were laid down for specific allocation of credit and inputs in favour of the weaker sections. Farmer Service Societies (FSS) were introduced in order to give a special place to small and marginal farmers in the management of societies. Small and marginal farmers and agricultural labour agencies were established to provide loans to the small and marginal members to become members of co-operatives and subsidies were made available for lending to those groups. Later the programme of small and marginal farmers were merged into a programme of integrated rural development under which poorest 600 families in every block are assisted to bring them above the poverty line every year. Thus in the country as a whole this programme was designed to help about 15 million farming during Sixth Plan period.

The national rural employment programme was meant for the landless to provide them employment in the shape of physical labour. However, even here if the work done could create durable agricultural assets, they could also contribute to increased agricultural production.

Land reforms were also expected to eliminate absentee landlordism and give security of tenure to the actual cultivator. Some states also introduced land reforms for making the actual cultivator the owner of the land. It was also envisaged that land ceiling would be enforced and surplus land would be available for distribution among the landless. However, the land reform legislation was evaded and the reforms did not meet with all the objectives. Even today the dichotomy between social mobilisation approach and purely technical approach continues. Purely technical approach concentrates on those farms and areas which can give maximum return. The social mobilisation approach on the other hand, emphasises the distribution aspect and in any case believes that unless large majority of the marginal and small farmers are mobilised, agricultural development would not take place.

Economic Incentives

Technical support, social mobilisation and economic incentives constitute the pillars of the agricultural triad. Unless incentives are provided in the form of higher prices, for agricultural commodities, farmers would not produce. Hence the importance of remunerative prices. Agricultural prices often fall immediately after the harvest. Even otherwise, without sustained incentive of higher prices, sustained increase in agricultural production would not take place. The Agricultural Prices Commission was therefore established to recommend minimum agricultural prices. In respect of several commodities in short supply like pulses and oil seeds, the open market prices have always been much higher than the minimum prices recommended by the Agricultural Price Commission. But in respect of foodgrains like wheat and rice, the support prices have definitely proved attractive. The Food Corporation of India and the Cotton Corporation were established to purchase foodgrains at the stipulated prices.

However, the agricultural price policy has not only to provide remunerative price to the producer, it has also to provide foodgrains at reasonable prices to the consumer belonging to the weaker sections of the society both in rural and urban areas. Hence the concept of the public distribution system supported by the buffer stocks of the Food Corporation of India. The operation of the Food Corporation of India has imparted a measure of stability to the agricultural and consumer economy. The Cooperatives have played a role as procurement agencies of the Food Corporation of India and as a machinery for retail distribution to the consumers. For commodities not covered by these corporations like fruits, vegetables, potato, onion, ginger or forest produce, cooperatives linked at various levels have been playing a role in providing remunerative prices to the producers.

Thus agricultural administration is characterised by multiplicity of programmes, policies and agencies. Their success depends on high level of efficiency of each organisation and a high degree of coordination between all of them.

12

Agricultural Marketing

In 1973 I wrote an article in which I said "If agricultural production was India's concern in the sixties, agricultural marketing promises to be the major concern of the seventies. The Green Revolution, which was the name given to the successful efforts on the front of agricultural production, has already shown that the "cornucopia" of abundance can also open the pandora's box of marketing problems. Indeed, agricultural marketing could be called the second generation problem of the Green Revolution. While the gains of the Green Revolution will have to be consolidated, expanded and diversified to all regions and in respect of all crops, there have already been sufficient warnings that unless we are able to make adequate arrangements for marketing, our agricultural production efforts will themselves receive a set back causing widespread frustration among the agricultural producers".

Agricultural Marketing — All Important

These predictions have come true. The Green Revolution has spread to other parts of the country beyond Punjab, Haryana and West Uttar Pradesh, and crops other than wheat. Production of fruits, flowers, milk and eggs has substantially increased in different parts of the country. Sometime back, there was a news in Bombay newspapers that there was such a surplus of milk in Maharashtra that it had to be thrown away into the sea. Whatever be the truth about this news item, it illustrates that marketing of agricultural products has become all important. Agricultural has made the transition from a way of life, as subsistence agriculture was, to a commercial proposition and is throwing up surpluses at national, regional and local levels which are to be properly handled through adequate marketing arrangements.

Era of Liberalisation

While I had rightly predicated that problems of agricultural marketing would emerge as the most important problem in the years to come, I could not have anticipated the change that was to take place in the macro economic scene of our country in the nineties. In the seventies, we still followed the Nehruvian model of economic development. That model was based upon the concept of planning of economic activities rather than leaving them to the vicissitudes of the market forces. It envisaged the direction of economic forces through State intervention and dominant position of the public sector in the national economy. That model now seems to have been almost totally abandoned. This change in macro economic policy has been caused by various factors including the radical change in world economic scenario, the culmination of which was the recent adoption of the new world trade arrangements known as Dunkel proposals. These have now been adopted as a general agreement on tarrif and trade. These new arrangements envisage open economies permitting free flow of goods and services, and inclusion of intellectual properties amongst commercially traded articles covered by the general agreement.

In the new policy framework that we have now adopted, planning has been replaced by marketisation, public sector by privatisation (beginning with disinvestment of State share in public enterprises), control and command economy by liberalisation and deregulation and autarky by globalisation. The new model aims at ushering in a competitive economy in the country. In the absence of competition in the past, thanks to customs barriers to promote import substitution, Indian economy had become a high cost economy based on the outmoded technology. Indian goods could not compete in the world market. Exports lagged behind imports thereby creating an adverse balance of payments position putting strain on foreign exchanges position. Subsidies proved to be artificial cruches of economic activity not justified in terms of profit and loss calculus of the market economy. The public enterprises had to be propped up with budgetary support. Private enterprises started relying on licences and permits. Vested interests grew depending more on political manipulations and influence rather than on competitive performance. The policy makers came to a conclusion that non-competitive goods stand nowhere in the modern world.

No Special Place for Cooperation in the New Set-up

The logic of the new policy would apply to all forms of economic enterprises including the cooperative enterprises. In the early years after independence, cooperatives were given a special place in the economy. Jawaharlal Nehru fully supported the cooperatives. He wanted to "convulse India with cooperation". He envisaged for India a mixed economy consisting of public, private and cooperative sectors. But it was the cooperative sector which was given a special position on ideological grounds. Cooperatives, it was felt, combined the values of freedom and initiative of private enterprises and social concern and accountability of the public enterprises. He had also high hopes about the public enterprises and wished them to hold the commanding heights of the economy. Later years were to show that his hopes were not fully justified.

In the new dispensation, cooperatives are unlikely to be given the role that was accorded to them in the early years. Talking of the specific field of agricultural marketing, the state policy was to intervene in the market mechanism to-undertake price support operations, and protect the farmers and consumers from the vicissitudes of the market. State marketing intervention agencies like Food, Cotton and Jute Corporations of India were brought into existence. The cooperatives were often called upon to join hands with these State agencies to undertake agricultural marketing. Cooperatives were also considered agencies readily available to Government in times of crisis. Thus Union Government called on NAFED to purchase onions in the Nasik market when the prices of onions fell. When similar crisis situation arose in case of commodities like ginger, jute, etc., cooperatives were called upon by the State to undertake marketing operations. Apart from such ad hoc operations, permanent schemes were also devised like the monopoly procurement of cotton in Maharashtra which was entrusted to cooperatives. As a result of this, cooperatives came to be looked upon as part of the Governmental system.

Needed a New Approach

This approach will have to undergo a total transformation in the context of the new economic policy. Cooperative enterprises will have to play their role in the field of agricultural marketing not as agents of the State but on their own as autonomous marketing agencies and business institutions. The implications of the new approach have to be fully worked out by the cooperative marketing system.

The cooperatives will also have to shed functions often thrust on them by the State to act on behalf of consumers of agricultural products or as importers of consumer goods like dates which are not part of their work as genuine agricultural cooperatives.

Autonomous Role —Not Agency Role

It is necessary to clearly distinguish the "autonomous role" of cooperatives in the field of agricultural marketing from the "agency role" of the past.

In the agency role risk-taking was assumed by Government; when NAFED undertook the purchase of onions, Government bore the risk and bore the financial loss incurred by NAFED through subsidy. Government is unlikely to bear the loss in future because the new policy aims at elimination of subsidies. The cooperatives would be expected to undertake agricultural marketing bearing the risk attendant to these operations.

New Colour to Cooperative Agricultural Marketing

This puts an altogether new colour to the character of cooperative agricultural marketing operations. The cooperatives cannot undertake agricultural marketing operations in an ad hoc manner or in crisis situation at the behest of the State. In the new context, cooperatives as autonomous marketing organisations will have to look at the marketing scenario on their own and in the interest of the protection of interest of their members viz. farmers, chalk out their new role. They will have to respond to marketing opportunities in such a manner as will enable them to undertake viable marketing operations, justified in terms of competitive business. Can the cooperatives do so without the support of the State?

The new economic policy looks at the agricultural sector as a dynamic source for exports. Indian agriculture, therefore, will have to turn global.

In the new environment, cooperative institutions engaged in agricultural marketing will have to establish their competitiveness not only within the economy, but also on a global scale.

In the past, exports were often canalised through the State or cooperative agencies. Government policy now is to make a clean sweep of the concept of canalised exports. Cooperatives will have to compete with private export agencies for their share of export market.

Prepare for Competitive Marketing

Cooperatives engaged in agricultural marketing will have to therefore do basic thinking to prepare themselves for successful and effective agricultural marketing in the context of this new policy and environment.

The basic goal is to build up competitive capabilities. This would require much more effective organisation, much better planning and much more systematic operations. It might well need a major change in the cooperative marketing institutions. The cooperative marketing sector would have to undertake this task as early as possible.

Market Survey

The first task will be for the cooperatives to take note of the major features of the diversification of marketing today and in the years to come. The cooperatives would have to undertake a survey of the total agricultural scene to identify the possibilities of export of agricultural commodities, and the internal movement of agricultural commodities from one State to another and finally, within the state. In the light of information from such survey, they will have to work out these marketing operations.

The task is complex and covers a wide range of agricultural commodities traded in the country including foodgrains, oilseeds, pulses, jute, cotton, spices, plantation crops like rubber, arecanut, coconut and copra, tea, coffee, cocoa, spices and perishable commodities like vegetables, fruits, eggs and dairy products.

Long Run Scenario

This is essentially a long term scenario here knee jerks decisions to manage a crisis situation will be inappropriate. The cooperatives will have to build up their organisations and personnel in the context of long term scenario. This does not, of course, mean that cooperators should overlook the seasonal character of agricultural operations. Agriculture is still dependent on monsoons though for the last six years, India was fortunate to have good monsoons. Besides technological and infrastructural progress has made it possible for Indian agriculture to be less vulnerable to the vaguaries of nature. Cooperatives will have to adjust marketing operations to short term seasonal changes; but that has to be done as a part of a long term strategy.

Information Service

For working out such long term strategy of agricultural marketing, cooperatives should have at their disposal comprehensive information service at various levels. The cooperatives at all levels must have at their disposal upto date management information system regarding the trends of production and prices in the domestic and world market. The initiative will have to be taken by the State and National Cooperative organisations to set up such efficient information network. We are today living in an "information age" ushered in by fantastic development of computer technology. Cooperatives should fully avail of this so that market intelligence and information is instantly shared by cooperatives at all level. In the light of that information, marketing operations will have to be planned by cooperatives at all levels. The computerised database should provide timely and accurate information for decision making at all levels including the farmer's level.

Organisation

The cooperatives are organised in a three tier pyramid consiting of the primary agricultural cooperatives at the tehsil level, the State cooperative Marketing Federations at the State level and the NAFED at the national level. It would be necessary to make the cooperative marketing institutions at all the three level function in an effective, cohesive and organised manner. At present, there are far too many organisational weaknesses, far too little integration of activities of cooperatives at various levels and consequent inability to work in a coherant and effective manner. The weakness is considerable at a primary level where out of 3000 cooperative enterprises, a large number do not take cooperative marketing operations. The linkages between the national, State and primary levels should be strengthened. All of them should work in a coordinated manner in order to provide strength to the farmers to stand in the competitive market, by improving their holding capacity and bargaining strength.

Financial Management

Agricultural marketing operations by cooperatives must be undertaken in such a manner that the organisations do not incur losses. The State in future will not come forward to make good the losses. Surpluses alone can build the capital that is required for expansion of marketing business. But that does not mean that the goal of agricultural marketing cooperatives is simply profit maximisation. John Wood, Commercial Consul at US Consulate in Bombay recently said in an exclusive session with the Economic Times "The US is not against Cooperatives. But they should be run with profit motive in mind. Only then can they compete in a free market". This appears to be a mistaken view. For competitive performance in a free market, cooperatives do not have to lose their identity nor do they have to be indistinguishable from private enterprise. "Not charity, not profit but service" should continue to be the goal of cooperatives. The service to the member should be in terms of maximum benefit to the members. They must get remunerative price for their products. But this does not mean that cooperative should incur losses or should not build up surpluses or operations should not be carried on in a most cost effective and efficient manner. That is necessary for cooperatives to survive and grow and cooperatives should evolve their own norms of highest business efficacy.

Infrastructural Development

Effective agricultural marketing operations are not possible without infrastructural support. Storage and transport facilities are required. Apart from cooperative godowns, storage facilities are provided by Food Corporation of India, and the Ware House Corporation. These could be availed of by cooperatives. As regards transport, the cooperatives have to depend more on railways or private truck transport. Cooperative transporting business have yet to come into existence in a substantial manner. Specially manufactured vans are necessary for transporting fruits, vegetables, milk and poultry products for transporting them over long distances. Specialised storage facilities will be required for storing perishable commodities like fruits, potato, onion, flavour milk etc. Storage and transport facilities will have to be developed and modernised. Agricultural marketing operations are carried out in the regulated markets. There are more than 6000 wholesale assembling markets and 22000 primary rural periodic markets. Many of them are devoid of basic infrastructure like auction platforms, cart packs, water facilities, rest houses, metalled roads, etc. The markets should also have all the technical service for weighting and grading of commodities. False weight and measurement have to be completely eliminated. Also grading services should be provided in an adequate measure. At present, few commodities have come in the orbit of grading standardisation. In the modern sophisticated market, goods which are not properly graded according to size and quality will not be acceptable to the consumer. Grading operations will have to be provided on scientific lines. Facilities for strictest quality testing will have to be provided since it is not easy to put the goods in the world market without fulfilling these tests.

It is also necessary to eliminate defects in the existing market system in the rural areas like use of defective weights, existence of a large number of intermediaries, and large deductions made from farmers who sell their produce. Regulated markets are run by the Regulated marketing committees. It is for them to remove defects and provide the facilities mentioned above. But cooperative marketing institutions should firmly establish themselves in these markets, provide a countervailing power to that of the omission agents and traders and play a leading role in the modernisation of the marketing facilities and eliminating market imperfections.

Another important aspect of modern marketing management are the use of modern marketing techniques for packaging and preservation of commodities. New and better types of packaging both for preservation of commodities and attracting the buyer have become necessary.

Quite a different approach would be needed for the development of organised rural markets in a tribal economy. Cooperatives would have to reach the remote interior areas to procure agricultural and minor forest produce from the tribal farmers.

Agricultural Processing

Marketing of goods can be facilitated by processing. In the wake of economic development, there is an increasing demand for processed agricultural products. There is also considerable potential in export market for them. There is a great demand for example, for processed fruits and vegetables. These facilities could be taken in the cooperative sector and there should be a nexus between cooperative processing enterprises and marketing cooperatives.

Cooperatives should Gear Themselves Up

Thus information service, infrastructural facilities and improved technical operations of marketing are key to the success in the field of cooperative marketing. The cooperative marketing organisations have to gear up themselves for these new tasks.

Efficient Personnel and Enlightened Farmer Members

The field of agricultural marketing is getting very sophisticated and agricultural cooperatives will have to employ qualified, trained and efficient personnel to undertake such operations. They should be well versed in economics, management and technological knowledge about various kinds of agricultural commodities. They should also have business acumen. But they should also be good cooperators and know the essentials of a cooperative enterprise and how they differ from those of private enterprise. Then alone would they be able to establish firm links between the growers and the cooperatives. Training should not be confined only to executives in the cooperatives. Even the farmer members should be provided training on various aspects of scientific marketing. This should form part of the programme of cooperative education.

Cooperative Marketing in New Agricultural Policy

Government of India has formulated its new agricultural policy. Agriculture has many dimensions. It is an interdisciplinary subject. The general statement of agricultural policy as formulated by the Government does refer to marketing. But this hardly does justice to the subject. It is necessary that the general statement of agricultural policy must be supplemented by detailed policy statement about each of the major aspects of which marketing is one of the most important. The ideas discussed here could find place in the policy statement on agricultural and cooperative marketing in the country. This is very necessary for the future of cooperative agricultural policy in the country.

13

Agricultural Census in India

Population census is a widely known operation. The census of agricultural holdings is not. The population census is connected with the counting of heads; the agricultural census is connected with the counting of agricultural holdings. A holding for the purpose of agriculture census is defined as "all land which is used wholly or partly for agriculture production and is operated as one technical unit by one person alone or with others without regard to the title, legal form, size or location". A technical unit has been defined as "that unit which is used under the same management and has the same means of production such as labour force, machinery and animals." The main objective of the agriculture census is to collect information about the number of operational holdings of different sizes, the area irrigated and the source of irrigation, number and area of holdings by tenure and area under different land uses and crops.

This information is of extremely great importance for agriculture planning at various levels - national, regional, block and individual farm levels. The agriculture census provides essential information for formulating correct policies and programmes relating to land reforms, supply of agricultural inputs and increase in agricultural production. Thus, for evolving a correct strategy for increasing agricultural production, we ought to know which types of farmers have adopted the high yielding variety programmes. In order to ensure that irrigation, agricultural inputs and credit are equitably available, it is essential to make a close study of the relationship between them and agricultural holdings.

Realising the importance of agricultural census in relation to the agriculture economy, countries like United States of America and Japan have been carrying out the quinquennial agricultural census. Thus, the United States of America started with decennial agricultural census as early as 1840 and switched over to the quinquennial census from 1920 as the demand for more frequent agricultural data became pressing. However, in India, the first agricultural census was undertaken only in the year 1970-71. It is not as though the need for agriculture census was not realised earlier. As far back as 1945, the Famine Enquiry Commission suggested that for every village, there should be a record of agricultural holdings. We should distinguish between various occupancy rights and adopt a basis of classification distinguishing between small, medium and large holdings. However, due to various reasons, these recommendations were not given effect to. In 1948, the Food and Agriculture Organisation requested India to participate in the World Agricultural Census Operation. A Technical Committee on Coordination of Agricultural Statistics was set up by the Ministry of Agriculture. The Committee recommended that the opportunity provided by the Food and Agriculture Organisation Census should be utilised for overhauling country's machinery for collection of agricultural statistics. Following this, the Government of India requested the National Sample Survey Organisation to undertake the survey of land holdings. The National Sample Survey brought out a number of reports from 1952 onwards. However, it was only in 1970 that Government of India decided, at the instance of Food and Agriculture Organisation, to participate in the World Census on Agriculture which envisaged the collection of data for all individual holdings. For States with comprehensive land records, the data was collected by retabulation method whereas for those without such comprehensive records, namely, West Bengal, Kerala and Orissa as well as what were that the Union Territories, namely, Manipur, Meghalaya, Arunachal Pradesh, Goa and Lakshadweep, etc. independent sample surveys were carried to provide information on all items.

The second census with agriculture year 1976-77 as reference period followed more or less the same approach. The census with 1980-81 as the reference year, is also more or less on the same lines. A special feature of the second and third census was the survey of agricultural inputs in addition to the main census of holdings.

The analysis of the results of the agriculture census operations provides significant information for planning and policy formulation. The following three tables give a comparative picture of the distribution of agricultural holding according to size :

Table I

Size Class	*No. of holdings (in million)*				*Percentage*			
	1970-71	*1976-77*	*1980-81*	*1985-86*	*1970-71*	*1976-77*	*1980-81*	*1985-86*
Marginal (Below 1 ha.)	36.20	44.53 (+23.0)	50.01	56.14	50.9	54.6	56.4	57.8
Small (Between 1-2 ha.)	13.43	14.70 (+9.5)	16.07	17.92	18.9	18.0	18.1	18.5
Semi-Medium (Between 2-4 ha.)	10.68	11.64 (+9.0)	12.45	13.25	15.0	14.3	14.0	13.6
Medium (Between 4-10 ha.)	7.93	8.21 (+3.4)	8.06	7.91	11.2	10.1	9.1	8.1
Large (10 ha. and above)	2.77	2.44 (–11.9)	2.16	1.91	4.0	3.0	2.4	2.0
Total	71.01	81.52 (+14.8)	88.75	97.13	100.0	100.00	100.00	100.00

Table II

Operated Area

Size/Class	1970-71 (Mil.hec.)	Percentage to total	1976-77 (Mil.hec.)	Percentage to total	1980-81 (Mil. hec.)	Percentage to total	1985-86 (Mil. hec.)	Percentage to total
Marginal (Below 1 ha.)	14.56	9.0	17.50	10.7	19.73	12.1	22.04	13.4
Small (Between 1-2 ha.)	19.28	11.9	20.86	12.8	23.16	14.1	25.70	15.6
Semi-Medium (Between 2-4 ha.)	30.00	18.5	32.36	19.8	34.64	21.2	36.66	22.3
Medium (Between 4-10 ha.)	48.24	29.7	49.60	30.4	48.54	29.6	47.14	28.6
Large (10 ha. and above)	50.06	30.9	42.82	26.3	37.70	23.0	33.00	20.1
Total	162.14	100.0	163.14	100.0	163.77	100.0	164.54	100.0

Table III

Size/Class	Average size of operational holding				
	1970-71	1976-77	Percentage decrease in 1976-77 over 1970-71	1980–81	1985–86
Marginal (Below 1 ha.)	0.40	0.39	2.50	0.39	0.39
Small (Between 1-2 ha.)	1.44	1.42	.1.39	1.44	1.43
Semi-Medium (Between 2-4 ha.)	2.81	2.78	1.07	2.78	2.77
Medium (Between 4-10 ha.)	6.08	6.04	0.66	6.04	5.96
Large (10 ha. and above)	18.14	17.53	3.36	17.41	17.21
Total	2.30	2.00	13.04	1.84	1.69

Some significant conclusions emerge from the data. First, the number of holdings has gone up sharply from 70.1 million to 97.15 million. This shows that non-farm occupations have not increased in number large enough to prevent a substantial increase, much less to diminish, the number of land holdings. In the absence of a large scale transfer of people from farm to non-farm occupations, and also in the absence of the law of premogeniture in our country, the sub-division of land has gone on unabated. Secondly, while the number of land holdings has gone up substantially the operated area has remained stagnant at about 163 million hectares. The result is an inevitable fall of the size of average holdings from 2.3 hectares to 1.69 hectares - a substantial reduction which is symptomatic of the pressure of population on land. The third important conclusion which emerges from the data is the extremely inequitable distribution of land. Thus, according to the results of the 1985-86 cencus, while 59.49% were marginal holders, the area operated by them was only 13.4%. On the other hand, large holders who constituted only 2.00% of the number of land holders, operate as much as 20% of the area. Similarly, while the number of medium holders was 8.1% the area operated by them was more than 28.6%. What is worse, despite the land reforms, the number of marginal holders has gone up from more than 36 million to more than 57.8 million, thus, increasing their percentage in the total number of holdings from 50.9% to 59.49%. In fact, the largest increase amongst the holders of all the sizes has been that of the marginal holders. The class in which there has been a fall in the number of holdings was in the medium and large size which might be partly the result of sub-division and partly of land reforms. But it is obvious that the inequality of the land holding continues to remain of extremely high order. While the average holding of 59.49% of the land holders belonging to marginal size was 0.39 hec. that of the 1.96% of the holders belonging to large size was as high as 17.21 hecs. From the point of view of equitable distribution of land, this would clearly indicate the need for land reforms in order to bring about re-distribution of land. Thus, if the ceiling of land holding is pegged at 10 hecs. then the surplus land available from the large holders would be of the order of 18 million hecs., i.e. nearly the same as the total land held by all the marginal holders put together. This would enable the average size of the marginal holders to be doubled. Such a radical land reform measure would enable the large majority of agricultural holders to attain a size which, under the available modern technology, can well be considered an economic size. But while the census data would indicate the need for such a radical land reform, it is for the policy makers to decide whether such radical measure should be introduced.

It could be argued whether this would not adversely affect agricultural production and productivity. Apart from the social justice argument in favour of the marginal holders, there are some other points also in their favour. First, the 1970-71, data has shown that small and semi-medium holdings form the largest part of the area under rice cultivation, the role of large holdings in rice cultivation being only marginal. Secondly, the performance of small and medium holdings in the development of primary irrigation facilities has been the most impressive amongst all the size groups. Land reforms coupled with increased supply of agricultural inputs and credit to marginal, small and medium holders can well provide a strategy which could meet the ends of both social justice and increased production.

This is the overall picture of Indian agriculture as revealed by the agriculture census. There are, of course, regional diversities. Thus, the overall size of holdings is much smaller in some States as compared with others—the least average size of holding being in Kerala, namely, 0.70 hecs. followed by Jammu & Kashmir 0.94 hecs., Uttar Pradesh 1.16 hecs., West Bengal 1.20 hecs., Bihar 1.52 hecs., Tamil Nadu 1.45 hecs., Himachal Pradesh 1.23 hecs. and Assam 1.47 hecs. indicating the pressure of population in these areas. The average size is more than 4 hecs. in Madhya Pradesh and Rajasthan and more than three hectares in Maharashtra and Gujarat. But these areas are mostly un-irrigated and fall in the dry zone and hence, in terms of equivalence of productivity, do not amount to really any bigger size of holding. The policies and programmes regarding land reforms, supply of inputs and increased agricultural production must take into account these regional diversities.

If the relentless growth of population indicated by the latest population census is any pointer, there would only be an accentuation of past trends *viz.* continued dimination in the size of average holdings and increasing inequality of land ownership. This would make all the more urgent the neẽd for radical land reforms and policies for redirection of inputs and agricultural credit to an increasing number of small and marginal holdings.

— —

Part - IV

ORGANISATION AND ADMINISTRATION

14

Institutional Arrangements for Rural Development

More than three decades of experience has accumulated in the field of rural development in developing countries and time has now come to take stock of the experience, to draw out a balance sheet of success and failure and derive appropriate lessons for future action.

Most developing countries in the Asian region, since the very inception of their emergence as independents nation states, had realized the importance of rural development. A large majority of their people lived in rural areas and the hopes and aspirations of the rural people had to be reflected in their design for development. One of the earliest documents in the field of rural development—the report of the Rural Credit Survey Committee appointed by the Reserve Bank of India (1954) made the classic statement. "In India, development means rural development and rural development means agricultural development." Critics of the development process in the developing countries have pointed out that the importance of rural development was not always reflected in the allocation of investment but this seldom detracted from the policy pronouncements of the governments of the developing countries regarding the importance of rural development.

The external financing agencies — the World Bank (WB) and the Asian Development (ADB) - were initially reluctant to support development projects in the field of rural development. Rural development was considered to be a "soft" area which did not lend itself to "projectization", to formulation of bankable projects. Hence their initial support was to "hard" areas of industrial and infrastructural development. But later years saw a radical transformation in the approach of these agencies till a time has now come when rural development projects are not only accepted as "bankable" but are to be accorded a high priority and indeed to be considered as central or at the core of the lending operations. But not all projects have been successful or have yielded desired results and these agencies - WB (IDA) and ADB — alike are anxious to find out the conditions under which rural development succeeds in meeting the objectives and those under which it fails. And one of the most important of these conditions is the presence of appropriate institutional structure which makes or mars the success of the rural development projects.

In most countries, the rural development projects have been extensively documented. Planning and evaluation organization of these countries have themselves brought out a number of studies. Besides, rural development has widely attracted the attention of academicians, scholars and social thinkers and workers of developing and developed countries alike and there is a vast output of studies based on their researches. And there are any number of publications based on proceedings of seminars and conferences - both national and international - on the subject of rural development. The fruits of these studies, researches and seminars need to be garnered.

Rural development is a part of "development". "Development" has emerged as a major theme of the second half of the twentieth century. "Development Economics" has emerged as an independent branch of economics. Politics and sociology of development have also emerged in their own right. Major thinkers have "conceptualized" the process of development. In their publication "Pioneers of Development," the WB has brought out major concepts of development as explained by their originators themselves.

The pioneers are of course not unanimous as to what brings about "development". One conceptualization is that development process in the developing countries would be no different from that in the developed countries. It is the result of the operation of market forces. Market itself is the proper institutional framework for development.

The other approach is that the developing countries are caught in a low level equilibrium trap; they are caught in a vicious circle of poverty. And the only way they can get out of the trap is "a big push". In another formulation, the underdeveloped countries are at the "periphery" while the developed countries are at the "centre". That leads to dominance of the centre and the dependence of the periphery, if the market forces are allowed to have their own sway. In a third formulation, it is said that the developing countries require "complementary investments" to take advantage of the "external economics" which market cannot provide. Hence the process of development cannot be left to be the vicissitudes of the market. The State must intervene; it must initiate policies and programme of development; and it must establish, promote and foster appropriate institutions of development.

This is because development is not just a matter of investment. The simplistic formulation in the early years of conceptualization of development such as the Harrod-Domer equation that

$$g \text{ (growth rate)} = \frac{I \quad \text{(Investment)}}{K \text{ (capital output / ratio)}}$$ was soon found inadequate

Development is not just a matter of raising savings ratio from 5 per cent of 12 per cent as one "pioneer", Prof. W. Arthur Lewis thought in his *Theory of Economic Growth*. Even Investment and Technology together cannot do the magic. A third factor is required and that is "organisation". Without this third factor, investment would have poor yields and technology though available would not be "transferred". Hence the crucial importance of organization. And what is "organization" but a structure of appropriate institutions?

This conceptualization regarding "development" in general is relevant to rural development as well. If developing countries are peripheral in the world economy dominated by the developed countries, rural areas are peripheral *within* the developing countries themselves. The developing countries have a "dual economy" with dominating growth centres or enclaves of development in metropolitan areas, and a vast hinterland of backwardness in rural areas. Development in the developing countries must, therefore, be a process of structural transformation which would eventually put an end to this "dualism". But this cannot be done through indiscriminate process of urbanization or industrialization. More often than not, urbanization in the developing countries is the result of "push" factor rather than "pull" factor. The pressure of population in rural areas leads to a relentless process of migration from rural to urban areas. This is not development. It merely leads to slums, shanties, overcrowding and the growth of the so-called "informal sector" in urban areas. Nor can "industrialization" be an artificial process unrelated to agriculture or to rural areas. It has organic links with the development of agricultural and rural sector which must provide both the input in the shape of food and raw material and output in the shape of market for the products of industry.

So conceived, rural development is a part of general development but it does not simply follow general development in the sense that mere increase in general growth rate would necessarily or automatically generate rural development. It has to be distinctly understood and consciously promoted.

The earlier approaches to the promotion of rural development were conceived in general terms. Rural development has to be multipurpose, multi-focussed and multi-facetted. It has to include agriculture, rural industry, rural engineering, health, education and promotion of rural institutions. Various aspects of rural life are inextricably interlinked with each other and hence all aspects have to be taken up together in a general process of rural development. This was also the earlier approach of community development. The rural community should be energized for aided self-help with the machinery of government administration acting as a catalytic agent. Both the "general" approach and "community" approach were found wanting in the light of experience. The general approach led to a thin spreading out of resources which did not yield dividends in terms of increased agricultural production of food grains and raw material which became an imperative necessity. 'Hence a strategy of "selective concentration" had to be conceived of. And the community approach meant merely the perpetuation of the dominance of the elite groups in rural areas to the neglect of poor. Hence a strategy of "target group" orientation was called for.

The strategy of "selective concentration" led to single minded pursuit of agricultural modernization through

(i) Agricultural extension to transfer high yielding technology from lab to land;

(ii) Delivery system to supply agricultural inputs like hybrid, HYV seeds, chemical facilities, pesticides, insecticides and implements;

(iii) Agricultural credit, short term, medium term and long term for financing agricultural inputs as well for long term investment in the shape wells, pump sets or land development; and

(iv) Provision of incentives via (a) land reforms and (b) arrangement for marketing and processing.

A variety of institutional arrangements had to be devised, designed and established for this purpose. The following chart is illustrative of such arrangements.

Function	*Institutional Arrangements*
1. Agricultural Extension	1. Extension agency of the Department of Agriculture.
	2. Agricultural University/Agricultural Research Institutions
	3. Farmers' clubs; youth clubs

Function	Institutional Arrangements
2. Delivery of inputs	1. Government depots/seed farms
	2. Cooperatives
	3. Private agencies
3. Agricultural Credit	1. Cooperatives
	2. Agricultural banks
	3. Commercial banks
	4. Non-institutional credit
4. Incentive - Land Reforms	1. Abolition of land lordism
	2. Abolition of intermediaries
	3. Protection to tenants/share-croppers
	4. Ceiling on holdings
	5. Distribution of land to landless
	6. Establishment of land tribunals
5. Incentive - Marketing	1. Marketing cooperatives
	2. Commodity boards
	3. Price-support operations
	4. Warehousing arrangements
	5. Regulated markets
	6. Agro-processing enterprises - cooperative and otherwise
6. General promotion	1. Local setup of development administration
	2. Elected local government institutions
	3. Autonomous/voluntary organisations

Which arrangements have succeeded and which have failed? Some institutions succeed in some countries but do not in others. Much depends on the ethos of a country or the genius of a people. But institutions and their functions *can* be transplanned. Countries can learn from mutual experience. Hence the importance of a comparative study of institutions and of the conditions under which they work successfully and deliver the goods.

Agriculture though dominant is not the only sector of the rural economy. Anxiliary occupations like dairy, poultry and fishery, traditional industry and handicrafts and trade specially in the weekly fairs constitute other sectors and though smaller in size than agriculture are of considerable significance in the context of the sustaining and diversifying non-farm gainful occupations. Rural industry is in even more vulnerable position than agriculture in as much as it has face the competition of modern industry. It requires, all the greater institutional support than agriculture, though of the same type viz. for technological upgradation, supply of inputs and raw material, availability of cred:t and marketing arrangements. Similar institutional support is also needed for anxiliary occupations.

Infrastructural support and social consumption are the two other sectors of rural development. Inspite of decades of development, rural people still lack facilities for potable drinking water and health and educational facilities of adequate standard. Rural roads and electrification have so far covered only a part of the country side. How can these facilities be accelerated? One solution is to establish special organizations to be in charge of these tasks like Departments of Rural Health and Water Supply or Rural Electrification Corporation. Irrigation is another important part of the rural infrastructure though it is probably considered together with and as a part of agricultural development.

But even if all the variety of institutions and organizations mentioned above are established, one question still remains. Will they serve the poor and help them bring above the poverty line or will they be the instruments in the hands of the elite? If the latter be the case, the whole purpose of rural development will be defeated. What then is the way out? Can these institutions be reformed in the interest of the poor? Can the poor be given a dominant voice in the management of the affairs of these institutions? Or should some special exclusive institutions be established for the poor? Or short of that, could government prescribe norms and targets for the working of these institutions so as to ensure that the benefit accrues to the poor? If the poor are altogether out of the productive process, as is the case in many countries, these institutions ab initio would be of no relevance to them. The rural poor must first be provided with productive assets and other employment opportunities, may be on rural works programmes which can create productive assets in rural areas like rural roads of afforestration and for this special antipoverty programmes have to be devised. But the question still remains—even if special programmes of rural development are devised for the rural people, how do we ensure that the benefit go to them and are not cornered by well to do classes? Do we have institutions and organizations to ensure that our delivery system is such that the benefits accrue to the poor and there are no leakages? How do we ensure effective participation of the poor as "beneficiaries" of rural development?

It has been suggested that in the ultimate analysis it is a matter of organizing the poor and making them aware and articulate of their "rights" and rightful claims. But who will organize the poor and provide them leadership? Should government provide funds for "organizing" the poor or should it be left to political parties, voluntary organizations or social workers" or the poor themselves would throwup the leadership. This brings us to an understanding of the whole political and social process of development.

What is outlined above is a brief scenario of a complex institutional process of development in general and rural development in particular. Not enough emphasis has been laid on institution building. A priority should be given to support institution - building. But institution building on what lines? The answer can be given in the light of a comprehensive study of the functioning of the institutions in the field of rural development in different countries. A study of the institutional arrangements in different countries must cover both macro and micro aspects, the general system as well as the inner working of the individual institutions. Such a system would have much to offer to provide basic insights for effective institution building for diverse purposes and aspects of rural development.

15

Ensuring People's Participation in Rural Development Programmes: Revive Local Institutions

From the very inception of the rural development programmes introduced in the country after the attainment of Independence, great importance was attached to people's participation in these programmes. Indeed, the community development programme introduced in the year 1952, went to the extent of announcing that the goal was to develop the programme from the stage of people's participation in governmental programmes to that of governmental participation in the people's programmes. The very concept of community development was based on the idea of people's participation. Community development meant that the community itself must be able to identify its felt needs and work out programmes and projects through which it could meet its felt needs. The community should be able to evolve its own mechanism and techniques of development.

In actual fact, however, the concept of people's participation had a much more limited connotation. In the early years of community development, the emphasis was on construction of school buildings, dispensaries, panchayatghars, open drainage, approach roads etc. and the concept of people's participation in relation to these brick and mortor programmes took the form of "Shramdan". "Shramdan" meant that in the execution of the programmes, people would contribute their share by way of physical labour and supply of local material and provision of services like carting. In the rural areas, Monday is treated as a holiday and so people's participation was in the shape of Monday labour provided by the members of the local community on the local projects. The concept of Shramdan was also used to revive certain old traditions and practices. Thus, the late Shri V.T. Krishnamachari, the first Deputy Chairman of the Planning Commission, used to lay great emphasis on 'Kudimaramat' that is the traditional obligation of the villagers to maintain old tanks and irrigation works by regular contribution.

Though the concept of Shramdan as a method of people's participation in community projects evoked great degree of enthusiasm in the initial years and provided many examples of the upsurge of popular enthusiasm and participation, soon the initial enthusiasm gave way to scepticism and even cynicism, when it was discovered that the application of the concept of Shramdan led to two abuses. First, the people, who were called upon to contribute their labour were the very ones who had nothing but their labour to offer! To expect them alone to contribute their labour amounted to nothing but begar or forced labour. To expect them to give free labour was to ask them to work on empty stomach. Shramdan, therefore, degenerated into exploitation of the weaker sections. Secondly, even a worse abuse of the concept of Shramdan had been crept in when in order to accommodate people's participation, the work estimates started getting jacked up. Thus, if 25 per cent was described as the extent of people's participation in any work, the estimate was escalated by a like amount, thereby the contractor accounting for people's participation only on paper and deriving the full amount of the cost of construction! Soon the occurrence of the abuse became widespread and the very concept of Shramdan was brought into contempt and gradually abolished. Today, the concept is totally forgotten and its revival has become almost impossible as people have come to expect the government to bear the full share of every possible construction activity.

This was particularly noticed under the major irrigation projects. These projects were constructed by government at heavy cost. Reservoirs were formed by constructing dams across rivers and major distributories and canals brought water to the villages through channels upto 3 cusec capacity. But even then, irrigation development would not take place because the assumption that the field channels taking off from the 3 cusecs channels constructed by government would be provided by the farmers was not borne out in practice. The farmers expected that even the field channels would be constructed by government. Government anxious to develop irrigation potential brought into existence by the irrigation projects decided to construct the field channels also; thus, once again, abandoning the hopes of people's participation.

After the early brick and mortor emphasis of the community development, the attention shifted to the more demanding programmes of agricultural production. Increasing agricultural production required millions of farmers to participate in the adoption of new technology. This was sought to be done through various methods of agricultural extension. The approach in the initial years was that the new technology would first be communicated to the "leaders" in the farming community or in other words, to the progressive farmers who, it was expected, would then inspire others to follow their example. The progressive farmers were expected to be the multipliers of the modern technology. They were provided with the package of improved practices and services. This approach, however, led to deepening of disparities in the rural society. The large and the well-to-do farmers quickly absorbed the new technology and derived the benefits of the supply of inputs and cheap agricultural credit, while the large majority of small and marginal farmers were left out, thereby increasing the distance between the large and the small and marginal farmers in the rural areas. Soon the government realised that from the point of view of increased agricultural production as from the point of view of justice and equity it was necessary to modify the approach of agricultural extension in order to ensure that the benefits of rural technology and facilities of input and credit are not confined to small and well-to-do but were extended to large majority of small and marginal farmers. The new approach, therefore, involved an attempt to identify the small and the marginal farmers and bring them in the fold of various programmes of rural development.

This was attempted through the small farmers development agencies and the marginal farmers and labour agencies which were recommended by the Rural Credit Review Committee in the year 1966. Under these agencies, the first step after the identification of small and marginal farmers was to enable them to participate in the activities of the co-operatives by enrolling them as members of the co-operative credit institutions. A number of steps were taken to ensure the participation of the small and marginal farmers in the co-operative activities. First, loans were given to enable them to purchase shares in the co-operative societies. Second, a certain percentage of lending was earmarked for the small and marginal farmers. Third, about one fourth to one third of the loan was given in the shape of subsidy. Fourth, the purposes for which agricultural loans were given were diversified giving greater emphasis to auxiliary occupations like dairy, fishery and sheep rearing. The new technology being neutral to scale it was expected that given the measures mentioned above, the small and marginal farmers would be able to participate in agricultural development. To some extent, these expectations have been fulfilled and the share of the small and marginal farmers in the supply of agricultural credit and input has gone up substantially.

There was, however, another section which was completely left out and that was that of the landless labourer. For enabling them to participate in rural development was devised the concept of "Food for work", now known as the programme "National Rural Employment". There were many other precursors of the scheme including that of the crash scheme for rural employment; an advanced version is that of the 'Employment Guarantee Scheme of Maharashtra'. These schemes have ensured even those families in rural areas who have no assets of their own would be able to earn their purchasing power by working on construction programmes of government in rural areas.

Thus, the original concept which was that of evoking people's participation in a general way in rural development has given way to devising specific programmes for different sections of the rural society to enable them to participate in programmes of rural development.

The need has now come to make a definite attempt to see that the well-to-do sections in the rural society not only do not try to grab the benefit of government's scheme meant for the rural poor but themselves contribute their share to the development of those people in rural areas who are below the poverty line. There are many who feel that such a voluntary self-denying ordinance can hardly be passed by the affluent sections of the rural society. They feel that the only way of ensuring the participation of the poor in the rural development programmes is to organise them on a militant basis so that they will assert and get their legitimate share in the additional incomes generated in the rural areas. The rural people could be organised in the shape of militant trade unions. However, such militant organisations would create conflicts in the rural communities. It would give a setback to rural development generally.

In fact, there are two models which are before us for consideration. One is that of Punjab where modernisation of agriculture or the 'Green Revolution' as it is called, has led to the increased production and prosperity of the farmers or the land-owning classes but also, at the same time, despite mechanisation, has generated greater demand for agricultural labour, as a result of which not only has local labour started getting high wages but even outside labour from distant Bihar and Eastern U.P. have migrated to Punjab to take advantage of the demand for agriculture labour at higher wages. On the other hand, trade union type of activity organised amongst the agriculture labour in Allepy District in Kerala has only led to stultification of the progress of agricultural development. We can only command the Punjab model rather than the Kerala model because, in the ultimate analysis, all round prosperity in rural areas can only come about as a result of all round increase in agriculture production and productivity. Trade unionism would only create rigidities. On the other hand, a deliberate attempt to extend technology, services and credit to the poorer people in rural areas through co-operatives and other organisations is bound to lead to more equitable development. In some academic circles there is a tendency to look with scepticism at all such attempts since they feel that bureaucracy is hardly the instrument to bring about social and economic change in rural areas. However, as things stand today, the only instrument which can act as agent of change in rural areas is bureaucracy in the shape of thousands of village level workers, extension agents, employees of co-operative institutions, bank employees etc. Institutions like Co-operative Credit Institutions, Co-operative Dairies, Co-operative Marketing Societies, Regional Rural Banks, Agricultural branches of commercial banks and people working in these institutions can surely bring about a change in the shape of greater participation of the rural poor in various development programmes.

The Panchayati Raj institutions conceived as principal agencies of rural development were set up at three tiers in the year 1959 following the recommendation of the Balwantrai Mehta Committee Report. In the initial years there was a euphoria in favour of these institutions. It was felt that the elected representatives of the people in the panchayati raj institutions namely village panchayats, samities and Zilla Parishads would kindle popular enthusiasm and participation in rural development. These earlier expectations, however, soon gave way to frustrations when Panchayati Raj institutions were seemed to be involved in local factions and became centres of power struggle rather than instrument of rural development. Also, the politicians at the state level started looking at panchayati raj institutions as rival centres of power. Their growth, therefore, was stiffled by various state governments who refused to hold elections to these bodies and allowed them to remain in a state of suspended animation. No wonder that the Asoka Mehta Committee found the panchayati raj institutions in a moribund state but despite this they did recommend the revival of panchayati raj institutions. Recently, steps have been taken by some of the state governments to hold elections to the panchayati raj institutions. 73rd amendment of the Constitution has now made timely elections mandatory. This is a move in the right direction.

There is no doubt that in a large country like India, rural local government institutions have to emerge as the institutions of grass root planning and development. Pandit Jawaharlal Nehru had great faith in the panchayati raj institutions, since he felt that these were the institutions, which were nearer to the rural people. What is, therefore, needed today, once again, is to give a new fillip to planning and development at grass root level through the revival and strengthening of panchayati raj institutions. The General Body of the Village Panchayat known as Gram Sabha should be taken seriously. The rural people of India have long traditions of self-government which should be revived. Several schemes of development like social forestry or developing local water resources or making economic use of water resources through scientific techniques of water management or programme like Dairy Development could best be promoted through the agency of panchayati raj institutions. What is needed, once again, is to revive the old spirit of rural development as the voluntary and spontaneous movement of the people, but this time people, essentially in the sense of the poorer sections of the rural society.

16

Rural Development Administration: Alternative Approaches

Two alternative approaches have clearly emerged during the last three decades and a half of our experimentation with rural development administration. The first is the multi-purpose integrated approach and the other is the specialised subject matter approach.

The first approach came in the wake of introduction of the programme of community development. The programme aimed at dealing with all aspects of rural life including agriculture, animal husbandry and allied occupations, rural industries, education, social education, rural engineering and development of Panchayats and cooperative institutions. Above all, it aimed at energising the entire community in the process of aided self-help. Underlying the approach was the assumption that all aspects of community life are inextricably linked with each other and therefore only an integrated approach can deliver the goods.

In the wake of a greater urgency for increasing agricultural production, particularly food production, it came to be believed that the generalised community development approach was not adequate and specialised approach concentrating on the task of increasing agricultural production was inescapable. The approach was strongly advocated by the Ford Foundation team in 1959 and as a result a specialised machinery for agricultural development was created in the districts selected for intensive agricultural development programmes.

A further change towards specialised approach came about following the recommendations of the Ram Subhag Singh Committee Report (1963). On the basis of the recommendations of the Report the Development

Commissioner was designated as the Agricultural Production Commissioner, the BDO was selected from the cadre of Agricultural Officers, and the village level workers required to spend 80% of their time on agricultural work.

Then followed the introduction of the T & V (Training & Visit) system of agricultural extension, and consequently a further concentration on agricultural extension. Many of the village level workers were removed from the block administration and assigned to the Department of Agriculture for working in the TV System.

Thus progressively the integrated structure of rural development administration created in the wake of the programme of Community Development got eroded and the machinery of development administration was considerably weakened.

A new development took place in the seventies when it was realised that the approach for intensification and modernisation of agriculture had led to the neglect of small and marginal farmers and landless labourers. It was decided to set up a special machinery to cater to pay attention to their needs in the shape of new organisations like Small Farmer Development Agency (SFDA) and Marginal Farmer and Agricultural Labour Agencies (MFALA). These agencies were registered societies but they consisted of officers and some non-officials and were presided over by the Collector or the Commissioner. They had a limited nucleus staff which was only to serve as a catalytic agent and get assistance of the staff of various departments like agriculture and cooperation for the implementation of their programmes. With the introduction of the integrated rural development programme in which were merged SFDA and MFALA programmes, a new agency called district rural development agency (DRDA) was set up replacing the earlier agencies.

Thus we have today three elements in the set up of rural development administration, namely, the departmental setup, the attenuated development block setup and the DRDA setup. The departmental approach is not often linked with the integrated approach which was adopted first by the community development block and later on by the DRDA. The DRDA is entrusted with the task of dealing with problems of poverty. This requires cooperation and coordination amongst several departments which is often not forthcoming. As was the experience in the days of the community development, the traditional departments do not take kindly and do not lend full support to catalytic or coordinating mechanisms such as those of development block or DRDAS. Unfortunately the departmental approach with limited objectives is not always consistent with the integrated approach and the problem has arisen as how to combine specialised approach of the departments with the integrated approach of community development or the anti-poverty programme approach. Studies of anti-poverty programmes have shown that they would not succeed without a full back-up support of the entire administration machinery concerned with rural development. They cannot be the concern of an adhoc agency like DRDA often looked upon as outside the mainstream of departmental administration. Indeed the entire rural and agricultural development machinery would have to be reoriented and geared to the complex, difficult and gigantic task of raising fifty per cent of the rural people above poverty line.

Obviously, a new attempt is required to evolve a new machinery of rural development administration which can combine accomplishment of overall tasks and the discharge of specialised functions.

Rural development approach has also to be combined with the approach of district and block level planning to which renewed attention is now being paid.

Then there is the question of the relationship between the machinery of rural development administration and the democratic institutions of rural local government. On the basis of the recommendations of the Balwantrai Mehta Study team, a three tier set up of Panchayati Raj institutions was brought into being consisting of village panchayat, panchayat samitis at block level and Zilla Parishad at District level and the Block Development Machinery was placed under the control of Panchayat Samiti. In States of Maharashtra and Gujarat even district rural development machinery was made responsible to Zilla Parishad. But soon enthusiasm for Panchayati Raj Institutions waned. Anti-poverty programmes and district planning were placed outside the pale of Panchayati Raj Institutions. Thus a chasm has developed between Panchayati Raj and the Rural Development machinery of administration. Where should be the link between Zilla Parishad and the DRDA?

What is required is to set up a comprehensive machinery for rural development administration which could incorporate within it the DRDA and the block organisation, which would have a greater weight so as to be able to coordinate the efforts of various development departments as well as agencies like banks and cooperatives and which would be linked up with Panchayati Raj institutions and mechanisms and processes of decentralised planning.

17

Development through Participation

When the country embarked on planning in the year 1951, it was clearly understood that our system of democratic planning was different from the totalitarian system of planning prevalent in the Soviet Russia and other communist countries. Totalitarian planning implied compulsion while democratic planning was based on consent. While Stalin heading the totalitarian system in Soviet Russia had no hesitation in saying that Soviet plans were instructions, Jawahar Lal Nehru heading the democratic planning in India often said that the democratic planning aimed at development through popular participation.

The concept of popular participation in development has, however, undergone a change over the first three decades of planning in our country. In the '50s, in the context of newly introduced community development programme, popular participation meant that the rural people would bear a share of the cost of local community development projects like approach roads, school buildings or drinking water wells. The popular participation would be in the shape of voluntary labour called "shramdan", provision of local building material like stones and wood and services like cartage. However, while in the initial years of the programme of community development there was a great deal of enthusiasm for 'shramdan', slowly it fell into disfavour for a variety of reasons. Firstly, it was found that it was only the poor who gave their labour while the well-to-do only supervised. Secondly, it was found that community projects were only a mask for what was in fact a contractual work and the contractors who took responsibility for the people's share often abused it by inflating the cost estimates in collusion with the project authorities. When instances of such abuse came to notice, the very sanctity of the concept of popular participation was destroyed.

In the '60s, popular participation came to be associated with the participation of the rural people in institutions such as Panchayati Raj and co-operative institutions. While the village panchayat was the political democracy at the grass root, the village co-operative constituted the economic democracy at the grass root. In the Annual Meeting of the Gram Sabha the entire body of the village citizens was expected to meet and discuss the village development plans. Similarly, primary agricultural co-operative (PAC) was expected to have universal membership and all the rural families are expected to meet at the Annual General Body Meeting of the co-operatives in which they were expected to take an active part and elect their representatives on the board of directors of the co-operatives. These expectations did not materialise and the meetings of the Gram Sabha and the general body of the co-operatives hardly functioned as direct democracy. The village people did not take active interest in them and the meetings of these institutions were arranged by the officials to fulfil the statutory requirements rather than treating them as opportunities for the articulation of a vibrant and direct democracy. Soon the panchayati raj institutions fell into the state of suspended animation because in several States elections were not held and their work was entrusted to the official machinery. Thus, the concept of popular participation in development through institutions was also eroded over a period of time.

In the '70s, there was a change in the approach to development. It was realised that the benefits of development in the past accrued to the more well-to-do sections of the community and a large majority of the under-privileged like the small and marginal farmers, landless labourers and artisans were not able to participate either in the development programmes or in the institutions and benefits of development did not accrue to them. This led to growing dispartities between the well-to-do and under-privileged and hence attention was focussed on formulating programmes which would directly benefit the people at the low end of poverty in the country side through the programmes like the SFDA (Small Farmer Development Agency) and MFALA (Marginal Farmer and Agricultural Labour Agency). These programmes required identification of the small and marginal farmers and landless labourers, and their enrolment as members of the co-operatives. 25% of the loans from co-operatives to the small farmers, $33^{1/3}$% to the marginal farmers and 50% to the tribals were treated as subsidies. Under the integrated rural programmes introduced subsequently, the approach was to identify some 600 poorest families every year in every block and help them to rise above the poverty line through creation of some productive assets in their favour. The national rural employment programme was also intended to create gainful employment for the poor who were outside the pale of the production system. It is not clear to what extent these programmes have enabled a sizeable sections of the poor to rise above the poverty line.

There was yet another fundamental concept of popular participation which was germane throughout the three decades of development planning. That concept was the participation of the people in the formulation of the five years plans. In our system of democratic planning an idea was often expressed that our planning should be from bottom upwards and that higher level plans ought to reflect the grass-root plans which must embody the felt needs and aspirations of the people. These grassroot plans at village, block and district level must be prepared by the people themselves. However, the concept of planning from below could not take a practical shape and our plans continued to be formulated at the national and State level and then disaggregated for the purpose of implementation at the district and village level. Thus at the local level the people had little say in the formulation of plans and programmes. To be sure, at the meetings of the development committees at local levels, popular elected representatives did give suggestions for the location of projects and schemes in their constituencies. However, this was far short of the concept of the formulation of grass root plans by the people or any consultation with the people. At the grass root level, planning still mean the implementation of stereo-type schemes with uniform features with limited scope for adaptation or modification. A local plan taking into account local resources, local needs and local popular opinion has yet to become operational.

Efforts, therefore, need to be made for providing active scope for popular participation in development planning in our country. Popular involvement in development planning is not possible unless the developmental programmes are such that people feel that they would benefit by participating in them. If the programmes are stereo-type or generalised or not modified to the needs of the local people they would provide little scope for popular participation. Thus it was found in one block that TRYSEM (Training for Rural Youth in Self-Employment) provided for training courses in weaving whereas the local youth of the Jatav community were interested in their traditional occupation of shoe making in which new skills could have been provided. In another area it was found that while land was distributed among the landless the land was of the inferior soil and the resources required for land development were not made available. These instances will show that the people cannot participate in a developing programmes unless all the conditions for worthwhile participation are fulfilled. Moreover, people will not be able to participate unless they know what the programmes are and how participation in them would be to their benefit. Communication is a vital pre-condition for popular participation in development.

Grass root institutions like panchayati raj and co-operative institutions and voluntary associations are of course excellent media for popular participation. But these institutions need to be nursed and nurtured for long periods of time. Again people should be informed about the manner in which their participation in these institutions would benefit them in the long run. If the people consider that these institutions are only parts of administrative machinery and they have no decision making authority, they are unlikely to be interested in participation in these institutions. The local people will also need to be motivated and trained for participation in the programmes. Human resources development is a starting point of development through participation.

Finally, while administrative machinery must promote popular participation in grass root programmes and institutions, they should be averse to continously "sitting on the back of the people". The old colonial approach of "Mabap" Sarkar ought to be given up once and for all. Administration should try rather to unleash the energies of the people and give them maximum scope. From this point of view, it has been rightly suggested that a part of the development funds should be made available through the local institutions for freely undertaking development programmes without any prescriptions or conditions attached to them.

The approach suggested above would bring development plans closer to the people and evoke popular participation.

18

Adaptation of Administration to Indian Rural Development

Supply of agricultural credit and agricultural inputs like fertilisers, seed, insecticides and improved implements and marketing of agricultural output have an extremely important place in the Indian strategy for agricultural development. Progress in agriculture is not possible without substantial increase in fertiliser consumption, use of high yielding and hybrid variety of seeds and use of pesticides and insecticides.

Increased utilisation of these inputs require additional resources. Traditionally, indebtedness has been a chronic feature of the rural economy in India, so eloquently articulated by the off-repeated sentence in the Indian economic literature - "the Indian agriculturist is born in debt, lives in debt and dies in debt". He has been traditionally in the grip of the land-lord-money-lender-trader who provided money at usurious rate of interest against landed security and resorted to foreclosure of loan on the failure of the agriculturists to the debt. Sometimes accounts were falsified which along with usurious rate of interest made it virtually impossible for the farmer to repay his debt.

With such poverty of resources, traditional Indian agriculture had a very low level of cultivation. The utilisation of inputs like fertilisers and pesticides was very poor.

In the absence of requisite research, high yielding and hybrid seeds were also not available. The wooden plough was the traditional implement which merely scratched the surface rather than turning the soil. Indian agriculture was, therefore, considered more a way of life than a commercial proposition.

Ever since Independence continuous attempts have been made to modernise Indian agriculture to raise its technological standard and make it progressive and productive. Firstly, a beginning was made with the establishment of a nation wide Agricultural Extension Service in 1952 and over years it has been continuously strengthened. The objective of the Agricultural Extension Service is to extend agricultural inputs and credit improved package if services and practices to the very door of the farmer. The Agricultural Extension Service guided from the State Divisional and district levels has now been established it at the block headquarters, with several specialists who support the village level workers and other field level agricultural functionaries in providing extension services to the far- mers. Secondly, Agricultural Research has been able to evolve new varieties of high yielding and hybrid seeds of wheat, maize, paddy, cotton, groundnut etc. Through the integrated programme of national demonstrations and local demonstrations the farmers have been made aware of these improved varieties of seeds.

As regards supply of inputs, in the beginning, the State Departments of Agriculture were responsible for supply of fertilisers and other inputs. Soon, it was realised the administrative/departmental organisation must concentrate on extension, leaving the actual supply of inputs and credit and other agricultural inputs to business agencies and institutions.

Of these, cooperatives were considered to be the most important. The report of the Rural Credit Survey Committee appointed by the RBI (1954) provided the blue print for integrated cooperative development. According to this blue print, large size primary cooperative societies were to be established throughout the country and were to be supported by the District Cooperative Banks and State Cooperative Banks. The Reserve Bank of India was to provide concessional credit facilities. While the primary cooperative societies at the village level supported by the credit institutions, at the higher level were to provide short-term and medium-term credit, long-term credit for purposes of agricultural investment like wells, pump sets, land reclamation etc.,was to be provided by the Land Development Banking Structure at the tahsil and State level supported by the Agricultural Refinancing Corporation, (since replaced by NABARD) an affiliate of the Reserve Bank of India in the year, 1963. This set up of cooperative credit institutions from village upwards has by now become established in all the States though in several states there are many weak primary and district level institutions and continuous efforts are being made to make them viable through programmes of amalgamation and rehabilitation.

The crop loan scheme recommended by RCS report envisaged that credit should be linked with production and marketing. Part of the credit should be given in kind in the shape of fertiliser and other inputs.While the primary cooperative credit societies were to receive resources from the District Cooperative Banks for lending purposes, supply of fertilisers has t be obtained through the tahsil cooperative marketing societies affiliated to the State Cooperative Marketing Societies. At the zonal meeting decisions are taken for the allocation of fertiliser to various agencies including State Marketing Federations.

The operation of this crop loan scheme has been continuously improved. Nearly, 50% of the farmers have become members of the primary cooperative societies, and the amount of the short-term and medium-term credit disbursed every year has gone up from 20 crore rupees to Rs. 2176 crores of short term credit and Rs. 317 cr. of medium term credit during 1990-91. Also the Land Development Banks have been able to disburse investment finance of more than Rs. 803 crores during 1990-91. These are impressive achievements. But the following problems have arisen from the point of view of people's participation and decentralised management.

People's Participation

(1) Half of the farming families are still outside the fold of cooperatives; specially it is pointed out that the small and marginal farmers, and Scheduled Caste farmers do not get their due share.

(2) Nearly 30% of the total short-term credit is provided by the cooperative system. However with the modernisation of agriculture the need for agricultural credit has enormously increased and credit gap has developed.

(3) The Management Committees of Cooperative are dominated by vested interests.

Attempts have been made to solve these problems through the following measures :

(i) A systematic drive has been undertaken for the enrolment of the small and marginal farmers.

(ii) Provisions have been made in the Cooperative Laws for a proper place being given to the representatives of small and marginal farmers and the Scheduled Castes in the Managing Committees.

(iii) Special programmes and agencies like SFDA and MFALs have been established to provide increasing participation of the small and marginal farmers in the benefit of the cooperative credit institutions.

(iv) New agencies like Nationalised Banks, Commercial Banks and Rural Banks have been established to supplement cooperative credit.

Decentralised Management and Administration

(a) The staff of the primary cooperative societies are not always up to the mark. To deal with this problem, it has been suggested that proper cadres of the secretaries of the primary societies should be established at the District Level and they should be properly trained. Training facilities available at the junior cooperative training centres should be fully utilised.

(b) Credit is not always properly linked with timely supply of agricultural inputs and its proper utilisation is not ensured. There is a need for better synchronisation and supervision. There is sought to be done through District and Block level planning machinery.

(c) Proper godown and storage facilities are not always available. Only about 20000 primary societies have their own godown facilities. The National Cooperative Development Corporation has schemes to avail all the primary cooperative institution to have their own godowns.

(d) The staff of the Land Development Banks are not always trained in project planning. Necessary training programmes have been arranged for the purpose.

The cooperative system of supply of inputs is supplemented by the public sector system of agro-industries corporations which are established in all the State. These corportations have their own custom service centres which make available the agricultural inputs. However, their network is not as wide-spread as that of the cooperative sector.

One of the recent developments is the distribution system established by the IFFCO, the cooperative society engaged in the manufacture of Urea and NPK, It is a unique cooperative enterprise to which are affiliated 27000 primary and state level agricultural credit and marketing societies in the country. It sells fertilisers mainly through cooperative marketing federations. Besides it has provided a variety of promotional and extension services to the farmers like training of sales personnel of cooperatives at the district and primary societies level and making available packages of inputs and improved practices to the farmers through Farmers' Service Centres established in various States. It has adopted twenty districts under the intensive district development programme of Government of India. With a view to assisting the cooperative to lift fertilizer stocks from the nearest warehousing point, IFFCO has opened warehousing points in most of the States in the country.

The marketing of farm output is a complex problem. The farm output is broadly divided into food crops and commercial crops like cotton, jute, oilseeds, areanuts and other plantation crops etc. In case of some of these crops procurement and marketing is done through public sector institutions like the FCI, Cotton Corporation of India and the Jute Corporation of India. They purchase substantial quantity of farm output through the cooperative institutions. The Food Corporation's procurement centres at the village level are run by the primary cooperative societies.

Cooperative marketing system is comprehensive with some 3,200 marketing societies at the tahsil level affiliated to the State Cooperative Marketing Federations which in turn are affiliated to the National Marketing Federations. The total farm production handled by the cooperative marketing system is of the order of Rs. 7,000 crores of which roughly 1/3 is accounted for by foodgrains, 1/3 by sugarcane and the rest comprises cotton, jute, etc. The Sugarcane marketing is done as a part of the working of cooperative sugar factories which are 220 in number. Foodgrains marketing is done as a part of the link-up between the cooperative system and the food corporations. There is a large scope for expanding the scope of cooperative marketing in respect of agricultural commodities like cotton, jute and oilseeds. As the arecanut cooperative marketing society has shown, a strong cooperative marketing system will be able to stabilise the price of agricultural commodities including fruit and vegetables.

Twenty thousand milk cooperatives affiliated to eighty cooperative dairies have also been able to provide good marketing facilities to the milk growers. The Kaira District Union's Amul Dairy and similar other dairies in Gujarat have shown how their activities can substantially raise the level of living of farming families. Almost half the income of every farming family is derived from sale of milk through the cooperatives. The total milk handled by the cooperative sector is worth Rs. 180 crores. Similarly fishery and poultry cooperatives handle products worth about Rs. 5 crores.

The following are some of the problems of people's participation and decentralised management :

1. The farmers are rather reluctant to market their products through cooperatives and are still dependent on the commercial agencies.
2. The cooperative marketing societies have yet to develop an integrated network and proper techniques of marketing. The cooperative personnel will have to be trained to handle a much large business of marketing of agricultural produce.
3. The public corporations (existing and to be established in respect of other commodities) will have to lend much greater support to the cooperative for stabilisation of agricultural prices and giving remunerative price to the agriculturists.

19

Decentralisation for Rural Development: An Operational Framework

Decentralization can be broadly defined as the transfer of planning, decision making or management function from the Central Government and its agencies to field organisations, subordinate unit of government, semi-autonomous public corporations, area wise or regional development organisations, specialized functional authorities or non-governmental organisation. The World Bank defined Rural Development as a strategy designed to improve the economic and social life of a specific group of people viz the rural poor. The term Rural Development, thus connotes a distinct approach to interventions by the state in the economies of under developed countries.

Decentralization may be considered as an important instrument for generating people's participation at the grass root level. Decentralization has been seen as a "way of increasing the effectiveness of rural development programmes by making them more relevant and responsive to local needs and conditions, allowing greater flexibility in their implementation and providing means of coordination the various agencies involved at the regional or local level." To put in brief, decentralization signifies a release of control from time to time by the higher authorities through the downward flow of power and gradual simplification of administrative process. It is a means for improving the national planning and implementation by delegating the power to the lower level.

The study of decentralization for rural development is a vital subject of importance which has thrown light on the problem of local planning and pattern of development. It is universally recognised by the policy makers that a close association of people with decentralized management is very useful.

In India the growing acceptance and utility of decentralization can be traced back from the Gandhian philosophy of development. Soon after the Independence, the policy of democratic decentralization called for the establishment of effective local government in villages. The practical orientation of this policy of democratic decentralization is outlined in details in the Report on the Team for the Study of Community Projects and National Extension Services. Based on the recommendations of National Development Council, the Committee on Plan Projects known as Balwantrai Mehta Committee (1957) pleaded for establishment of people's elective representatives institutions to ensure 'democratic decentralization'. It is hoped that this would strengthen the public policy in India and would fulfil the aspirations of creating 'economic swaraj' for the common man. To achieve this objective, civil servants and political leaders have been entrusted the task of strengthening public policy and formulating and implementing the development programmes through a process of democratic decentralization. In order to achieve the goal of national development, civil servants and political leaders are supposed to play a vital role in the decentralised planning process. They have to work in accordance with the norms of prescribed decentralised political system and within the prevailing constitutional framework, social environment and cultural ethos of the people.

With the increasing growth of democratic decentralization, exposure to modernisation, technological innovations and social change in India, the role and functions of bureaucratic and political elites above assumed critical importance for development. The decentralised administration calls for an increasing important role of different agencies, associations, organisations and institutions operating at the local level and their organisational linkages in the management of different schemes and programmes connected with rural development. Therefore, in order to achieve the development goals an innovative approach of democratic decentralization has been adopted in India.

Past Experiences

During the last three decades attempts were made to have governmental interventions for making he traditional system more responsible to the changing need of rural mass. Community Development (1952) and Panchayati Raj (1959) experiments were made to have more community movement and more people's participation in administrative decision making. Technocratic directions were imposed at the time of Integrated Agricultural Development Programme (1960). In March 1964, Ministry of

Home Affairs set-up a Machinery for Administrative Reforms and consequently, Administrative Reform Commission (ARC) was set up in January, 1966 which laid considerable stress on decentralization administration, delegating administrative and financial power to all decision making level, simplifying rules and procedures. A serious effort to decentralised the planning process was started during the Fourth Five Year Plan (1969) by allocating task of planning to the state governments and districts. After the Fourth Five Year Plan (1969) the Planning Commission emphasized on formulating district plan and also provided guidelines for district planning and suggested that.

> "The first objective of the formulation of district plan is to set forth a long term perspective indicating the economic activities to be established in different sub-regions of the district and the measures to be taken over the next 15 to 20 years to develop and conserve natural resources, build-up infra-structural facilities and social services and foster the growth of town and eities in a manner that would help the district to develop in the predetermined direction. The second objective is to prepare an integrated programme of action for the next five years or one year period on the basis of careful analysis of the existing conditions and a realistic assessment of the immediate problems, short term priorities and available resources".

Based on the recommendation of Rural Credit Review Committee (1969) Special Agencies such as Small and Marginal Farmer Development Agency (SFDA), Tribal Area Development Authority (TDA) were created to percolate the benefit to the specific area of specific class of people. It was clearly stated in the report that

> "there should be a committee in each district for advising and assisting the agency in determining the policies and procedures. The Committee should include in its membership the district officers of the various development departments connected such as agriculture cooperation, irrigation, animal husbandry, the president of Zila-Parishad or a comparable Panchayati Raj institution, the Chairman of the local district central cooperative bank and the chairman, of the local primary land development bank if the area is served by its branch." (No. 65. Summary and Recommendation).

In order to introduce the required decentralization of administration for Drought Prone Area Programme Command Area Development Authorities (CDA) were created. In some states, Tribal Development Corporations, Dairy Development Corporations, Sheep and Wool

Development Corporation were also created. One of the significant measure in decentralized administration has been the scheme of development of Small Scale Industries throughout the country. For the development and small scale and cottage industries. District Industrial Centres (DIC) were created.

In the year 1972, a Task Force on Integrated Rural Development was constituted by the Planning Commission to spell out the strategy of IRD, to work out the suitable pattern of investment and institutions connected with rural development programmes and suggest way and administrative arrangement, modification and synthesis into an integrated programme of rural development. In 1977 a Working Group of the Department of Personnel and Administrative Reform was set up to examine the administrative structure and procedure for decentralised development, especially the multiplicity of functionaries at the village level. Consequently, in order to strengthen a decentralised system of planning and development, Government of India set up a Committee on Panchayati Raj Institution (December, 1977) under the Chairmanship of Ashok Mehta. In his report (August, 1978) the Committee recommended that decentralization would commence with the district and Zila Parishad will handle all the decentralized state programmes and Panchayats will handle the implementation work. The Working Group on Block level planning under the Chairmanship of M.L. Dantwala in his report (1978) recommended certain structural and institutional changes for strengthening the organisation for rural poor. In fact, it was an important administrative reform in the field of decentralization of planning process. The Working Group has recommended the placement of planning team at District Headquarter for integration of the block plan with the district plans. During the Sixth plan period (1978-1983) under the Integrated Rural Development programme, emphasis was given on decentralisation of planning process to the district and block level. Accordingly, Area plans were prepared with full participation of voluntary agencies, professional institutions and public. In the district planning process; representatives of elected institutions, financial institutions and public were involved who have sufficient understanding in the local socio-economic problems.

For the improvement of administrative machinery, the Report of Working Group on Block Planning has mentioned the following:

> "Planning and implementation machinery will be further strengthened at all levels. In particular, the emphasis will have to be more on strengthening the administrative machinery for planning and implementation at the State, district, block and village level in view of further decentralization of the planning and implementation process, increased outlays on rural development,

agriculture and fulfillment of minimum needs. Though area level planning and involvement of voluntary agencies and the beneficiaries in the preparation and implementation of plan schemes at the area level, the decentralization process will be made effective. The existing local power structures such as those which in many area come in the way of successful execution of plan schemes relating to land reforms, would need to be dealt with suitably. Village level committees of the kind of proposed for improving the implementation of land reforms may also require to be set up to deal other schemes which seeks to benefit selectively the poor sections of the rural and urban population". (p. 121).

As a further examine to promote the concept of integrated, area planning, planning commission set up a Working Group on District Planning in September 1982, under the Chairmanship of Hanumantha Rao to assist the State Government in development plans/schemes, decentralization of planning decision making and evolving a methodology for local level planning for operationalization.* On May 1984 Report of the Working Group on District Planning was submitted to Planning Commission, New Delhi. The report has rightly pointed out the advantages of decentralization which "enables a better perception of the needs of local areas, makes better informed decision-making possible, gives people a greater voice in decisions concerning their among programmes, enables the felt needs of the people to be taken into account, ensures effective participation of the people, serves to build-up a measure of self-reliance by mobilising resources of the community in kind or money, making development self-sustaining and enables better exploitation of local resources and growth potentials of the local area for improving productivity and production. For the successful and effective management of the development, the report suggested that "all these would be possible only in the planning and decision making processes are decentralized to the regional and local levels particularly to the districts and blocks in the country."

The problem of decentralization has to be viewed in the conceptual and theoretical framework relating to the distributive and welfare activities of the state, and the basic assumption of public policy i.e. growth with social justice and the performance of bureaucrats and political leaders which is considered as a key for a solution of reorganisation and reconstruction of society in the democratic functioning of the country. In order to have a comprehensive and clear understanding regarding the role of administration in the implementation of decentralised development, various dimensions and different facets of development administration i.e. the need for

---

* The author was a member of this working group.

decentralised administration, forms and evolution of decentralised administration, nature and pattern of innovations and interventions, problems of implementation-issues of decentralized administration should be looked into. It is necessary to explore the administrative problems and practices connected with the rural development programmes with special reference to field problems of development administration at different levels-district block and village. It is also necessary to examine as to how far the innovations and interventions has affected the dynamics of participation at grass roots to promote decentralization in the achievement of effective admin- istration. Decentralized planning process calls for an increasingly important roles of different agencies in planning coordination, reviewing and monitoring the socio-economic plans and programmes connected with rural development.

In order to assess the effectiveness of democratic decentralization, efforts should be made to find out the weakness of the organisation and constraints that come-up in the way of administrative machinery in carrying out the task of implementation of rural development programmes and their solutions chalked out by policy makers and programme implementation.

20

New Thrusts in Decentralisation

Decentralisation has been the key note of reforms in many countries with a wide variety of socio-economic and political environment. It is at the heart of reforms in China under the leadership of Deng Xiaoping and was so under the leadership of Gorbachev in Russia. Thus in China, political, governmental and administrative and economic authority was concentrated in the same hands. In the reformed system Governmental and administrative authority would be separate from and to an extent independent of the political party while the manager of an economic enterprise would be independent of both. Each would have its own sphere of activity. As a result of these reforms, economic decision-making by managers in charge of economic enterprises has been liberated from Government and administrative control and intervention. Managers in charge of economic enterprise are now free to arrange for supply of inputs and sell the finish products in the best interests of the enterprise of which they are in charge. Thus the subservience to authority is replaced by price cost calculation in economic decision-making. In Russia the new concept of 'Perestroica' (reconstruction) and 'Glassnost' (openness) started dissolving the old rigidities and inefficiencies in the economic system. The socialist economies gave up their commitment to the social ownership of the means of production and have opened one increasing opportunities for private enterprise. After the disintegration of USSR & collapse of socialism, the picture has entirely changed.

Reforms of this type going by the name of decentralisation in China and Russia may not be quite applicable to the Indian conditions. However, decentralisation has been and continues to be of crucial importance in reforming our own system.

Decentralisation in India has both politico-administrative and economic implications and connnotations. I would consider these in turn.

We in India have rightly adopted the federal constitutional system. The word 'Federation' does not figure in the Indian Constitution but it embodies the federal principle of division of functions, powers and finances between the Centre and the States both of which are coordinate participants in our federal system. The Constitution has three lists; the Central List, the State List and the Concurrent List. It also identifies the source of revenue some of which are shared between the Centre and the States while others are exclusively available to them.

While all the constitutions which follow the system of the division of powers and finances between the Centre and the States are entitled to be called federations, some federations tilt towards the Centre while others tilt towards the constituent states. In the former the Centre is supposed to be powerful and strong while in the latter it is the States which can be so described. However, the formal division of functions in the Constitution is one thing; its actual working may be quite different and it has been noticed that thank's to the very logic of the development of the economic and political system, a tendency is noticed even in a country like United States, which owed its existence to coming together of 13 independent states, for the Centre to assume more power. In India the fathers of our Constitution, the Members of the Constituent Assembly went in for a constitution with a strong Centre. They did so because of the need to design a constitution which would ensure the survival of the Indian nation state based on a strong sense of unity and integrity. They were extremely suspicious of centrifugal tendencies threatening the integrity of the nation. Indian Constitution, therefore, consists of many clauses including those relating to emergency and President's rule in the States which makes for a strong centre in relation to the Constitution states. The revenues of the Centre are far more ample and elastic as compared with those of the States. Because of this strong centralisation built in our Constitution, Indian federation was even described as quasi federalism. In practice the centralisation tendency became even stronger in the early years after independence thanks to the same party in power at the Centre and in the States, specially when it was also the party which led Indian to freedom. Besides this, India had the rare fortune of having for the first seventeen years of independence the towering leadership of Pt. Jawaharlal Nehru which ensured close working of the State with the Central Government. Thus India functioned in practice almost like a unltary state despite its federal Constitution. Strong unitary tendencies developed in the working of in our federal system. This was facilitated by the existence of All India Services whose members functioned in key positions both in the Central and State Governments.

However, this was almost an ideal situation which could not be expected to last long. Governments with different political complexions were bound to emerge in the constituent states. This happened first in a conspicuous manner in 1967 and then recurred several times. Now the phenomenon of different political parties in power in different States can no longer be considered to be very unusual.

However, despite the political complexion, the States and the Centre have to function together within the framework of the Indian Constitution in a smooth and harmonious manner. Difference of opinion on specific issues or even policy approaches might well arise but have to be resolved through the mechanisms available under the Constitution. Irrespective of party complexions, the States often feel that they do not have the necessary authority to play their role even their own sphere of activity nor do they have adequate resources. At the same time, there is also a tendency in the States to look to the Centre not only of financial support but also for administrative support in many forms even in spheres like poverty alleviation or agricultural development which lie within the State list. Programmes in the States consist of employment and poverty alleviation schemes introduced by the Central Government. There is a strange co-existence of demand for autonomy of the States and at the same time greater dependence on the Centre. However, full scope for autonomy within the sphere allotted by the Constitution is one thing. Quite another are concepts such as those embodied in Anandpur Resolution which advocate that the role of the Centre should be confined to external affairs, defence and currency and coinage while all the rest should fall within the ambit of the States. This was the type of concept forwarded in the constitutional proposal brought out by the three members of the British Cabinet in the parlies that took place before independence but at that time Indian sub-continent was conceived as a single political entity. After the partition of the country, a weak Centre with authority limited to the three functions could hardly be envisaged.

Such has been the persistent clamour for greater autonomy to the States, that the Centre found it necessary to appoint the Sarkaria Commission to go into the question of Centre State relations. It is clear that a balance which would satisfy the need for centralisation or decentralisation in the Indian polity is not quite easy to accomplish.

The logic of decentralisation however, cannot just stop at the state level. It has to go down to the local level as well, through the establishment of urban and rural self-government institutions. A beginning was made during the British days as far back as in 1877 through Lord Mayo's resolution on decentralisation and Lord Rippon's charter of local government 1882. However, in the absence of national self-government, local self-government had limited significance but even then municipalities, district boards and panchayats not only provided some limited scope for development but also became nurseries for democratic experience and constructive leadership in public life.

After independence, started the era of planned development. In the rural areas the innovative programme of community development based on the concept of popular participation was introduced. However, the evaluation of the programme of community development by Balwantrai Mehta Study Team appointed by the Committee on Plan Projects showed that in the absence of elected local government, the programme was left entirely to the administrative machinery of Government which could not inspire popular enthusiasm for rural development. The Team therefore, recommended establishment of three tier set up of Panchayat Raj institutions and the accountability of rural development administration to the elected representatives of the people in Panchayat Raj institutions. The recommendation of the Committee for the three tier set up of Panchayat Raj was accepted by Central and State Governments and Panchayat Raj was ushered with great fanfare in Rajasthan and Andhra Pradesh. While in these two states, Panchayat Samiti at the block level was the effective unit of local development, the pattern introduced in Maharashtra and Gujarat provided for greater measure of decentralisation at the district level which became the more effective units of local development.

However, the initial enthusiasm for Panchayati Raj soon petered off and Panchayati Raj institutions fell in a state of suspended animation not only because of paucity of finances but also because elections when fell due were not held. District rural development agencies were set up for implementation of poverty alleviation programmes and Panchayati Raj institutions were by-passed even in State like Maharashtra. Separate planning authorities were set up marginalising the role of Zila Parishath in local planning. The Ashok Mehta Committee in 1977 reviewed the situation and made a strong plea for the revival of Panchayati Raj institutions as democratic institutions local development. They introduced the concept of Mandal Panchayat for a group of villages. However, there was hardly any effective follow-up of the recommendations of the Committee and Panchayat Raj institutions continued to be a low ebb. A group was constituted under the chairmanship of Dr. L.N. Singhhivi to prepare a concept paper on Panchayati Raj.* The paper submitted by the group to Government was both a philosophical and constitutional document. From the philosophical point of view, it went back to Mahatma Gandhi's concept of 'Gram Swaraj' as the foundation of Indian democracy. Mahatma Gandhi talked of concentratic circles of social and democratic institutions at the core of which were the village pachayats. Unfortunately, Mahathma Gandhi's concept of 'Gram Swaraj' was not adequately reflected in the design of the Indian Constitution. It contained only one article viz. Article 40 which state the Directive Principles of the Constitution that the State shall promote village

---

* The author was a member of this group.

Panchayats as units of local government. The concept paper stated that this was inadequate and the Constitution itself should provide for the three tier structure of rural local governments with a local list of functions and resources. In order that the elections to these institutions are held in a timely manner it recommends that the Election Commission should be entrusted with the responsibility for timely elections to Panchayati Raj institutions.

The concept paper was considered at a meeting of the Chief Ministers of the States. Barring a few, most of the States had their own reservations regarding constitutional amendments to provide for Panchayati Raj institutions. In the absence, however, of a constitutional place for local governments there was no guarantee that Panchayati Raj institutions would not suffer the neglect that they have suffered all these years. Rajiv Gandhi therefore, proposed a constitutional amendment which was passed by the Lok Sabha but rejected by the Rajya Sabha. The present Prime Minister took the initiative again and the bill was passed by the Parliament.

If devolution of authority through the establishment of local self-government institutions is one form of decentralisation, administrative deconcentration is another. The latter stands for delegation of powers to administrative agencies at the field level. In the absence of such delegation to the administrative agencies at the field level personnel directly dealing with the people are unable to take decisions or deliver the goods. Proposals have to be sent to higher authorities who go on raising queries and making back references resulting in delay and frustration. The right approach, therefore, is to lay down general guidelines and then leave it free to the "man on the spot" to take decisions. Such action oriented administration is a pre condition for an effective delivery system. Unfortunately sanctioning powers are often unduely centralised rendering field agencies ineffective causing wide spread frustration and delay. Even when the powers are delegated they are often not exercised and sanction of higher authorities are nevertheless solicited. With the multiplication of schemes and programmes of development, field agencies have proliferated in number creating a need for necessary coordination. The need is, therefore, for an integrated system of development administration with adequate delegation. This was what the CAARD Committee (Committee to review the existing administrative arrangements for Rural Development and Poverty Alleviation Programmes) recommended.* All branches of development administration would be brought together in a unified district secretariat headed by senior officer who would also be the Secretary of the Zila Parishad. The officer would be of 15 years field experience and senior to the Collector. The Collector would be concerned only with revenue and magisterial function while the entire development work will be under the authority of the Chief Executive of the Zila Parishad under whose

* The author was associated with the work of this Committee.

leadership the entire district development administration would be at the disposal and accountable to the Zila Parishad. The deconcentration of administration on the above lines together with the devolution to the local government institutions has been done only in one State - Karnataka. In this State, the Chief Executive has been designated as the Chief Secretary. The Karnataka model evoked a lot of interest all over the country. Did it succeed ? Did it create a system of development administration which was efficient and at the same time responsive to the people? Did it elicit popular participation in the development process? Unfortunately with the change of political government the approach was reversed and the questions remained unanswered.

So much then for the politico-administrative implications of decentralisation. We may now turn to economic connotation of decentralisation.

A perfectly competitive free market economy is a model of a decentralised economy. The model stipulates that there will be innumerable consumers and innumerable producers as well as owners of factors of production who would all be engaged in a free market in a process of maximising returns over costs in pursuit of self-interest. As a result of their individual decisions, the invisible hand of market mechanism will provide optimum answers to all questions which an economy has to solve - questions as to what to produce, how much to produce, for whom to produce, where to produce, when to produce, and how to produce? However, such a model has no relevance to reality where it is found that the bargaining positions of various participants in the economy are not the same and a few participants are in a dominant position to dictate terms and impose decisions on those who are dependent on them. What exists is not perfect but imperfect competition - monopoly and oligopoly. Rather than full employment of manpower and other resources and their optimisation with price equal to no more than average cost of production what exist are unemployment, under-employment, disguised unemployment, monopoly restriction of production, monopoly gains arising out of the restrictive practices, profiteering and even the evils of black economy. On the top of this is the systematic neglect of social costs and social returns which the market does not take into account since it is concerned with private costs and private profits. As a result, the market economy often gives rise to what Galbraith has called private opulence co-existing with public squalor - neglect of public assets like air, water and forest. Social cost in the shape of pollution, over crowding and development of slums and impoverishment of the quality of life. It then becomes necessary for the State to intervene on behalf of the society through measures like control of monopoly, industrial regulation and control over investment. A series of such public interventions are inherent in the logic of the concept of a planned economy which stands as a contrast to the market economy. When it is felt that the economic fotunes of the masses cannot be left to the vicissitudes of the market forces but have to be the result of well directed purposeful social effort, the case for planning is well established.

But State intervention and planning necessarily lead to centralisation. In a planned economy, the planners' choice superseeds the market choice though the planners' choice is no doubt in the name of the society. To ensure that the goals and targets of plans are accomplished, the planner has to resort to panoply of measures such as directed allocation of investment, regulation of credit by financial institutions, fiscal incentives and disincentives, licences, regulation of monopoly, industrial regulation, and public investment in strategic sectors of the economy.

Planning is often equated with socialism but they are not necessarily synonymous. Socialism stands for social ownership of means of production while planning stands for purposeful arrangement for the future. Even monopoly enterprises in the private sector will have their corporate plans and if these enterprises are in the nature of monopoly, these plans are bound to regulate the economic behaviour of many others. The question is whether it is planning by monopoly of large scale private enterprises or by the State.

We in India decided to have a planned economy without a wholesale social ownership of means of production. We rather made a choice for a mixed economy giving scope for public, private as well as corporate sectors. Agriculture was mainly n the private and cooperative sector where as basic and strategic industries and infrastructure in the public sector. The field of consumer goods industry was left to he private enterprise.

When we made a choice in favour of the planning economy, it was well understood that there could not be planning without the regime of controls; but over a period of time the controls proliferated; they became clumsy and counter-productive. They brought into being any number of administrative agencies to control every economic activity which administered these controls on case to case basis.

It is this realisation which led in the recent years to a policy of liberalisation. A large number of enterprises were delicensed. The levy quota for industries like sugar, paper and cement were reduced with a view to their ultimate elimination. The scope of Monopoly and Restrictive Trade Practices Act was confined to enterprises with assets above rupees hundred crores. The objective of these united measures was to give greater freedom to productive effort and improve the profitability of investment.

A large public sector also leads to a measure of centralisation. These enterprises are ultimately accountable to Government and to Parliament. The Ministries of Government therefore necessarily start exercising control over the public enterprises in their charge. This often leads to back seat driving leading to loss of initiative on the part of managers of these public sector enterprises. As a result the enterprises do not function as successful commercial concerns and often accumulate huge losses. They suffer from employment of excessive manpower or excessive inventories and are unable to take quick decision.

One way of course would be the privatisation of these enterprises. This is the path followed in Britain and Japan. Under Margaret Thatcher, Britain went ahead with a systematic policy of privatisation.

In India such a decision could not be taken because of the ideological commitment to the public sector and also the mis-givings about the private sector as also the unwillingness of private enterprise to enter into the fields like infrastructure and basic industries which above a long gestation period. Under the new policy of liberalisation, the State has now started divesting its shares in public enterprises.

Commercial flexibility in public enterprises needs managerial autonomy. How can managerial autonomy be reconciled with public accountability - that becomes the major question. The answer to this has been found in terms of the mechanism of Memorandum of Understanding between the Ministry and the enterprise. The MOU lays down the obligations of the enterprise in terms of fulfilment of certain physical and financial targets including target of production, efficiency and social obligations. In return the MOU provides for commitments of Government in terms of provision of investible resources, supply of essential materials and foreign exchange. The assumption behind the concept of MOU is that once it has been signed, there will be no ad hoc directions from Government. The management of the enterprise would be left free to pursue its plan. Full authority would be delegated to the management. It is only at the end of the period of MOU that the Government will review to what extent the enterprise has fulfilled its obligation. Autonomy will be balanced with accountability. The experiment of MOU has just made a beginning. Its success depends on the extent to which the concept is understood and followed up by the Government and the enterprise.

A fresh examination of the Central State relationship through a commission, a concept paper for providing constitutional basis to Panchayati Raj institutions, the establishment of a full fledged integrated administrative set up at the district level, accountable to local government, liberalisation of the regime of controls, greater autonomy to public enterprises through the mechanism of MOU - these are some of the new thrusts towards decentralisation. Decentralisation is a means to bring about more efficient decision-making as also more responsive decision-making — responsive to the people. Decentralised structure also additionally helps in multiplying the centres of initiative and capability for decision making and widening the area of freedom and flexibility. As against this concentration by sheer weight of monolithic rigidity has a risk of falling with its own weight. The new thrusts towards decentralisation are, therefore, only to be welcomed. The results cannot be immediate but can be seen over a long period.

21

Power to the People

When India attained freedom on 15th August, 1947, the political power was transferred from the British rulers to the Indian people. The Indian Constitution provided for a federal polity in which the legislature and executive power was divided between the Central Government and the State Government. It also provided for a Parliamentary system of Government under which the power was exercised by the elected representatives on behalf of the people. Under this system the leader of the party which commands majority in the legislature becomes the Prime Minister at the Centre and Chief Minister at the state. The Prime Minister and Chief Minister constitute the cabinet or the Council of Ministers consisting of members of his or her party in the legislature whom he or she selects to join his cabinet. The cabinet constitutes the political executive and exercises/ political power on behalf of the people.

The political executive is expected to exercise the power to translate the hopes and aspirations of the people into a concrete reality. It is also expected to devise policies and frame plans and programmes so as to satisfy the aspirations of the people.

The political executive has to rely on the members of the civil service in its task. The civil servants help the political executives in the formulation of plans, policies and programmes. They also implement them at various operational levels both in the State and Central Government.

The State in independent India is expected to work as a welfare State. The welfare State is expected to undertake a whole spectrum of developmental activities for the welfare of the people. These include a wide range programmes for rural and agricultural development, promotion of industry and developmental including irrigation, electrification, transport, communication, education, health etc.

In 1951, the nation embarked on a planned process of economic development. A nation wide community development programme was ushered in through the medium of 5000 Community development blocks. Each block had a machinery consisting of Block Development Officer and a team of extension officers for subjects like agriculture, animal husbandry, rural industries, rural engineering, social education, cooperation, etc.

After few years of working of the Community Development Programme in the country, it was evaluated by the Balwantrai Mehta Study Team. On the basis of an indepth analysis, the Balwantrai Mehta Study Team came to the conclusion that the success of the Community development programme depends on the participation of the people and such participation would not be forthcoming, unless the block development administration was placed under the elected representatives of the people at the local level. They, therefore, recommended a three tier system of Panchayati Raj Institutions with Panchayat at the village level, Panchayat Samiti at the block level, and the Zila Parishad at the district level.

Soon the recommendations of the Study Team were accepted by the Stateand Central government and Panchayati Raj Institutions were set up in different states in India, beginning with Rajasthan and Andhra Pradesh. There were many local variations in the pattern suggested by Balwantrai Mehta Study Team. There was initially a great enthusiam for the Panchayati Raj set up. It was hailed as a "transfer of power" to the people - as a change from people's participation in Government's programme to of Government's participation in people's programme.

However, after few years it was realised that for a variety of reasons the Panchayati Raj Institutions did not make a success in many states. Firstly, the elections to the Panchayati raj institutions were not held regularly. After their terms were over, the administration of these institutions was entrusted to the administrators consisting of the civil servants. Secondly, where they continued to function, their scope of activities was progressively curtailed. Thirdly, in many Panchayati Raj institutions, there was excessive politicisation leading to rivalries between factions which hampered the work of the Panchayati Raj institutions. The positions of the Panchayati Raj institutions were used more for acquisition of power than for the service to the people, thus defeating the very objective of establishing Panchayati Raj institutions. The whole system came into dolldrums.

It is in ths context, that it was felt that it would not be allright to leave the Panchayai Raj Institutions as on creatures of the State Government. The State Government cannot be left free to meddle with the Panchayati Raj institutions or supercede them at will. In a large country like India, the development programmes and indeed governmental power cannot be concentrated at the Central and State level. There has to be decentralization of power and demolution of functions which should be transferred to the local levels viz. district, block and the village.

For such decentralisation to be effective, it was felt that the institutions at the District, Block and village levels should be recognised as constitutional entities i.e. the local call self government institutions should have the same constitutional section as the government at the state and Central levels. This led to the revolutionary concept that Panchayati Raj institutions should find a place in the constitution itself. In other words, the constitutional authority should be divided between central, state and local governments as coordinate entities.

This concept was given expression by the 73rd amendment to the Indian Constitution which has been passed by both the Central and the State legislatures. Now, the Panchayati Raj institutions have become the organs of the constitutional scheme of the country.

Let us understand the implications of this change — Firstly, the 73rd. amendment envisages a "local sector". Hitherto there were only three lists of constitutional powers and functions viz. the central list, the state list and the concurrent list. Now there is the fourth list, the list of local government powers and functions. Secondly, to ensure timely and orderly elections to the Panchayati Raj institutions the amendment envisages a separate Election Commission for the Panchayati Raj institutions just like the Election Commission for the Parliamentary and state legislative elections. Thirdly, to ensure proper allocation of finances to the local bodies, the local finances commission has also been envisaged.

With the secure basis provided by the Indian constitution, the Panchayati Raj institutions can emerge as effective local self-government institutions. However, it has to be realised that a constitutional mechanism by itself cannot achieve the objectives envisaged. A constitution will deliver of goods only if the institutions created under it function in a manner they are expected to function. In other words, the Panchayati Raj institutions even though regularly elected and clothed with necessary power and supported by finances of their own, cannot succeed unless those who are elected to the Panchayati Raj institutions are aware that the power given to them has to be used for the benefit of the people and not for personal or partisan interests. The Panchayati Raj institutions have also tobe a efficient and effective bodies. If they become hot beds of local politics and dens of corruption, then the very objective of "power to the people" will be defeated.

It is rightly said that eternal vigilance is the price of libery. It is for the people to be awake and see that the Panchayati Raj institutions work with dedication, objectivity and sense of commitment for the welfare of the people. It could be expected that the Panchayati Raj institution being nearer to the people, would be more answerable to them. It is only an enlightened body of citizens who can ensure the answerability of the local governments to them.

One can hope that the 73rd amendment will usher in a new era of Panchayati Raj in the country and ensure fulfilment the concept of "power to the people" through decentralised democracy.

22

Decentralisation and Rural Development : Asian Experience

The principle of decentralisation has been adopted by several developing countries as a basis of the strategy of socio-economic developmen It has been found particularly appropriate in the field of rural developmer and this for many reasons. First in the very nature of the case, rura development has to be spread over large number of dispersed rural communities and it is only through a decentralised approach that it would b possible to reach them. Secondly, while a centralised approach reflects th priorities of the planners, it is the decentralised approach which enables th reflections of the local needs and priorities and the felt-needs of the peopl Thirdly, it allows the participation of the local people and the mobilisatio of the local resources for the task of development. Fourthly, it builds up loca institutions which provide an enduring base of national developmen Finally, it builds up leadership and enterpreneurship in the rural communities by working as a school of education in the art of decision making an administration.

The form which decentralisation has taken, however, has varied fror country to country. In India, it has led to the establishment of the three tie set-up of Panchayati Raj institutions. Of course, panchayats have been a ancient institution in India even from the Vedic times. Sir Charles Metca called them a "little republics" able to hold their own against external force and lasted when nothing else could last. After the adoption of the principl of decentralisation the British rules also passed legislation for the establishment of the panchayats and the local boards. The establishment c Panchayati Raj Institutions in recent times however was a sequel to th community development programme in India. While evaluating th community development programme, the committee on Plan Projects headed by Shri Balwantrai Mehta obserbed that unless the development administration was placed squarely under the local representatives of the people, it would not be possible to kindle local enthusiasm for local development. Two patterns of Panchayati Raj Institutions emerged. In one represented by Andhra and Rajasthan, block became the real point of decentralised development administration whereas in the States of Maharashtra and Gujarat, district was chosen as the unit of decentralised administration because it was felt that it was only at that level that decentralisation could be real and substantial. These were the developments in the field of decentralisation in the 60's but during the 70's, disenchantment set in. The State Governments gave a short shrift to Panchayati Raj institutions. Regular elections were not held and they came under the rule of the Administrators appointed by Government. The Ashok Mehta Committee appointed in 1977 made a plea for the resuscitation of the panchayati raj institutions since they had a dynamic role to play in the field of rural development. Recently, the 73rd amendment at the Constitution has made Panchayati Raj institutions a constitutional entity. Decentralisation was also promoted through, the idea of planning at the local level, namely,the block, and district levels but this local planning has been more in the shape of dis-aggregation of the state plan rather than formulation of an autonomous plan aimed at mobilisation of the local resources by harnessing the skills and energies of the local people.

It is in neighbouring Sri Lanka that the principle of decentralisation has gone further. Firstly, under the scheme of decentralisation a specific decentralised budget has been placed at the disposal of ever district which would be free to spend resources according to local plans and priorities. Secondly, every district has a Minister who finds a place in the Cabinet for the whole Island. The Cabinet thus has these district Ministers in addition to the functional Ministers. Thirdly, a District Secretariat for the Minister is provided by the local administration headed by the Government agent. Law on agrarian reform has envisaged the establishment of a District Development Council headed by the Local District Minister. Fourthly, with the help of international agencies and aid-giving countries, Sri Lanka has worked out comprehensive development projects for several of its twenty four districts. While these steps taken by Sri Lankan appear to go far in the direction of decentralised development, the weakness of Sri Lankan approach to the decentralisation lies in the absence of self reliant local institutions. The Local Government institutions stand superceded while the cooperatives remain isolated and being very large have very tenuous links with the local people. Thus, decision making tends to be centralised in the District Minister rather than in the local communities or autonomous institutions at district and sub-district levels.

In Bangla Desh, the principle of decentralisation received a new impetus through the establishment of "gram sarkar" as grass-root institutions. These have been launched under the inspiration of the President himself. The Swa-Nirbhar Gram Sarkars have to be organised in 68,000 villages of Bangla Desh by December 1980. A Gram Sabha had to be constituted for each village. It has to choose a Gram Pradhan. These Gram Sarkar institutions were to be incharge of the crucial programmes of canal digging, mass literacy and family planning and population control programmes. In implementing these programmes, the District Administrators was given the coordinating role in organising the masses and officials into work teams. They were to be ultimately responsible to the President for the successful completion of the projects. At the District level, 20 District Development Coordinators had been appointed by Government from amongst the Members of the Parliament with the rank and status of Deputy Minister and had been placed in their respective districts with specific responsibility in relation to the three crucial programmes mentioned above. This is a development somewhat on the lines of the Sri Lankan approach. Thus Gram Sarkar was a new decentralised approach to develop viable village level organisations.

In Malaysia, there are 13 States divided into 74 districts each incharge of a District Officer. Besides the district level administration, there are the municipalities and the regional development authorities. It is more and more realised in Malaysia that national development cannot be achieved by public agencies or government efforts alone and that semi-public and private sector agencies have also to play a very significant and crucial role. The lowest tier of the planning and development machinery are the village development committees. During the hay day of the Red-book system of 1960, the village development committees were full partners in the bottom of planning process. However, even today, the planning capacity or authority at the district or sub-district level have been extremely limited. It is frankly acknowledged that there is no happy marriage of top-bottom and bottom–up planning in Malaysia and, in practice, it is more top-bottom. The district and local organisations do not have planning capacity nor the resources. The local organisations are under-developed and neglected. Most development programmes and projects are based on sectoral planning rather than spatial location.

In Thailand, the administrative tradition has been that of centralisation. Most industrial activities have traditionally concentrated in and around Bangkok Metropolitan area. Budgets provide for programmes and projects on narrow sectoral considerations rather than on requirements of different regions. It is only when the Prime Minister noticed that his own homeland was an area of backwardness that the first step was taken towards the formation of regional development committees for the backward regions. The regional policies thus introduced aimed at establishment of regional centres, decentralisation of economic and social services and also of industries. In 1977, a bottom level development planning scheme taking province as a focus was undertaken as a measure to diffuse development. In 1979, the village development scheme was inaugurated to cover about 5,000 impoverished villages. Ten years ago, the Government gave out-right grants to of lakh Bahts to each commune throughout the country with the purpose of decentralising development responsibility to rural people. This set off new trend of decentralisation of development responsibilities. In Thailand, the provincial units or other units are only the units of the Central Government and almost all programmes or decisions to allocate funds are initiated by the line departments in Bangkok. The Provincial Governors are supposed to be the coordinators at the provincial level and the Chief District officials at the district level but they have limited scope for coordinating projects of the Central Government since the officers incharge of field units report directly to their superiors in Bangkok. The hope to have a provincial plan which has its own identity and which covers all the development projects which are operated in the area has so far achieved only a little success. The provinces receive guidelines from the Prime Minister, the various Ministries and the various Central committees which sometimes ssue contrary and inconsistent policies and guidelines. Recently, the provincial development planning scheme has been designed under which unds are directly channelled to the provinces in terms of its potential and or reducing the economic and social disparities. However, the responsible organs of planning and implementation at the provincial level lack expertise and administrative resources.

In China, big reforms have been introduced in economic management ystem in order to provide scope for considering the needs of localities and ndividual enterprises. This has made relaxation in the system of centralised ontrol over production and distribution. These relaxations have been deliberately introduced out of a realisation that under central planning it is ot possible to reflect the dynamic change of economic activities and to chieve optimal economic results. Under the new system, the State owned nd collectively owned units can run their business independently. To the nd of June 1980, 6600 such enterprises of large size have undergone eforms. Under the new system, the planned economy is integrated with the narket economy and the individual enterprises have to expose themselves o the forces of a competitive market economy. Like individual enterprises, ndividual regions have also to utilise and develop their resources. Thus, the reforms of decentralisation are considered to be crucial to reach the targets of four-fold modernisation, i.e., in industry, agriculture, defence and science and technology by the end of the century.

Indonesia is a unitary state. It has regions, provinces and smaller regions which, however, are not independent entities but are an inseparable part of the republic of Indonesia. However, Indonesia has introduced de-concentration for purposes of regional development. Development activities are transferred to regional offices from the Central Government. The programmes are coordinated at regional and sub-regional levels by Governors and Bhupatis. Regional development programmes are subsidised by the Central Government. There is a basic pattern of regional development. A national consultation is held for harmonising sectoral development with regional development. There are Development Planning Boards at the national and regional level which assist the President and the Governor in development planning and evaluation. Since sectoral plans are too strong, regional planning is still very weak. The Regional Planning Board are unable to include all programmes into a single development plan. Moreover, the provincial budget is too small compared to the sectoral budget.

In the Philippines also, decentralisation is really a form of administraties deconcentration. The country has been divided into standard regions for administrative as well as planning purposes. For each region, Regional Development Council is organised. Regional development has been identified as one of the major objectives of the development effort. One of the objectives of regionalisation is to reduce the disparity among different regions. The country is divided into 30 administrative regions. The determination of the geographical boundaries of the regional areas has been based primarily on the river basin project but also taking into account the economic and socio-economic profiles of the regional areas. Various Ministries have been asked to establish regional offices which serve as extensions of the Ministries in the regional areas. The administrative authorities have been directed to delegate powers to the regional offices including those for the formulation of the Regional budget estimates.

It would thus be seen that almost all the developing countries in the South-East Asian region have attempted to give a practical expression to the principle of decentralisation specially for the programmes of rural development. They have recognised that top-down approach does not always work and there is an area of development where bottom-up approach is more appropriate. But it is obvious that the advantages of decentralisation cannot be reaped without the establishment of a strong and capable local institutions with adequate resources and trained personnel. In the absence of these, the bottom-up approach has little chance against the traditional top-bottom approach.

Part - V

SECTORS OF RURAL DEVELOPMENT

23

Command Area Development Programme

Ever since the country embarked upon the process of planned develop-
nent in the year 1951, sustained attention on a priority basis has been paid
the harnessing of the copious water of India's river system for agricul-
ıral development. Traditional Indian agriculture had been a gamble in
in, especially in areas of low and uncertain rainfall. These were known as
in-shadow areas. Very often these areas were in the immediate neigh-
ourhood of mighty rivers and yet they have been known as a drought
one area of our country. The district of Raichur for example is a doab lying
tween the rivers Krishna and Tungabhadra, and yet the district itself was
dry parched land till the mighty Tungbhadra reservoir brought the life-
ving waters to it which turned the district into a large producer of food and
mmercial crops. Similarly the district of Bijapur has the Krishna river
wing through it with its several tributaries, and yet the district has been
toriously and chronically drought-prone. Waters of these rivers, instead
providing life-giving support to the soil were flowing down into the
ean. Ambitious projects were, therefore, taken up to construct dams
ross these rivers and to store water into mighty reservoirs to be
annelised in large tracts of agricultural land. Thus the first batch of the
ghty irrigation projects taken up in the fifties included the Bhakra
ngal, Damodar Valley, Mahanadi and Tunga-Bhadra projects. These
re followed by other mighty projects like the Naga-Arjun Sagar Project
Andhra Pradesh, Jayakawadi Projects on Godavari in Maharashtra, and
jects in Krishna and Cavery Basins in Karnataka. These projects were
scribed as temples of modern India by Jawaharlal Nehru. They were
ected to increase rapidly the country's irrigation potential and to provide
ble and productive agriculture in the hitherto parched tracts of the
ntry.

While the completed reservoirs stood as a witness to the mighty effort of the nation, it was soon realised that these investments would not yiel returns unless the water stored in reservoir was actually used by the farme on his field. And experience showed that this could not be taken for granted In other words, there was a considerable gap between the creation and th utilisation of the irrigation potential. Such a gap not only delayed desire development but also meant idle investment which blocked country' precious resources without an adequate return from investment in th irrigation projects. A country as poor as India could not afford anything bu the quickest utilisation of the irrigation potential created by the river valle projects.

The Irrigation Commission as well as a Committee of Ministers i charge of irrigation in several states went into the whole subject and mad recommendations for decreasing the gap between the creation of th irrigation potential and its utilisation. The main idea that emerged out o these recommendations was that the utilisation of irrigation potentia should not be taken for granted, and conscious and deliberate efforts wer required for the development of the Command Area under the irrigatio projects. This is the genesis of the idea of the Command Area developmen

Soon it was given a concrete shape. The Agriculture Commissio (1970-75) made recommendations for the establishment of Command Are Development Authorities incharge of the command areas under variou major irrigation projects in the country. Separate departments of wings c departments were established at the level of the State government and th Central government to be incharge of the subject of Command Are Development. There are, as at present, about 85 Command Area Projects i the country and one of the most important tasks of administration today to see that command area development takes place in a speedy manner.

There are many reasons why the Command Area Development do not automatically take place after the construction of the reservoir. First all, it was the experience in the initial years that while the reservoirs we constructed, the water conveyance system was not complete. In the earli years, the water conveyance system constructed by the authorities co sisted of the main canal and distributoris, but the field channels we expected to be constructed by the farmers themselves. The canals ended the level of three-cusec water courses but the further work of wat conveyance was expected to be undertaken by the farmers themselves. Th assumption was not found to be justified. The water flowing in the can only passed down the drain because the farmers were not able to use t water for irrigation their fields. Thus the absence of field channels tend to jeopardise the entire irrigation facility in terms of the results. It wa therefore, decided that the construction of the field channels must be integral part of the provision of the water conveyance facility.

Mere construction of the water conveyance system is not adequate. The water has to spread uniformly over the soil, and this requires a programme of land levelling. Land levelling could be undertaken either manually through bullock power or with the use of ordinary tools, like buck scraper or a leveller where the gradient is low, but where it is more, use of tractors is very necessary. Therefore, it is either necessary to introduce the programme of supply of land levelling implements and bullock power to individual farmers or else provide tractor service to the farmers in command areas. The tractor service can be provided either through a corporation or a cooperative. All this requires tremendous effort.

The problem of water conveyance is not just one of construction of field channels. It is also that of water management. Often while abundant water in available at earlier reaches, the tail-enders suffer. An economic and judicious use of water is necessary both for making the maximum use of water as also for getting the highest yields. Excessive water at earlier reaches and deficient supply at the tail-end are equally undesirable from the point of view of higher yields. For equitable distribution of water, the system of Warabandi was recommended. The objective of the system of Warabandi or roster of water supply is that water is available to various crops according to prescribed requirements say 4-5 times at the various crucial stages in the development of crop. This requires a certain amount of discipline in the use of water. Often in the absence of the social discipline, the well-to-do people take the lion's share of the water while the poor and the weaker sections of the farmers suffer. No doubt the Irrigation Departments have their own lower-level functionaries often known as Patkaris incharge of the water distribution. But more often than not, the Patkari is in collusion with richer sections of the farmers, and there are complaints of corruption. The best way of ensuring equitable distribution of water is for the farmers themselves to evolve a fair and efficient system under the auspices of either an irrigation Panchayat or a water cooperative. The water cooperatives have been tried in Gujarat and have been found successful, and the concept needs to be followed up in other parts of the country.

An equally important problem requiring social discipline is the conformity to the prescribed pattern of localisation of crops. The Command Area under the irrigation project has, first of all, to be systematically brought under comprehensive soil survey to show the appropriateness of various kinds of soils for the cultivation of various types of irrigated crops. Thus, for example, in the heavy black cotton soil, crops like paddy and sugarcane are inappropriate and would only lead to water-logging. These lands are more suitable for irrigated cotton or wheat or oil- seeds. On the other hand, lighter soils are more appropriate for paddy or sugarcane. It is not enough for the technologists to survey and analyse the soils and prescribe the pattern. The pattern has to be acceptable and accepted by the farmers themselves. Often the farmers are not educated into understanding the rationale of localisation of crops and they tend to violate the prescribed cropping pattern, and no amount of attempt by the revenue authorities to fine the delinquent farmers serves avoid violation of cropping patterns. This is indeed a ticklish problem. If the farmer realise the benefit of the prescribed cropping pattern in terms of their own self-interest. It is likely that the prescribed cropping pattern would be followed and optimum benefit derived from irrigation.

Indeed an important hurdle in irrigation development is the acclimatisation of the farmers to irrigated agriculture. Farmers used for centuries to the non-intensive cultivation of dry crops are hardly in a position to provide intensive labour, skill, knowledge and investment required for irrigated agriculture. This is a case of taking the horse to the water and then being faced with the problem of how to make the horse drink water. The transition from dry agriculture to irrigated agriculture is seen to be not only an agricultural change but a cultural change - a total change in the way of life of the farmer. In many cases, the shortage of manpower in irrigated area is sought to be made good by the colonisation of people from other districts and areas into irrigated tracts. Such schemes of colonisation of people in irrigated areas did not always succeed. On the other hand, what did succeed was the spontaneous immigration of people as e.g. the immigration of the farmers from Sarkars in Andhra Pradesh long used to irrigation into Raichur district of Karnataka. These immigrant farmers sold away their lands at high prices, bought larger tracts in the newly irrigated area of Raichur district at comparatively low price and were able to grow abundant crops of cotton and paddy, and thus were responsible for the total transformation of the entire economy of the area.

While immigration is the market solution to the problem of deficient low skill and entrepreneurship. Command Area Development Authorities introduced programmes for the training of local farmers in irrigated agriculture at either training institutions or through extension programme in the field. Thus skill formation in irrigated agriculture is another important component of the programme of Command Area Development.

But this has to be followed by organisation of additional inputs. Irrigated agriculture makes a much greater demand on improved or hybrid seeds, fertilizers and credit than dry cultivation, and often the cooperatives and other extant institutions are not able to arrange the delivery of these essential inputs. Strengthening of the delivery system therefore emerges as an important component of Command Area Development.

In anticipation of the increase of various crops in irrigated areas, it is necessary to build up the post-harvest facilities in the shape of the arrangements for quick harvesting of crops, building up scientific storage, transport, marketing and processing facilities. A series of godowns need to be constructed at the village and market levels. Strong marketing cooperatives needs to be organised with trained manpower. These cooperative institutions whether in the field of credit or supply of inputs or marketing or processing do indeed provide attractive and gainful employment opportunities to the educated rural youth. Without a network of credit cooperatives to supply short-term, medium-term and long-term credit as well as inputs like seeds and fertilizer, the programme of command area development would not get off the ground. Without the presence of strong marketing cooperatives, despite increased agricultural yield, the farmer will not get higher returns. Intermediaries may exploit the farmer by buying the agricultural commodities at as low a rate as possible and selling them later at the much higher rate in the terminal market. Properly organised marketing cooperatives can pass the benefit of the higher prices to the farmers. Inspite of the undoubted advantages of marketing cooperatives, they have not had an all-round success, and indeed many of these 3,200 primary cooperatives in the country are not quite effective in marketing of agricultural commodities. The marketing cooperatives or specialised cooperatives can also undertake agro-processes through enterprises like sugar factories, flour mills, oilseeds extraction units or the ginning and pressing of cotton bales. Development of market yards in the rural area and other marketing facilities under the auspices of regulated markets are an important component of Command Area Development.

Agriculture has to be supported by subsidiary or auxilliary activities like dairying or fishery. Irrigated area provides possibilities of increased supply of feed and fodder for cattle and this opportunity should be fully utilised for upgrading the standard of cattle and marketing of milk. Similarly the reservoirs could be stored with fingerlings. Increase in fish products could be very enormous. Along the canals and distributaries, trees could be planted and a systematic programme of afforestation taken up.

These are some of the principal components of the programme of Command Area Development. It is now well recognised that such an integrated Command Area Development Plan has to be prepared and implemented in a systematic manner in all command areas in the irrigation projects. Irrigation development is the work not just of the engineers. It is a work which requires participation of various development departments, including agriculture, horticulture, animal husbandry, cooperation, marketing and so on. Command Area Development is indeed an inter-discipline. The officers incharge of these various departments have to work as members of one administration which has to be headed by a Command Area Development Commissioner who must have a broad perspective regarding the work involved in Command Area Development and who should be capable of orchestration of the efforts of a very large number of individuals belonging to various institutions as well as departmental agencies.

Though Command Area Development work is of a high significance and national importance, often it tends to get sidetracked or ignored by the established agencies of government. It requires technical knowledge, and perchant for farmer education and organisation rather than exercise of authority or power to which the departmental officials are often addicted. It is, therefore, necessary to give adequate recognition to the work of Command Area Development in the country. It should not be allowed to be routinised or belittled.

With the establishment of agencies at the level of State and Central Secretariat, attention has been given to the preparation of the Management Information system related to the Command Area Development. Because of the multi-dimensional nature of Command Area Development, the establishment of a Management Information System that works is not easy. A group was constituted in the Planning Commission to work out the Management Information System for Command Area Development.

24

Drought and Development

During the year 1987-88 India was in the grip of a severe drought which was described as 'the worst in the century'. It affected several parts of the country, some of which like Rajasthan and Gujarat suffered from third or fourth successive drought. The nation was hard put to it in tiding over the situation. Addressing the nation from the ramparts of the Red Fort on August 15, 1988 the then Prime Minister, Rajiv Gandhi congratulated his Government for its performance in successfully dealing with the drought situation "without going with a begging 'bowl', to any other country in the world. Fortunately the year 1988-89 turned out to be a year of excellent monsoon which brought copious rains almost all over the country. Both Kharif and Rabi were good season. A record crop of 172 million tonnes of food grains was reported[1] exceeding by 26 million tonnes, the last peak of 152 million tonnes reached in the year 83-84. [The break-up for individual crops 49.55 million tonnes of wheat. 74 million tonnes of rice, 9.54 million tonnes of groundnuts and 204.63 million tonnes of sugarcane.] The performance during 1989-90 was still better. This has been hailed as a great revival of Indian agriculture. The optimism has been sustained by seven succesive good monsoons raising food production to more than 185 million tonnes and available food stocks to more than 35 million tonnes.

While the sense of gratification in tiding over a difficult situation and resuming tne process of agricultural growth is understandable, any sense of complacency would be a great danger. Droughts may recur in the future as they have occurred in the past. Moreover, there is evidence that droughts have been causing successively large variations in employment and rural incomes.[2] Inspite of this, one has the feeling of deja as one witnesses a mood of complacency. The Bihar drought of the year 1966-67 was followed by an excellent season and bumper crop which wiped out all concern for drought and the desire to draw lessons from the drought experience.

With it slackened the determination to take resolute steps to prevent th recurrence of distress that the drought caused and to continue the type o development activity that was initiated during the drought years The phenomenon of complacency replacing concern was repeated in th aftermath of Maharashtra drought during the years 1970-73.

Drought— A Part of Climatology

Droughts are bound to recur because they are after all a part o climatology. India has suffered from droughts from times immemorial. Except for small pockets in the North East, there are no areas in India no affected by drought one time or another. For every seven good seasons there are at least two or three bad seasons in India.[4] Droughts have occure in India towards the middle and end of each century.

Droughts have afflicted different parts of the globe as well. The Sahe belt in Africa lying between the world's largest tropical desert, the Sahar and the tropical rain forest of Africa is a drought prone region. Anothe drought prone area is Ethiopia whose drought pattern has links wit droughts in Sahel belt.

Even developed countries in the world are not free from the onslaugh of drought. During the summer of 1988, the food bowl of USA was in th grip of drought described as "the worst in half a century". At the same, tim drought ravaged large parts of Central and Eastern China.[5] As a conse quence of these droughts the world stock of food grain, was expected to fa from 402 million tonnes constituting 89 days supplies to no more than 25 million tonnes enough to last 54 days.

In the context of this historical background, India cannot slacken it concern regarding the drought situation just because 1988-89, 89-90 an 90-91 have been good agricultural years. Even in the good year 1988-8 droughts had been reported from Bihar, Kalahandi in Orissa and Chhatisgar in M. P. Though there was excellent rainfall in the country during 1990, i some tehsils in Bikaner District, there was hardly any rainfall and famin conditions prevails. Cattle have died, there is high incidence of malnutritio among children and people who have not yet migrated are starving. Peopl have to walk 20 km to get drinking water.[6] Moreover, despite the bumpe crop during 1988-89, procurement had been below expectation an replenishment of depleted food stock was not upto expectation. In th meanwhile prices of food grains and sugar rose oddly in the year of goo monsoon and bumper crops inspite of two good years 1988, 89-90 and goo crop expected for 90-91 there is no slackening of food prices. This makes necessary that the good years do not dilute the national concern about an attention bestowed on the strategy of dealing with the drought situation

Strategy of Dealing with the Drought Situation

A—Laissez Faire Strategy during Colonial Times

During the British period droughts led to famine and mass starvation. The colonial period began with drought and famine in Bengal in 1770 during which 1/3 of the population of the province perished.[7] The colonial era ended with the great Bengal famine of 1943, not entirely due to drought, in which 3 million people perished.[8] Between 1770 and 1880 as many as 27 scarcities and famines were recorded. During the 50 years 1850 to 1900, 20 million lives were lost in about 20 famines. Amongst the serious droughts and famines were those of 1837-38 (Allahabad area), 1860-61 (Agra - Delhi belt), 1860-65 (Western and Northern provinces, Bengal and Bihar, and 1868-69 (Bengal & Orisa), 1873-74 (Bengal, Bihar, Bombay and Madras) and 1876-78 (Bengal, Bihar, UP, CP, Madras and Bombay).

During 1837-38, and 1860-66, Government remained indifferent and people died on the road side and in the fields not only due to starvation but also disease and epidemics. The Government took the view that its only responsibility was to give employment to able bodied labourers at as a low rate of daily wages as possible with a fixed quantum of work demanded in return. The relief to helpless and infirm was considered to be a business of the charitable public. It was only during 1868-69 drought in Western and North Western provinces and the Bengal Bihar famine of 1873-74 that the Government aimed at "preventing loss of lives at any cost". However, this humanitarian approach was abandoned in dealing with famine relief operation in the course of Bengal Orissa-Madras-Bombay Deccan famine of 1876-78 on the ground that 'effect of indiscriminate help of government was far worse than the effect of famine.' The recommendations of Famine Commission of 1880, 1898 and 1901 led to a more considerate approach and the modification of the laissez faire strategy. Suspension and remission of land revenue, protective irrigation, extension of railway network, land tenure improvement and rural financing under the Taccavi and Agricultural Lons Act were added as positive elements in the strategy for dealing with droughts. Famine codes based on the recommendations of the Famine Commissions provided authoritative guidelines to local administration for anticipation, recognition and relief of famines. Inspite of these recommendations and personal supervision by the Viceroy Lord Curzon, so severe were the droughts of 1897 and 1899 affecting 28 million people that despite relief to 4.6 million people, a million perished.

Droughts continued to occur in the first 2/3 decades of the 20th century but they did not lead to mass starvation. This may be attributed to the modified strategy. Sir Theodore Morrisson[9] and Prof. Mc-Mácalpin[10] however, attributed it to improvement in transportation through the railway network which facilitated transport of food grains surplus to drought stricken areas as also to the commercialisation of agriculture in response to rise in prices in agricultural commodities with corresponding reduction of the burden of land revenue.

It is of course a moot point as to why these factors did not prevent mass starvation during the great Bengal famine in 1943.[11]

On the whole, the colonial approach to drought management may be described as the policy of the masterly inactivity based on the laissez faire approach which continued till the Great Bengal famine of 1943. Criticising such an approach, Mahatma Gandhi observed "Famines in India are not a calamity descended upon from nature but created by rulers. None but a representative national government can cope with it."[12]

The laissez faire strategy of dealing with drought is indicated in the following chart.

Diagram 1

Drought Management Strategy — Laissez Faire

Food	:	Free Trade
Employment	:	Relief Work on Test
Gratuitous Relief	:	Charity
Indirect Relief	:	Inadequate
Infrastructure	:	Irrigation and Railways

Food

Following the principle of laissez faire, Government took responsibility neither for supplying food nor for fixing of prices. The colonial government found it expedient to follow the advice of the classical economists like Adam Smith and J.S Mill who condemned the policy of direct price control. They believed that heigher prices reflected scarcity rather than collusive practices and speculative hoarding. Adam Smith had observed. "When the Government in order to remedy the inconvenience of dearth, orders dealers to sell food grains at reasonable prices, it either hinders them from bringing it to market which sometimes may produce a famine even in the beginning of the season, or if they do bring it, the people are encouraged to consume so much as necessarily to produce famine before the end of the season." Unlimited and un-restrained freedom of trade is, according to this theory, the only effective measure for preventing the misery of famine. But the theory miserably failed and resulted in mass starvation.

Employment

Behind the policy of employment on famine works was the theory of establishment in England at that time viz poverty was largely the fault of the poor who should never be given something for nothing. As a result, the government did "too little and too late." Employment on works' programme was not available until millions of people were too weak and too debilitated to work and thus perished. And when, at long last, it was provided, it was subject to serve tests viz (1) **Distance test** : The works were at far off places requiring the people to go to far off places. (2) **The residence test** : They were required to stay at work sites away from family life and (3) **Labour Test** : Subsistance wage in return for hard manual labour. The worst case was "Temple ratio" of lb be per day. Wages were never paid daily.[13]

Gratuitous Relief

The colonical regime suffered from puritanical prejudice against the provision of gratuitous relief which was given only to those who could not work, on the basis of strict discretionary selection.

B - Positive Policy in Post Independence India

Drought continued to occur in post independence India resulting in crop failure almost every year in some part of the country of the other. To cite recent examples. 156 districts in Bihar, U.P., West Bengal, Rajasthan, Gujarat, M.P., Mysore and Maharashtra were affected by drought in 1965-67, 227 in Maharashtra, Rajasthan, A.P., Gujarat & W.B. in 1971-72 & 72-73 and 240 in 1979-80 almost all parts of the country.[14] 1982-83, 1984-85 & 1986-87 were also years of drought. However, the strategy for dealing with drought adopted after the attainment of independence as compared with that during colonical period was conspicuously successful in preventing mass starvation and death. As compared to the laissez faire policy of colonial times, the policy after independence could be described as positive as indicated by the following comparative chart :

Diagram 2

Drought Management Strategy-Positive

Food	:	Public Distribution System
Employment	:	National Rural Employment Employment Guarantee

Gratuitous Relief	:	In coordination with Voluntary Agencies
Indirect Relief	:	Rural Institutional Credit (Conversion of short term cooperative credit into medium term)
Infrastructure Development	:	Protective Irrigation, Rural Electrification

Food

During the Bihar drought of 1965-67[15] the Public Distribution System made supplies of food grain available at reasonable prices, at distribution centres known as fair price shops. Similarly, during Maharashtra drought[16] a state-wide network of about 25000 fair price and ration shops was by and large able to respond to the needs of the time. On an average one fair price shop was available within a radius of 5 km.

Employment

While during the colonial days large works formed the bulk of the relief efforts, after independence as during the Bihar drought, employment was made available to small and dispersed village works such as (1) construction and renovation of irrigation projects, (2) Minor irrigation works, (3) Reclamation of waste land, (4) Soil conservation measures, (5) Sinking of kutcha wells to relieve water shortage for both men and cattle, (6) improvement of water supply (7) Schemes to improve sanitation and public health such as removal of weed grass, water hyacinth, filling of ditches, removal of rubbish, (8) Construction and repair of village roads, (9) Repair and improvement of public buildings.

Though the Famine Code did not envisage employment on private works, in order to explore all avenues of employment, they were also included. Forest work also provided avenues for employment. These relief works were to supplement plan/departmental works. But due to the financial stringency, plan projects were curtailed and relief works became the main stay of employment. For indigent section, who by custom or constitution were incapable of doing hard manual work, light manual work such as net and rope making was arranged. As regards wages, instead of substistence wage prescribed by the Famine code, wages were revised upwards taking into account the price sprial and health and nutritional status of workers.

In Maharashtra drought, work was offered to those who needed it. At the peak nearly 5 million people constituting 50% of the total working population were employed on relief works. The employment opportunities were made available at a reasonable distance of about 5 kms from the homes of the affected people. Works were taken up departmentally and with the help of Zilla Parishad and not through contractors. Wage rates were fixed in such a manner as to enable a house-hold head and his wife working for a full day to purchase sufficient grain to maintain themselves and 3 dependents. The scale of daily maintenance for a household was of the order of 4 kgs of grains. Wages were paid in cash to enable labourers to purchase their food mainly from fair price shops. The unconditional provision of employment to all those who wished to join the relief works went a long way towards providing insurance against starvation.

Gratuitous Relief

In Bihar, this was not left to private charity but was organised by a number of voluntary agencies whose work was coordinated with the Bihar Relief Committee under the chairmanship of Shri Jaya Prakash Narayan. Those incapable of doing labour due to old age or physical infirmity were given grain and cash against cards or cheap breads in packets or through free kitchens.

During Maharashtra drought also similar doles were provided. 'Sukhadi' consisting of corn, soyabeen oil and milk were blended with jaggery and distributed through kitchens run by a philanthropic organisation.

Indirect Relief

Going beyond the limited strategy of famine code, subsidised loans were given to cultivators to save crops by resowing short term crops, construction of a kutcha well to tap the underground water resources and installation of electric pumps.

One crucial reason for the success of the post independence strategy in preventing mass starvation was the early response of administration, thanks to political pressure of the democratic system as against the delayed response of the colonial days when the government did not have to be responsive to the woes of the people.

C - Crisis Management vs Compensatory Development Policy

However, despite the success of post independence strategy in avoiding mass mortality, it has been similar to the pre–independence strategy in that it has been essentially "a crisis management strategy — adhoc and short run. It is "a fire fighting approach"[17] more oriented to dealing with an emergency like famine than with a persistent problem like drought exacerbating the persistent problem of mass poverty and malnutrition. What is required is reorientation of development planning itself in a long range perspective. At present, development plans look upon drought as an interruption in the process of planned development. If the development targets are not reached, specially in the field of argicultural production, droughts are blamed for the shortfall. But is it not necessary for the development plans to workout targets and strategies taking into account the facts that the droughts are a part of climatology and that they are bound to occur in any Five Year Plan period? Unfortunately, no plan document is expressly formulated on this basis.

The adhoc approach towards droughts is borne out by the fact that the task of drought management has been a matter of financing relief expenditure to be taken care of by the Finance Commission, rather than a problem of development to be taken care of by the Planning Commission. Successive Finance Commissions have held that financing relief expenditure in times of natural calamities like droughts and floods is the responsibility of the State Governments, and the Centre can only provide assistance to the States. The Central Ministry of Finance accused the States of making unnecessary and unjustifiable demands on the Union Government and asked the Finance Commission to evolve 'a scheme for financing relief expenditures which would curb the present abuses.' This way of looking at drought expenditure seems to have distorted the perspective required to view drought in relation to development rather than in terms of emergency relief.

To make the strategy of dealing with drought an integral part of development planning, there has to be a development theory which integrates the phenomenon of droughts with the process of development. Development theory, as it has grown in the last forty years, has drawn attention to crucial factors in development such as capital formation, technology and organization. A proper combination of the three, given proper attitudes and institutions would bring about development and growth in a cumulative manner at an evenly accelerating pace. That good seasons and bad seasons would result in ups and downs of development and would crucially influence the process of development, and hence need to be systematically woven into development theory is generally overlooked.

The analysis of upswings and downswings in economic life, of prosperity and depression belongs to theories of Cycles which were so fashionable before the advent of the Keynesian Revolution. With the advent of the Kenesian theory, businesses cycle theories went out of fashion. Cycles o prosperity and depression no longer worried economists and policy makers since keynesian theory had provided the managers of the economy with the tool of compensatory fiscal policy. However, compensatory fiscal policy can not take care of deficiencies of natural seasons. These call for Compensatory Development policy.

Such compensatory development policy should be based on a more scientific understanding of causes and consequences of seasonal variations.

III (A) Chain of Causes

Drought is a phenomenon which slowly unfolds from one phase to another-meteorological drought, hydrological drought and agricultural drought.

Meteorological drought is a situation when there is significant decrease from climatologically expected and seasonally normal precipitation, over a wide area.

Meteorological drought if prolonged will result in hydrological droughts with marked depletion of surface water and consequent drying of reservoirs, lakes, streams and rivers, cessation of spring flows and fall in ground water levels. This may necessitate curtailment of hydro power generation and affect industry as well as agriculture.

Agricultural drought occurs when soil moisture and rainfall are inadequate during growing season to support healthy crop growth to maturity and cause extreme moisture stress and wilting in the major crops of the area. An agricultural drought may exist even when meteorological drought may not and vice versa. For example even if total rainfall is in excess the gross water requirements of the whole crop periods, if soil moisture is deficient during critical periods of growth, there is agricultural drought.[18] In other words, for agricultural drought not to occur, rains have to be not only adequate but also timely.

The transition from meteriological drought to hydrological drought and from that to an agricultural drought is a slow process. Often it takes two successive meteorological droughts before the hydrological drought sets in. And then it slowly leads to the agricultural drought. The slow unfolding of the phenomenon of drought, the slow process of conversion of meteorological drought into agricultural drought could be illustrated with reference to the documentation of 1965-67 Bihar drought and 1970-73 Maharashtra drought.[19] Agricultural operations by millions of farmers are planned in anticipation of the normal meteorological cycle. The success of these operations is crucially dependent upon fulfilment of these anticipation. Thus in India the traditional agricultural cycle is as follows. The autumn crops are sown in June and July and ripen in October and November. If the seasonal showers (known as Southwest monsoon) do not fall during July, August and September the autumn crops (known as Kharif crops) fail. The spring crops (known as Rabi crops) are sown in October and November and ripen in March and if seasonal showers (the winter rains) do not happen to fall during December and January they fail, save what are artificially irrigated. A good monsoon means a year of plenty, a weak one a year of scarcity, more or less acute according to average annual rainfall. Traditionally the Kharif crops have been the more important ones providing staple food stuffs of the year-rice, Jowar (sorghum), bajra (pearl Millets), gram (chick-pea), barley and other cereals. The Rabi crops consist of wheat and oil seeds, gingley, safflower and linseed. Rabi crops are supported by winter rains and moisture left by earlier rains and hence less vulnerable than the Kharif crops.

Average rainfall in India is 105 cm and is considered to be the largest anywhere in the world for a country of comparable size. But it fluctuates widely - it is either delayed or ends earlier, or in between there are long breaks or it concentrates on one part and shuns another.

While no regular drought cycle can be established, conditions of drought do occur over large areas once in four or five years. Without copious and timely rains no crops can either be raised or brought to maturity. Good Monsoon rains replenish tanks, raise water level and enable irrigation to be practiced. A weak monsoon throws out of cultivation thousands of hectares of land and decreases production of food crops all over the affected parts. Drought is described as nature's way of 'Declaring a lockout in the agricultural industry". Rains and water play such an important part in Indian agriculture that life giving rain and life giving streams and rivers have been deified.

Increase in area under irrigation, greater preparation of area under Rabi crops and introduction of short duration varieties has made agriculture in India less of a "gamble in rain," less vulnerable to seasonal vagaries.

(B) Impact of Drought : Chain of Consequences

Agricultural drought is not the end : it is but the beginning of the slow but sure process by which it permeates through the economy and makes its impact on the ordinary lives of the mass of people.

There is a 'sequential pattern' in which impact of the drought manifests itself. The consequences rising in crescendo are :

1. Decline in crop acreage.
2. Set back to agricultural production (crop production, milk production).
3. Fall in employment in the agricultural sector due to slowing down of agricultural activity.
4. Fall in purchasing power of those engaged in agriculture.
5. Scarcity of drinking water; fall in water table.
6. Scarcity of food grains.
7. Rise in prices of food grain and other commodities.
8. Scarcity of fodder.
9. Distress sale of cattle.
10. Loss of cattle life.
11. Low intake of food.
12. Malnutrition specially among children.
13. III health and spread of diseases like diarrhea, dysentery, cholera, famine scab and ophthalmia caused by starvation.
14. Distress sale and mortgage of land, jewelry and personal property.
15. Migration of people in search of employment; depopulation of area.
16. Death due to malnutrition/starvation/diseases.
17. Fall in effective demand from the agricultural sector leading to dislocation of productive processes and slowing down of the economic activities in the secondary and tertiary sectors.
18. Low morale of people.
19. Social stress and tension, disruption of social institutions and relationship and social crimes, e.g., looting of grain shops.
20. Growth of fatalism; reliance on heavenly powers.[20]

Diagram-3 gives a graphic presentation of the chain of these consequences.

While droughts are bound to affect the economic and social life of the people, the severity of the impact depends on the intensity of the drought, the manner in which it is handled and the strength and resilience of the economy and society.

Nor is the impact the same on all sections of the society. It is, of course, greater on the more vulnerable sections, i.e., those with hand to mouth existence and with very little margin or staying power. They include the landless and the marginal farmers and the artisans like the weavers whose

Diagram - 3

Consequence of Drought

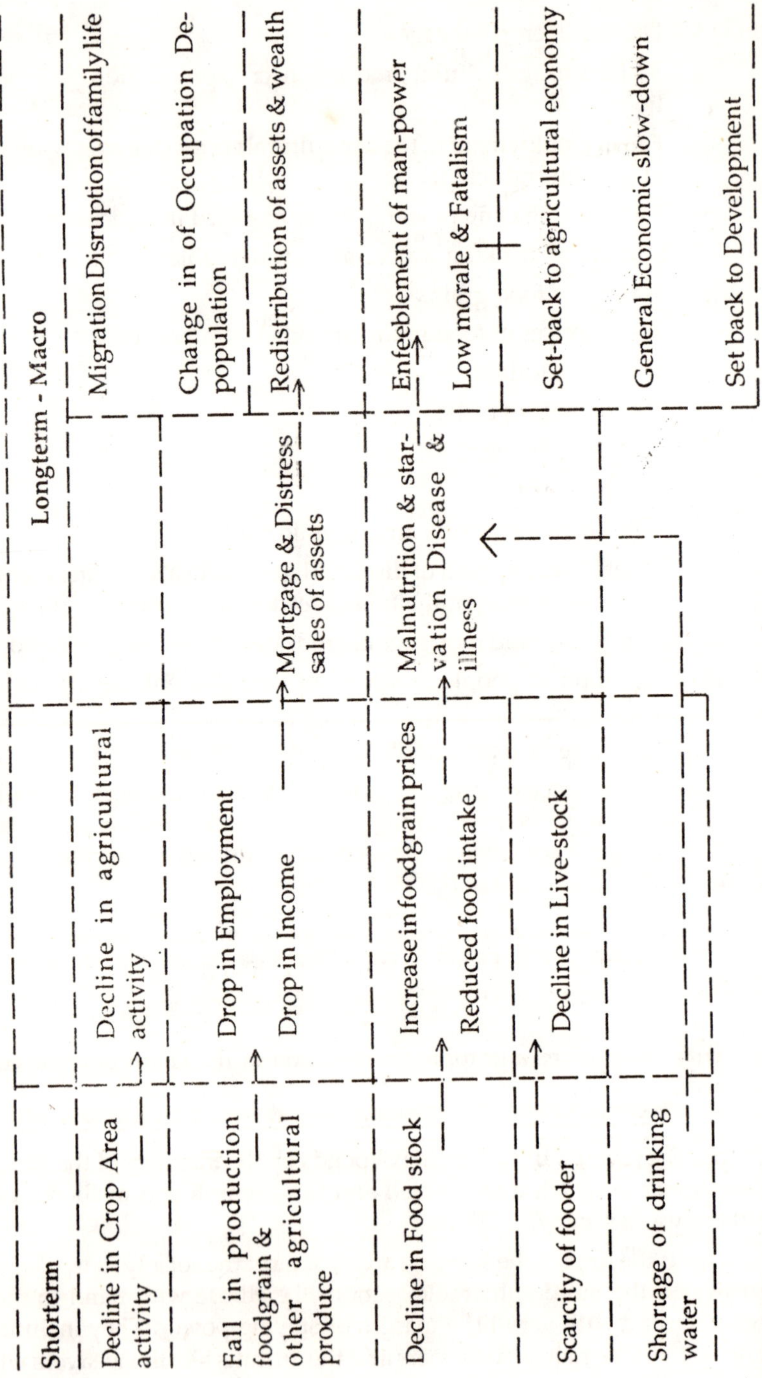

ivelihood depends on local demand for goods and services. They are the ones whose stocks, if any, are quickly exhausted, who have to eat their seeds and who are compelled to sell or mortgage their meager belongings to the well to do. A succession of bad harvests can plunge small and marginal armers in a vicious circle of poverty dragging them down from the status andowner to landless, penniless, powerless condition. This is illustrated in diagram (4).

Diagram 4

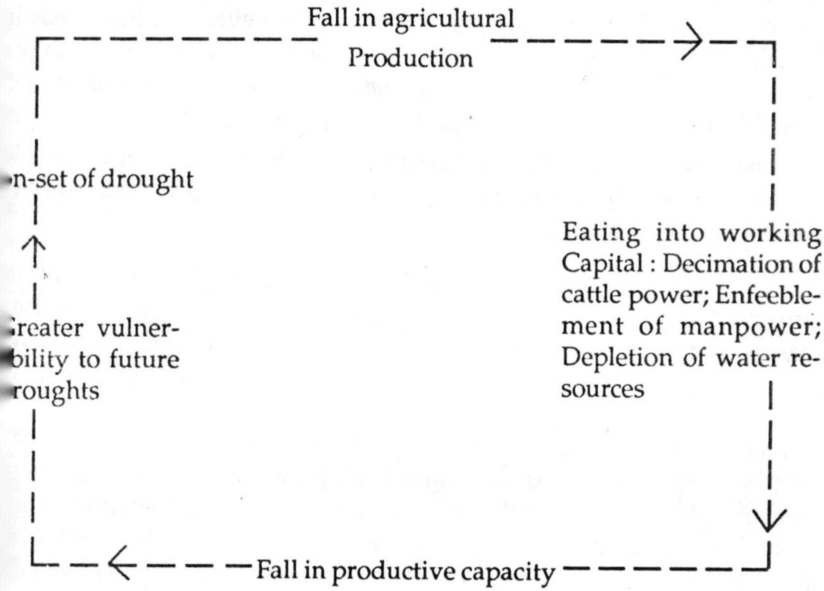

On the other hand, the well to do would not only survive but could nerge even stronger. Taking advantage of scarcity and high prices of od grown they could make a fortune out of their surplus stocks. They uld lend money against the land mortgaged by the small/marginal rmer and later taking advantage of their weakned economic position of d inability to repay the loan, could foreclose the mortgage. Thus, the termath of a drought could leave the poor poorer and the rich richer and greater measure of inequality and potential for exploitation.

Drought has both spatial and temporal dimensions.

Spatial dimensions : Drought may be a local phenomenon confined to egion of a country or it may envelop much the larger part of a country. it is local or regional, its impact depends on its relationship with the macro-economy of the country as a whole. In a large prosperous economy, with larger resources and greater resilience, the local drought could be contained with comparative ease, the farmers could be compensated for low production by higher prices, their incomes thus remaining the same or as in the case in the USA, farmers could be compensated to the extent of 65% of crops in cases where loss of production exceeds 35%. Those rendered unemployed in the agricultural economy could seek jobs in the secondary or tertiary sectors, thanks to greater degree of mobility of an advanced economy. Consumer goods shortages could be made up by larger inflow from outside the region. However, if the drought occurs simultaneously in different parts of regions of even a prosperous country, its ability to contain the consequences of the drought may be seriously impaired. The impac would be much greater on a poor, under-developed country.

The impact of drought may assume global proportions if it were to occur simultaneously in a number countries important from the point c view of agricultural production.

Temporal dimensions: Drought is a short term phenomenon but it impact is felt over the long run. Drought may occur over one or tw seasons—or even more. Rajasthan in India suffered in 1987 from fourt successive drought and Gujarat from third successive drought. A mil drought followed by a good season may not leave its mark. But if it is severe it can take a heavy toll of the human, animal and natural resources of th area coming under its direct impact. Men and women would be s enfeebled that their capacity to work may be seriously impaired and ma even be permanently damaged. Children may suffer from such malnutr tion and debility that they may grow up as substandard human beings. I extreme cases, the whole region may be depopulated. Animals may b decimated causing a long term shortage of drought and milch animals. Le perceptible but more devastating may be the adverse effect on natur resources in the shape of depletion, or nonrepletion of underground wat resources resulting in the water table going down. All these consequenc would be greatly aggravated by the cumulative impact of successi droughts.

Thus droughts, though a short term phenomenon may be a contrib tory factor in the long term process of progressive impoverishment o country; they may worsen the vicious circle of poverty which makes a pc country and a poor people poorer.

A series of severe droughts followed only by moderately good seaso would lead to a secular decline of the economy. The trend may be accen ated by indifferent drought management. On the other hand, milk droug followed by good seasons and effective handing of the consequences of drought, may not come in the way of secular upward movement of the economy. These two sets of relationship between short term impact of the drought and secular trends of the economy are illustrated in Diagram 5.

Diagram 5

Drought and secular trend in the economy

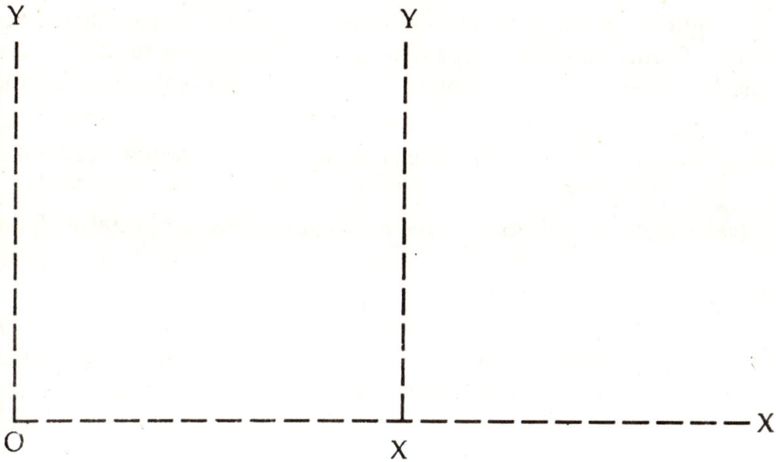

Year	Year
ecular decline as a result f successive severe drought	Secular rise despite mild drought

What is particularly significant from the point of view of long term npact of drought is the fact that while some consequences of drought may e easily overcome, others may prove to be irreversible, leaving a permaent impact on the economy. Thus good rains following drought, may wipe it shortage of drinking and scarcity of fodder. A good season of rain, may ing a bountiful crop replenishing depleted food stocks. A good agricultral season may herald the return of gainful employment opportunities in ral areas. But some of other changes may prove irreversible and enduring cause they may be entrenched in the shape of structural changes in the ral economy and society. Thus the redistribution of assests and wealth ay create inequalities which may only accentuate in the years to come. arginal farmers joining the ranks of the landless during period of drought ay remain landless for ever since they would have no means of recovering eir lands and other assets unless powerfully supported by strong interventionist public policy measures both legal and institutional. Emigration, depopulation and run-down infrastructure may permanently turn drought-prone areas (otherwise known as "rain-shadow) into depressed areas or backwards areas of a country attracting neither manpower, nor capital nor enterprise.

Drought Compounded by other Calamities

Drought is not the only cause of famine. Floods, its opposite may be another.[21] Scanty rainfall causes drought and excessive rainfall causes floods. And if both follow each other, they can cumulatively cause famine

However, floods could have some redeeming features in that they could augment both soil and water resources. Soil through deposite of fertile alluvial material and water resources by raising the water table.

Locust menace, on the other hand has no remeeding feature at all. Rains may encourage locust breeding and have a devastating effect on crops and vegetables.

Floods and earthquakes are phenomena which have sudden devastating effects. Droughts, in contrast, have consequence which slowly manifest themselves. They lead to a creeping crisis.

IV — Pro-Active Strategy

Crisis management of strategy adopted so far in dealing with drought has been a reactive management strategy. Reactive management strategy in dealing with drought mainly concentrates on giving relief to the victims of drought and to some extent tries to rehabilitate them. But a pro-active policy should go beyond relief and rehabilitation. It should seek to prevent the recurrence of drought through reorientation of the process of development

Such a policy would not just be confined to the dealing with the consequences of drought viz shortage of water, scarcity of food grains and their rising prices, the slowing down of agricultural activity and loss of employment and income to those who depend on it for daily livelihood, and their inability to secure needed intake of food for themselves and their families over a period of time leading to undernutrition, malnutrition and vulnerability to diseases and in extreme cases to mass starvation and death. It would go into causes of these consequences and seek to transform the given environment which contains this chain of causes and consequences of drought into the preferred environment where these are removed.

In his book "Poverty and Famines - an essay on entitlement and deprivation",[22] Prof. Amartyan Sen has made a penetrating analysis of the chain of causes and consequences of drought on the basis of an exhaustive study of data and statistics pertaining to four famines viz. The Great Bengal famine of 1943, the Ethiopian Famine of 1972-74. Drought and famine in Sahel during 1968-73 and famine in Bangladesh during 1974. The last was attributed to floods while the first to an inflationary situation rather than drought. Prof. Sen was concerned more with famine as such rather than with drought induced famine but for all the four cases, he has evolved the same framework of analysis and the same theory or rather approach for understanding the incidence and impact of famine.

He has come to the conclusion that the famine is caused not by any absolute decline in food but rather by collapse of entitlement of certain sections of the society which denies them any access to the available food supplies. In respect of the Ethiopian famines he says :

"Since the Ethiopians famine clearly was intiated by drought and since drought causes crop failure it may be easy to be predisposed towards accepting an explanation of the famine in terms of food availability decline." Prof. Sen does not accept this explanation. He argues that a drought causing as agricultural or pastoral crisis not only reduces food supply; it also cuts earnings of the agriculturist or the pastoralist affecting his command over food. "While the food output in Wallo province was substantially reduced in 1973, food prices in general rose very little. The inability of Wallo to command food was the result of low purchasing power in that province. The phenomenon of starvation can be understood in terms of extension of entitlement failures of various sections of the Wallo population. "As regards the pastoral population who belonged to nomadic and semi-nomadic group, they were affected not only by drought but also by the growth of commercial agriculture which displaced them from the traditional dry weather grazing land. The effect of loss of animal stock was compounded by servere worsening of the terms of trade. The pastoralist hit by drought was decimated by the market mechanism."

In the Sahelian drought of 1969-73, the per capita food availability did go down substantially. But according to Prof. Sen what caused famine was 'the dramatic shift in the purchasing power" in the drought years between the dry region i.e. Sahel and the rest of the regions i.e. Savanna in which the vast majority of the population of these countries lived. The famine victims were almost exclusively the nomadic pastoral from the dry region and the sedentary population of the Sahel region like agriculturalist and fishermen. The substantial destruction of crops and death of animals in these parts of the Sahelian countries, meant a sharp reduction in the ability of the affected people to command food, whether from one's output or through exchange of food, whether from one's own output or through exchange. It is this collapse of the entitlement to food that according to Prof. Sen in the cause of starvation.

Prof. Sen rejects the thesis of FAD (Food Availability Decline) to explain famine; instead he puts forth the FEE thesis (Food Exchange Entitlement) as the direct and proximate cause of starvation. The FEE thesis is particularly relevant to explain the Great Bengal famine of 1943 which seems to have greatly influenced Prof. Sen in formulating it. However the policy implication is not that decline of food does not take place during the drought period. In Ethiopian-Sahelian cases it has taken place. Nor that it is or no consequence.[23] The policy implication rather is that the most vulnerable sections of the society like the marginal farmers, the landless and the pastoral people are likely to be the first victims of starvation because of their inability to have access to food supplies. Administrative policy and strategy during the drought period must therefore, address itself to the task of making food available to the vulnerable section of the society. The employment in relief works, gratuitous relief and public distribution systems have been evolved as the programme for dealing with the problem of lack of entitlement.

But this is not enough. As mentioned above, the proactive policy must seek to transform the environment which gives rise to the chain of causes and consequence which converts.

1. the 'meteorological drought' into 'hydrological drought'.
2. the 'hydrological drought' into 'agricultural drought'.
3. the 'agricultural drought' into 'food drought' and
4. the 'food drought' into 'economic drought'

Preventing Conversion of Meteorological Drought into Hydrological Drought

The meteorological drought leads to hydrological drought when the decrease of precipitation is such as to lead to depletion of surface water and ground water. The objective of the administrative strategy should, therefore, be to minimize such depletion, through an extension program of water conservation. This has of course received attention in the development plans but needs a much higher priority and much greater mobilization of "social energy".

Mobilization of "social energy" for water conservation does not have to await plans and projects formulated by Government departments. People themselves, given leadership and organization, could undertake such projects despite unwillingness of administration to initiate them. A recent example is provided by an organization called "Mukti Sangharsh Vahini" in Sangli district in Maharashtra state, which symbolizes awakening of the people to be self-reliant.[24] Following path of self-reliance, the organisation undertook to construct a small dam across a dry river not with Government aid but through "Shramdan" (donation of labour) of villagers. The small river which had perennial water supply some year ago, was running dry on account of poor rainfall in recent years caused by indiscriminate cutting of trees. Agricultural lands were turning barren; the problem of unemployment was staring people in the face. People were deserting their villages and going to big cities to escape starvation. The dam project was a part of the movement for eradication of famine and would serve as a stimulus for further construction projects in drought areas.

Another such community organized development response to drought to took place in a drought prone village in Kolar district in Karnataka. The development response of drought prone village Yaavhalli in Kolar district has been documented by Morgan Maclachan.[25] The village faced terrible drought in year 1965-66 when there was only 12 inches of rain. And yet the village people came through the drought better than expected because they were well prepared to face the catastrophe as a result of the development of agricultural intensification through scores of irrigation well and garden dotting the landscape. This was the product of human labour and considerable initiative and enterprises. The intensification occurred as a response by farm people themselves to increased population density. The wells increased cultivation opportunities in times of drought and maximized production in lean years thus drought-proofing farming to some degree and famine-proofing the population to the same degree.

Ralegansiddhi village in Maharashtra (district Ahmadnagar) provides a successful example of water and soil conservation through community action.[26] Though the area receives only 15 inches of rainfall a year, the water conservation programme initiated by an Shri Anna Hajare in 1971 has been able to provide drinking and irrigation water even in summer. Nearly 1100 acres of land in the village is now irrigated, against only 50 acres in 1971. Growing grass on hills and planting trees has made the area lush green. In the next thirty years, the village will get income over Rs. 28 lakhs from the trees. Besides the trees have halted soil erosion.

Another striking example of success of this approach is the work done by Pani Panchayat in Maharashtra.[27] As a result of experimentation started in 1974 on 16 hectares of land at Naigaon in Purander taluka of Pune district, Shri Vilas Salunke a pioneering rural development leader, concluded that even in a region where rainfall is scanty, erratic and ill distributed over the season, there is scope for impounding run-off of surface water by constructing appropriately located small works like check on embankments dams, percolation tanks etc. at the village and miniwatershed levels. What is critical is to value water as a community asset to be distributed equally among all families. This new concept would reduce the severity of the impact of drought, especially on the weaker section of the society. So far small irrigation schemes at a total cost of about 6.4 million rupees have been constructed which irrigate about 1275 hectares of land belonging to 1641 farmers all living under extremely poor condition. This has enabled farmers to produce a substantially higher yield in cereal crops (from 120 kg per hec to 900-1200 kg per hec.) and increases the capacity of the farmers to withstand the drought condition reurring every two or three years.

Another example of a voluntary effort for soil and water conservation is reported from the Gogunda plateau in the heart of the Arawalis.[28] Massive deforestation, extension of cultivation on steep slopes and over grazing have inflicted severe damage to the soil and water resources which are unable to provide subsistence to the increased population even with the best of rains. Padayatra by Ambeshwar Vikas Mandal created awareness among the Bhils about the need to improve their land and water resources. They therefore, decided to join together and by turn take up the work in each others fields for improvement of their water resources. They have discovered their own 'shakti' for undertaking the work of soil and water conservation in a collective manner without any expectations, but with hope and faith. If this is sustained and further degradation, prevented their progress through self-help would be assumed.

It has been observed that while new major reservoirs have been constructed across rivers, the programmes of minor irrigation works like construction of small tanks is neglected, though this has been the traditional approach of water conservation in the past. For example in the old Mysore state (now part of Karnataka), a chain of anecuts were built across streams in the valley with waste weirs allowing surplus water to flow. These not only provided small irrigated patches scattered over the villages communities; they also helped to raise the underground water table. The traditional obligations of the people for maintenance of these village tanks works got into disuse leading to silting of those tanks. On the other hand, the availability of high power rigs has facilitated easy quick construction of deep wells and rural electrification has facilitated quick installation of pump sets both of which no doubt helped farmers in times of drought. But at the same time so indiscriminate has been this process that it has seriously depleted the underground water resources in some parts of the country.

As Bharat Dogra points out: "The trend towards indiscriminate exploitation of ground water has continued unabated. In areas consider suitable for tube well irrigation like Punjab and Haryana there has been such an excess of tube well installation that vast parts of these states consider the bread basket of India are now listed as danger zone from the point of view of ground water depletion. In areas considered not suitable for tube well irrigation - such as Malwa region of Madhya Pradesh alarming reports are pouring in regarding ground water depletion during the last two years as a result of tube well installed by well-to-do farmers. Other form of irrigation are available in Malwa region which do not deplete ground water, tank irrigation being the most widely prevalent in the not too distant past. By neglecting the social responsibility of collective management of these sources, the better off sections find it more profitable and convenient in the short run to go further ahead of others by growing water intensive crops using the more abundant privately owned water from the tube wells.[29]

The trend towards indiscriminate exploitation of ground water was observed by the National Commission of Agriculture more than a decade ago. "The present ground water development in the country is to a large extent uncontrolled. As a result there has been over-pumping in several areas. Overpumping results in permanent lowering of the ground water table... making ground water utilization ultimately uneconomic." There is a cutthroat competition amongst farmers for deeping wells adversely affecting each other because of depletion of ground water. The Commission recommended that in situation like this the state must intervene and rationalize the extraction and distribution of ground water." Yet in times of drought during 1987, in condition of emergency, the strategy was to give maximum assistance for deepening tube wells and exploitation of ground water.

Another factor that has adversely affected water conservation is the indiscriminate deforestation growing apace in the hilly regions. Forests, apart from providing woods and other products greatly help in holding and conserving the heavy precipitation during peak rainy season. On the other hand, indiscriminate deforestation depletes ground water by not conserving water and results in floods which cause havoc in lower region. Deforestation also has an adverse impact on the rainfall pattern. Preventing indiscriminate deforestation and active and vigorous conservation must receive high priority.

The approach to drought management should, therefore, be in consonance with water and forest conservation which are but elements of environmental preservation and sustainable development. A short term approach to drought management and development will only go to accentuate the process of conversion of the Meteorological drought into hydrological drought.

The drought prone areas could be divided into hydrologically identified watersheds. Water conservation through methods like farm ponds & small check dams and contour, bunding, ridge furrows, to store run-off water and social & farm foresty should be integral parts of micro-plans for watersheds management. Such micro watershed plans should aim at rational use of land, water, livestock and manpower resources and restoration of ecological balance. When successfully implemented these plan would create the needed social and economic infrastructure and generate employment.

The successes of these watershed development plans would depend on the involvement of the local communities and mobilization of social energy. This in turns require creation of social awareness of the links between meteorological drought and hydrological drought. Development based on watershed management plans could be the best defence against drought.

Watershed micro-development plans have to be prepared and implemented essentially on a decentralized basis. Microplans for integrated development for optimum utilization of resources water, lands, livestock and manpower have been attempted but they have been as adhoc collection of different sectoral schemes, many of which were left incomplete or implemented in a routine manner without analysis of information or motivation of the people.

Preventing Conservation Hydrological Drought into Agricultural Drought

While better watershed management can reduce the severity of the hydrological drought, it cannot altogether be eliminated. A development and administrative strategy is, needed to deal with the chain linking hydrological drought with agricultural drought. Greater the extent to which crops are susceptible to moisture stress, greater is the impact of hydrological drought on the agricultural drought. Thanks to the adoption of green revolution strategy, great stress has been laid and more reliance placed on high yielding varieties (HYV) crops. However, these require greater and assured input of water which is threatened in times of drought. Hence they are more vulnerable to drought. The approach to reduce crop vulnerability to hydrological drought is to lay stress on drought resistant varieties and crops like sorghum, pearl millets and finger millets, sunflowers, castor, especially in drought prone areas. Research and extension activities instead of concentrating attention only on HYV crop dependent on assured input on water, should also pay attention to development of drought resistant varieties and crops like pearl millets which make lesser demand on moisture. A deliberate strategy to change cropping pattern in favour of less water intensive crops as well as horticulture is called for.

Tree crops have a distinct advantage over agricultural crops in moisture deficient dry areas. While the millets crops can tolerate a 16 days dry spell period, a tree would be able to tolerate upto 25 days period without moisture stress. They have a "perennial life cycle" as contrasted with annual life cycle of agricultural crops.[30] Fruit yeilding species like ber, sitaphal, custard apple, pomogrenate grow well under rain fed conditions.

What tree-crops can do in transforming the economy of a drought prone areas has been shown recently in Solapur district in Maharashtra.[31] Due to chronic drought conditions farmers in this district had to sell their cattle-heads at throw-away price. Next step for them was to migrate in search of work. This had a destabilising effect on the socio-economic fabric of the rural population. Even in a year when rain was satisfactory, the poor quality of land did not yield much.

Under such circumstances a plan was chalked out under the extension scheme of the State Agricultural Development to put in circulation plant varieties developed by agricultural universities. Considering the poor quality of land and scarcity of water in Solapur district *ber* and pomogrenate were selected to be popularised with the farmers. Under this scheme during the past eight years, out of 83000 farming families in the district, 15000 have developed their own orchards. This has given employment to at least 2 lakh farm labourers for about eight months in a year. Orchards of ber, pomogrenate, custard apple, figs and grapes abound on either side of the road in 11 talukas of the district. This indeed is mini-miracle.

There is no dearth of finance. The State Bank of India and District Co-operative Bank have liberally financed the farmers.

Fruit grower cooperatives have come into existence. They organise the supply of inputs like fruit stalkgrafts and fertilisers. They also arrange periodic meetings of the farmers where they can discuss their problems in the presence of experts from Krishi Vidyapeeth and Government officers from agricultural department. Apart from supplying packaging material to the farmer and handling transportation, the co-operative also collect the sale proceeds and distribute the same to the farmers. Apart from domestic market, expert market in the Gulf countries, is being tapped. Proposals for fruit processing plant are also mooted.

If Solapur district has shown the way in developing horticultural tree crops; in Nasik district change in the traditional cropping pattern in favour of agro foresty has taken place. The lead has been taken by the Eucalyptas Grower Co-operative society in launching a successful campaign. The society has taken up jatropha plantation as a joint venture with the soap manufacturing unit of Godrej Industrial House. The effort has conferred economic as well as ecological benefits. Taking clue from the success of this experiment, similar societies have been formed elsewhere.[32]

Another important measure is the economic use of water available in the irrigation reservoirs. In times of drought, the level of water in reservoirs goes down and the water conveyance system consisting of canals and distributaries is unable to supply water to lower reachers unless a regime of rationing through rotational distribution is enforced. The tail-enders suffer and their crops wilted. Robert Wade has pointed out,[33] that under the

Valenican canals of Southern Spain and those of Taiwan there is a strict system of rationing under which the operating procedures for coping with drought are codified in elaborate detail. The delivery rule when water supply is abundant is a continuous flow; as water supply falls during times of drought, there is a switch from continuous flow to rotation between and down the length of distributaries in order to share the shortfall proportionally; as water scarcity worsens irrigation interval is lengthened and time limit per hectare are imposed. Wade found that in South India, the rules for responding to drought are uncodified and no attempt is made to implement a coordinate rotational delivery schedule for the whole canal system. An important duty assigned to CADAs (Command Area Development Authority) recently established under major irrigation projects is "Warabandi[1]" i.e. rotational delivery system. It is important that the system is strictly enforced with understanding and cooperation of the farmers. India has at great cost raised area under irrigation from 22 million to 60 million hectares through six-five year plans. By the end of the century, the area is expected to be 112 million hectares. The rotational system can ensure that this potential is not reduced in times of drought. The system requires cooperation and understanding between the farmers and the irrigation authorities.

Preventing Conversion of Agricultural Drought into Food Drought

The chain is conversion of agriculture drought into food drought caused by deficient supply of food in relation to normal requirements in times of drought. The strategy for dealing with this problem is carrying food stocks over time and over space. Despite debilitating effects of droughts, the drought years with considerable drop of agricultural production are often followed with a year of peak agricultural production. For example after the Bihar drought of 1965-67, there was spurt in agricultural production in 1967-68 thanks to additional investment in agriculture and irrigation during the drought years and of course the introduction of HYV. The strategy of dealing with 'food drought' is to carry over the surplus stocks arising out of bountiful crop of good years into lean drought years. I could call this "Joseph strategy"—the reference being to the Biblical tale of the strategy adopted by Joseph in the service of Pharaoh King of Egypt. During its seven years of abundance, the land produced plentifully. Joseph collected all the food produced in those seven years of abundance in Egypt and stored it in the cities. In each city he put the food grown in the fields surrounding it. Joseph stored huge quantities of grain like the sands of the sea. The seven years of abundance in Egypt came to an end and the seven years of famine began. There was famine in all other lands but on the whole land of Egypt there was food. Joseph opened the store houses and sold grain to all Egyptians. . . All other countries came to Egypt because the famine was severe in all the world." (Genesis 42.2).

This operation cannot always be left to private trade without risk of mass starvation as demonstrated again and again by recurrent droughts during times of British colonical rule in India. Private trade has a tendency to corner stocks at low prices during years of bumper harvest and withhold them from the market. The high prices in drought times could enable traders to harvest bumper profits. This could be rationalized by Adam Smith's economics as the equilibrating market mechanism but could hardly be acceptable in modern times if it involves mass starvation for those sections of society who are unable to have access to food stocks available only a high prices. That is why Prof. Sen has observed "the public sector would have to play a major role in the task of guaranteeing food of vulnerable sections."[34]

After repeated frustrations in dealing with private trade in times of food scarcity with stop-go policies of control and decontrol, the Government of India ultimately found an effective solution in the shape of Food Corporation of India, a gigantic organisation with nationwide operations starting in Jan. 1966. It was able to build larger stocks of food grains in a sustained manners through procurement operations in major food grain market centres. These food grain stocks known as 'bufferstocks' have provided remunerative prices to the farmers as well as food security in times of drought. The Food Cooperation of India had accumulated huge stocks of about 25 million tons which had started becoming an embarrassment what with locking up funds, storage space and possibilities of spoilage. But these came handy in 1987 drought for preventing near starvation. In 1966-67 Bihar drought India had to import 13 million tons under PL 480 with stiff terms imposed by President Johnson.There was not such contingency in 1987. Food and freedom could be combined. In contrast, in 1974 famine, Bangladesh had to compromise freedom of export of jute to Cuba, before good grains from USA could be secured!

Whether for reasons of politics, shortage of foreign exchange or shipping, transport and port handling capacity, a country cannot always depend on food stocks available elsewhere. Prof. Sen had, therefore, thought of "some system of international insurance" to make resources available for import of food abroad when domestic production fails and when the earnings of foreign exchange go down.

But even world food stocks can go down disastrously. 1988 drought in North and Asia (Chinese crop in trouble) cut down world grain supplies — wheat, corn and other cereals causing steepest decline in grain stock piles.[35] By early next year grain in storage around the world was expected to be no more than 250 million tons enough to last 54 days as against current stock of 402 million tones which constitute 89 days supply. In early seventies when world grain stocks dropped below 60 days supply, wheat prices more than doubled and corn prices tripled. The current drop in food supplies would, in all probaility, lead to a similar rise in food grain prices and sharply cut the amount of food shipped to poor and under-developed countries. Even in 1986-87 when grain production reached record levels and surpluses reached 458 million tons, millions starved and hundreds of millions of people were under-nourished. Every country has, therefore, to evolve its own strategy of food security in its fight against 'food drought'. Within a country also food stocks should be widespread than concentrated. The position in India from this point of view cannot be said to be satisfactory with bulk of its procurement coming from the green revolution belt of Punjab, Haryana and West U.P. This belt with a share of 21.3% to the gross cropped area, account for as much as 66% of public procurement of rice. Any bottleneck, whether caused by turbulent politics or transport bottleneck can easily upset the apple cart of the delicate balance between demand and supply in different parts of the country. Building a mechanism for *decentralized procurement and stocking* of foodgrains would be a good administrative strategy for providing food security.

Concentration of procurement is the inevitable result of concentration of production in green belt areas. Dispersed procurement is possible if there is dispersed production. Green revolution strategy has been the exact opposite. It has led to concentration of funds available for agricultural development including all subsidies—direct or indirect to all supportive inputs of the Green Revolution such as fertilizers (Rs. 1800 in 1984-85) irrigation, electricity, farm machinery and pesticide on the small green belt area (already relatively prosperous). As a result, 15% of area under food grains has contributed to as much as 56% increase in foodgrain production in post green revolution period while backwards areas accounting for 85% of the area contributed only 44%. Per capita food grain production if falling in these areas and correspondingly their dependence on grain belt areas in times of drought has increased. In future, green revolution style development has to be modified and greater attention paid to the development of backward areas.

Prof. V.M. Dandekar had proposed creation of marketing apparatus at District level in food grains trade which is amenable to a certain degree of social control, but which is nevertheless effectively autonomous and decentralized in its marketing functions.[36]

Even a more decentralized stocking of food grains would be possible through the strategy of setting up village grain banks. This was suggested by the late Vaikuth Mehta, during 1943 Bengal famine.[37] Treating India as one nation, we are all members of one family and it is our duty to see that none of the members of family is left to starve. At the same time there is the duty that rural producers owe to their immediate neighbors, and these two duties have to brought in harmony with each other. This is possible if in every village sufficient grain is stocked for next months for the entire population, workers as well as dependents. When there are properly provided for, the rest of the stocks should be available for use outside the village—to meet the deficit of other areas. Rural social workers who undertake the duty of assisting the rural population to form village grain banks have to do much spade work before the banks get going."

Preventing Conversion of Food Drought into Economic Drought

Even if food stocks were to be available, the poor may not have access to them in times of drought because of what Prof. Sen has called 'collapse in entitlements'. The accounts of drought have shown that it is the vulnerable sections of the society—the small and marginal farmers, the tenants and sharecroppers, the pastoral people and the artisans who are included in the category. They are the ones who, in times of drought, lose their entitlement. There is continuing evidence of low consumption levels among large sections of the rural population. Thanks to increased addition to government stocks, per capita availability turns out to be lower than per capita production. And in already poor regions, there is progressive loss of agricultural income. The poor in these areas, with low levels of normal consumption are highly susceptible to drought.

The employment on relief works linked with access to public distribution of food is intended to provide the poor with the needed entitlement. But this is only a drought time palliative. Cannot a durable strategy be evolved for preventing a collapse of their entitlement in times of drought?

The strategy has to ensure that the poor do not lose their assets in times of drought.[38] This is what has always happened. Drought gives opportunities to the well to do to strengthen, their grip over the weaker sections. Without any reserve of food grains to draw upon in the time of difficulty, the marginal farmers mortgage their meager land, and sell away their animals and the ornaments of their women, eat away seeds and join the ranks of the landless and the assetless persons. The cooperative credit system in India contains provisions for conversion of crop loans into medium term loans in years of scarcity. But that does not seem to be enough. Before the advent of cooperative credit, there used to be a system of taccavi loans which has been a discontinued. It seems necessary to make a provision of drought loans with the express purpose of ensuring that the poor do not lose their assets in times of drought.

Prof. Sen has brought out the entitlement losses suffered by the pastoral people as a combined result of animal loss and exchange rate devaluation.

There is a progressive tendency for the deterioration of grazing lands. Some times common grazing lands are permanently lost when they are illegally occupied by powerful and resourceful and owners. No systematic attention has been paid to the issue. Through measures like fencing and soil water conservation, the state of grazing lands could be systematically improved over a period of time.

At the same time, the overpopultion of cattle needs to be reduced. Prof. Sen has observed that the tendency to enlarge one's herd, causing overgrazing is stimulated as uncertainty grows. Organized cooperative dairying can reduce the uncertainty and tendency to keep more cattle then necessary.

An important source of entitlement of the tribal poor are the minor forest produce including fruits, flowers, leaves, roots, shoots and honey to which they had a traditional access. Deprived of an access to these under a strict regime of law and administration which in the name of forest preservation prevent this, the tribals must perish. The traditional tribal rights on the minor forest produce should be restored.

In general, the landless must be given a chance through public policy to obtain livelihood from resources in and about villages like forests, fisheries, minerals, stones and skins of animals.

A proposal for conforming entitlement on the poor consists of drastic land reforms, reducing ceiling and distributing surplus land to the landless and organization of cooperative farming. This is the solution suggested for the poor in Bangladesh.[39] Cooperation in agricultural production would enable peasants to undertake self-help development projects which remain impossible so long as agriculture on a fragmented individual basis. Through labour-intensive construction of irrigation facilities, drainage canals and embankments, the peasants could collectively begin to master the forces of nature in the face of which single individuals are powerless. Cooperative farming would also provide mechanisms for social security helping to ensure each family against personal illness and crop *fluctuation.* The certainty that peasants themselves would reap the fruits of their labour rather than village landlords, would release tremendous popular energy.

Jean Dre'ze has rightly observed that the concept of "entitlement" is much broader than that of food entitlement.[40] The protection of entitlement of the vulnerable groups requires substantial attention to health care and epidemo-logical control.

Diagram 6 is a representation of proactive multi-stage strategy outlined above.

Diagram 6

Multi-Stage Proactive Drought Management Strategy

State	*Preventive Barriers Through*	*Stage*
Meteorological	* Water conservation	Hydrological
	* Water-shed management	
	* Afforestation	
Hydrological	* Economic use of water	Agricultural
	* Changing cropping pattern in favour of less water intensive crops	
	* Drought resistant crops and varieties	
Agricultural	* Decentralized procurement Food and buffer-stocks	
	* P.D.S. for target groups	
Food	* Land reforms	Entitlement
	* Marginal farmer oriented technology and input service	
	* Works programmes related to infrastructure development-soil and water conservation; irrigation, afforestation	
	* Labour construction co-operatives	
	* Development of grazing lands	
	* Reduction of cattle population	
	* Minor forest produce for tribals and poor	
	* Minimum agricultural wages	
	* Health and nutrition programmes	

)rought Management and Development Strategy : :ompensatory Development Plan

In dealing with the chain of causes and consequences drought, ompensatory development strategy would look upon drought manage-ient as an integral part of sustainable development. i.e. pattern and process f development without erosion of the nation's stock of natural resources. roughts are not an aberration since they are a part of climatology.

The occur at regular intervals, though despite advance of technology and model building, the cycle of good seasons and bad cannot be predicted with accuracy. Development planning should allow for occurrence of droughts and provide for them. The approach to drought management should not be ad hoc, but long term. If this is not done, despite the success of post-independence in India in avoiding mass stravation during drought, the tragedy of colonical times might be repeated. The multi-stage strategy outlined above for the prevention of meteorological drought converting into hydrological drought, hydrological drought into agricultural drought, agricultural drought into food drought and food drought into entitlement drought for the vulnerable groups should have a priority in development planning. If this approach is adopted, drought would not be looked upon as an interruption of the development process and drought management as a departure from the development plan.

Rather drought management measures would be an integral part of the Compensatory Development Plan. The elements of such a plan would include programmes for the prevention of ground water depletion and its replenishment, water shed development through micro-planning, prevention of indiscriminate destruction of forests, restoration of forests through replanning and social foresty, change in cropping pattern from more water intensive to less water intensive crops through research, extension and price incentives, development of drought resistant varieties, dispersed production, procurement and stocking of food grains, improvement and protection of grazing lands, reduction of cattle population, access to tribals and poor people to minor forest product, land reforms and programme o public health and nutrition. As Dre'ze says "durable elimination of vulnerability requires promotional policies such as expansion of general prosperity, reduction of insecurity through economic diversification and creation o secure earning arrangement to the provide for both" secure lives and secur livelihood."

It is said that drought are made by God but famines are made by man But to an extent even drought are made by man.

Compensatory development strategy is a long term policy aiming a sustainable development[41] and poverty alleviation. Diagram 7 depict compensatory Development Strategy in contrast to crisis Managemer strategy. In its absence, future droughts may bring in their wake mas mortality, avoided so far in post-independence period, since its victims ar even in normal times victims of 'quite violence' — the quite process (exploitation, malnutrition and starvation.

Diagram 7

Model - I : Crisis Management

D1 Drought D2 Resumption

Relief — — — — — — — > Rehabilitation

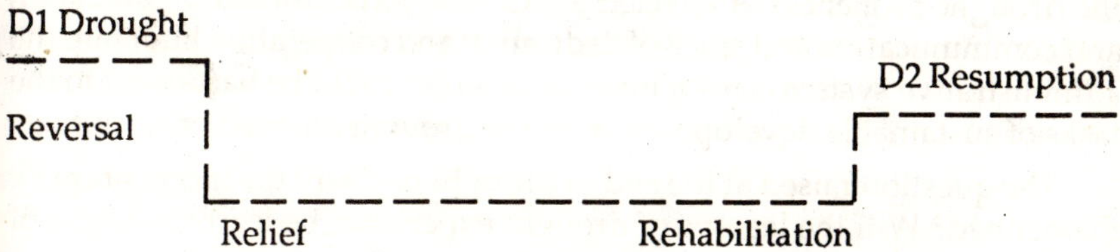

Development is resumed at lower level after relief operation

Model - II : Compensatory Development

D1 D2

Compensatory Development

D1 — D2

Compensatory Development

No drop in development because of
compensatory development strategy

During times of drought while the attention of administration and ›eople alike is focussed on crisis management, there is at the same time a learer preception of the chain of causes and consequences of drought, the .nks between drought and development and the need for reorienting levelopment so as to reduce incidence, intensity and impact of drought in ears to come.

Droughts are "agonising reminders" of vulnerability of agriculture, nd of the economic and social life, to seasonal vagaries of the monsoon. hus during the Bihar and Maharashtra drought, government was blamed ›r apathy, callousness and indifference in handling the problems of drought-prone areas in pre-drought period which were mainly responsible for the sufferings of the people during times of drought. "It has taken three successive monsoon failures" said a journalist "to awaken the authority from its death-like sleep." Drought provide a "Shock therapy" where development plans could have provided a 'preventive therapy'.

It is also realized that *programmes* taken on a crash basis during period themselves constitute a significant development effort which could reduce the drought-proneness of affected areas. Also stream-lined organization and communication and spirit of dedication and cooperation built into the administrative system during times of drought could be harnessed to the tasks of sustainable development after the drought induced crisis is over.

The question raised at the end of drought is - "will the momentum be maintained? Will the lessons of drought experience be learnt in terms of reorientation of development plans and policies?"

Unfortunately once drought years are followed by blessings of abundant rains, all the travails during the period of drought are forgotten. Instead of evolving a development strategy which takes note of drought, drought is blamed for the shortfall of plan targets, as though plan targets can be fixed as if no droughts would or should take place in the plan period. Clearly plans should be formulated on the basis of a compensatory development policy.

But the planner's response after 1987 drought does not seem to take into account the lessons of drought. The Special Food Grains Production Programme drawn after two years of drought and commended to the States by the Planning Commission and Union Ministry of Agriculture concentrated on 169 selected districts in 14 states for making up the shortfall in food grain production during drought years and raising it to 166 million tons in the current years (1988-89) and 175 million tons in 1989-90, final year of the Seventh Five Year Plan so as to come close to the plan target of 178-18[illegible] million tons of food-grains. But instead of building in the lessons of drought in the process of planning, the programme seem to be more of the same - the continuation of the 'green revolution strategy' of capitalizing the potentia[l] of green revolution area for immediate agricultural growth, instead o[f] broad-basing agricultural development strategy through effective implementation of land reforms, development of infrastructure of irrigation (as many as 500 major and medium irrigation projects are reported to be lagging behind at various stages of construction for want of funds) and programmes for drought prone areas and technology and input policies fo[r] small and marginal farmers.[42]

The various elements of compensatory development policy in relation to drought outlined above do find a place in the Seventh Five Year and earlier plans as well under different sectoral headings like Agriculture, Animal Husbandry, Rural Development and Rural Work Programme, Cooperation, Irrigation and Power. But there is no discussion of the causes and consequences of drought in relation to the course of development, the relevance of the impact of drought on the fulfilment of plan targets and hence no integrated long term strategy for dealing with drought such as indicated in the compensatory development plan outlined above.

If drought is looked upon as recurrent and normal phenomenon it should be taken care of through "compensatory development plan" such as the one suggested above. It should be built into the Development plan with a provision for augementing it when required. Such a strategy would not only be an antidote against wasteful expenditure on scheme hurriedly introduced under pressure of crisis caused by drought (during colonial times district officers were asked to keep a shelf of project ready for times of drought, since these were found wanting when crisis came; this happens even now!); it would also provide the perspective for seeing drought in relation to development and the course of development in such a direction, that the nation and the people (specially the vulnerable sections) would be able to deal with drought and absorb its consequences with greater resilience, order, preparedness and self-assurance.

The problem of drought would continue to haunt us even in the year 2000 A.D and thereafter. The strategy to deal with it is that of sustainable development.

Summary

The concepts and analysis of the paper can be summed up in the ten following propositions :

1. Drought are a part of climatology and cannot be abolished. They were there in the past; and would be there in the future.
2. Droughts should not merely be a matter of 'relief operations' or 'crisis management' as in the past; they should be seen in relation to Development.
3. Droughts have a series of consequences - economic and social, some of which are felt in the short run but some others can be irreversible and have long-term impact.
4. These consequences set back the clock of development.
5. Droughts in the past provided checks to population growth in relation to available resources.
6. Development can be a positive response to drought in maintaining a high level of living in the face of population pressure and adverse impact of droughts.

7. Such development requires "mobilization of social energy" which can be the result of people's own efforts given leadership and organization.
8. But it should be deliberate goal of public policy and planning.
9. Such plan and policy could be termed as Compensatory development plan and Pro-active public policy.
10. The components of such plan and policy could include:
    (a) water conservation projects and policies,
    (b) Drought resistant agriculture,
    (c) Dispersed production, procurement and storage of food buffer stocks, and
    (d) Increasing entitlement of the poor.

NOTES

1. Government of India, Economic Survey 1989-90.
2. See a Gopalkrishna Kumar, "Consumption Disparities, Food Surpluses, & Effective Demand Failures Reflection on Macro Economics of Drought Vulnerability, EPW March 10, 1990.
3. Historical account of droughts and famine in India can be found in Loveday-"History & Economics of Famine in India."

   BM Bhatia - "Famines in India : a study of some aspect of economic history of India - 1860-65. Asia Publishing House 1963, 1967; Mohiuddin Alamgir - "Famines in South Asia - Political Economy of Mass Starvation, Gunn and Hair Publishers Inc Cambridge Mass-a-chusettes, 1980.
4. Dr. M.V. Rao - "Crop Planning and Drought Management" Agharkar Memorial Lecture, Nov. 1987.
5. The following report about the Chinese drought was published in the Indian newspaper "Stateman" (July 1988) - "A drought reveging large tracks of Central and Eastern China. Drought began in May and hit 8 out of 30 provinces Reservoirs are bone dry; rivers run dry; drinking water wells contain nothing but mud; paddy field are perched; cotton stunted and corn dried on stock. Vegetable fields backed by sun have been abandoned. Buffaloes are dying of thirst. This is the first drought in the last fifty years. Such blight has not been since 1578."
6. Times of India, Sept. 17, 1990.
7. Hemendra Prasad Ghose - "The Famine of 1770". The Book Company, Calcutta.
8. Uppal, JN - 'Bengal Famine of 1943 : A man made tragedy" Atma Ram and Sons, 1984.

9. Theodore Morrison J. - "The economic transition in India"', London, 1911.
10. Mischelle Burge Mc Alpin - "Subject to Famine - Food crunch and economic change in Western India - 1860-1920, Princeton University Press 1983.
11. Jean Dre'ze - "Famine prevention in India "May 1988, World Institute of Development, Economics, LSE of the United Nations University. The author has expressed his reservation about Mc Alpin's conclusions "Improvement in communication could hardly account for the sharp reduction of famine in the twentieth century". National leaders like Mahatma Gandhi drew attention to the negative role of the Railways during the colonial regime in exacerbation of famines. Large scale exports of grain abroad during the famine period was a frequent phenomenon (Bhatia op. cit. has held this responsible for shortage for food supply) and railway played a role in facilitating exports from the famine stricken area. Bad harvests in England stimulated exports of grain from India.
12. Mahatma Gandhi - "Daridra Narayan - Our duty in Food and Cloth Crisis" Edited and published by Anand T. Hingorani, Karachi 1946.
13. For graphics account of these relief arrangements during widespread famine of 1897, see FMS Merewether, UHHA 1985 (First edition, 1898) also William Digby - "The famine campaign in south India", Langman Grean and Company, 1878 for an account of Drought and Famine in South India, 1876-78 in which four million people perished.
14. See N.K. Jaiswal and N.V. Kolto 'Development of Drought Prone Area.' NIRD 1981.
15. For information regarding Bihar famine see K. Suresh Singh - "The India Famine 1967 - a study in crisis and change. People Publishing House, New Delhi 1975; Wendy and Allen Scrafe "Triger on Rein - Report on Bihar Famines, Geofrery Chepman, London 1969; K.D. Gangrade and Siddharaj Dhadda "Challenge and Response - A study of famine in India", Rachana Publications, Delhi, 1973; Mussafir Singh - "People can Avert Famine" Central Institute of Research and Training in Public Cooperation, New Delhi 1970; also Dre'ze, op. cit.
16. For detailed account of management of Maharashtra drought see V. Subramaniam - "Parched Earth - The Maharashtra Drought - 1970-73, Government of Maharashtra, 1975 also Dre'ze op. cit.
17. The point has been made by Suhas Paranjape, R.K. Patil, K.R. Datye in their article - "Role of Non-agricultural Incomes and socio-economic aspects of Management of Drought."
18. See in the context Bharat Dogra - "Empty Stomachs and Packed Godowns - Aspects of Food System in India, New Delhi, 1987.
19. *See the works cited above.*

20. See for example Ann Grodzins Gold - "Fruitful Journeys - the ways of Rajasthani Pilgrims." University of California Press, 1987 villagers of Ghatiyali village in Rajasthan attribute powers to four village deities in times of drought. Their blessings are solicited to bring rains. The whole village joins indra-puja (worship of God Indra) to influence heavenly powers for rain.

21. Bangladesh famine of 1974 which took a tool of 100,000 was attributed to floods.

22. Amartya Sen — "Poverty and Famines - An Essay on Entitlement and Deprivation," Clarandon Press, Oxford 1987.

23. The point has been made by Jean Dre'ze op. cit as follows - While the entitlement approach asserts the inadengacy of food availuaability as the focus of the analysis of faminc, it does not assert its irrleievance. Improvement of food availability can play a critical role in preventing development of famine."

24. Reported in Times of India July 18, 1988.

25. Morgan D Maclachlan - "Why they did not starve : Biocultural Adoptation in the South India village," Institute for the study of Human issues, Philadelphea, 1983.

26. See my article - "Ralegansiddhi Saga", - Times of India, June 8, 1990.

27. B.M. Udgaonkar and V.D. Despande - "Meeting Drought : A Micro Watershed Development Approach" in Ambio, November 5, 1987 of Swedish Royal Academy of Sciences.

28. "Aravali Bhils Show the Way", IE Sept. 29, 1989.

29. See Bharat Dogra op.cit.

30. See Suhas Paranjpe et. al. op. cit.

31. "Treasure chest in Dry Land" Indian Express 4-5, 1990.

32. "Crop pattern changed for Economic Gain", IE May 25, 1990.

33. "Management Drought with canal Irrigation - A South Indian Case- Agricultural Administration, Elsevier applied Science Publishers Ltd. England 1984.

34. Sen, op. cit p., 126.

35. Report in New York Times, August 4, 1988.

36. V. M. Dandekar - "Food and Freedom", Karnatak University Dharwar, 1967.

37. This is referred to in K. Santhanam - "The Cry of Distress - a first hand description and objective study of the Indian Famine 1943, New Delhi, Hindustan Times, 1944 Delhi.

38. The poor lose their assets in normal times also. The process gets accelerated in times of drought.

39. Bety Hartman and James Boyce, "A quit violence - view from Bangladesh village, Zed Press, London 1983.

40. Jean Dre'ze - "Femine Prevention in Africa" March 1989 - Published under the aupices of the Development Economic Research Programme.

41. "Sustainable development" is defined as that process of development which seeks to raise living standards without depleting the production base of the existing stock of natural resources. See "Sustainable Development : Economics and Environment of the Third World" by David Fearce, Edward Barbier and Anil Markandya, London Environment Economics Centre, Edward Elgar Publishing Ltd. 1990 p. 217.

42. See editiorial "Agricultural Policies Fall in Line - "Economic and Political Weekly, June 18, 1988.

25

Coping with Seasonality and Drought

After three successive years of good monsoon, large parts of the country are once again under the shadow of a severe drought. It is reported that 29000 out of 40000 villages in Maharashtra are in the grip of drought. Gujarat, Rajasthan and Madhya Pradesh are also very badly affected.*

The occurrence of drought is of course, only to be expected. Two thirds of the cultivated area in India is subject to periodic droughts. After three years of complacency, once again attention is riverted on the strategy of dealing with drought. This is what makes the book under review of immediate relevance. It, is a study of strategies adopted by different types of households in a village in the semi-arid and chronically drought prone region of Gujrat State to cope with drought. The study is based on research carried out during 1987 which was the third year of a severe drought in the region.

The drought of 1985-87 was a real drought since it was spread over a succession of years. Many parts of Gujarat suffered shortfall during these years.' In all the villages of the area where the study was conducted, the 1985-87 drought was considered the worst in living memory.

Over the past three decades, Gujarat experienced wide spread drought over 8 years and localised drought every year. Maatisar village, located in – Dholka taluka of Ahmedabad district—a drought-prone region is severely affected by droughts every five years. Although the area under irrigation has expanded, monsoon crops are still grown under rainfed conditions and remain highly sensitive to rainfall. Ground water aquifers

---

* This refers to the year 1987.

need to be regularly recharged and are sensitive to shortfall in rainfall. Even though close to Ahmedabad city, the District remains relatively undeveloped.

The village had a feudal set up till recently. The situation changed after the introduction of Land Reforms during 1950 and 1960 and the institution of Gram Panchayats in 1963. The political power shifted from the socially higher caste to the numerically dominant castes.

The traditional economy of the village was organised on caste lines. Among the important caste are the Brahmins who cultivate lands, Thakkars are engaged in trade, shop keeping and money lending, Bharwads are engaged in animal husbandry, Prajapatis are engaged in potmaking, Vaghris are engaged in cultivation as wage labourers and hunting, Vonkars are engaged in weaving, and Koli Patels work as farm workers. The village has also service castes like carpenters (Sutars), barbers (Navi), geneologists (Barub), and priests (Pujaris).

Under the old jajmani system various caste groups rendered services to the feudal lords but in 50s these were abolished. In the early, 80s many household derived secured livelihood from the hereditary caste occupations but with increased population density and division of property, the hereditary occupation did not provide adequate sustenance. Thus many castes were forced to enter into the wage labour market.

The different households belonging to different caste and engaged in their traditional occupations have evolved their own strategies to cope with risks and uncertainty of arising out of seasonal changes. They have tried to build flexibility in their basic livelihood system in order to make mid-season and cross-season adjustments. One way of building flexibility was diversification of occupations and resort to various subsistence activities such as gathering of fuel, fodder and water which are carried on by women. Reduction of the consumption, drawing-down of inventories, entering into labour market, entering into and sharing group arrangement, drawing on social relationships, drawing on community resources like trees and grazing lands, pawning assets like jewellery and household utensils are the normal ways of coping with risks and uncertainty associated with seasonality and drought.

During 1987 drought, most landholdings and occupational groups reduced their consumption of foodgrains, milk and vegetables as the drought advanced. Festivals were celebrated with less expenditure. The bride price was lowered and the marriage cost were reduced. However, the number of marriages increased dramatically!

In adoption of various strategies, villagers depend on economic and social institutions. The traditional patron-client relationship, jajmani system and kinship and caste provide the traditional social security system which has been considerably eroded in modern times and consequently their ability to minimise the impact of drought on their economy. In the traditional system patrons were required to underwrite substantial consumption needs of the clients and provide protection in return for services, and respect and loyalty of their clients. With the introduction of cash transactions, the economic basis of the patron-client and jajmani system has gradually eroded. Market forces have replaced traditional modes of transactions in tenancy, labour and credit market which do not guarantee subsistence during the slack season for the period of uncertainty particularly in drought areas.

In the earlier years of drought, peasants were able to draw on the water supply to sustain wheat and barley cultivation. When rains failed, farmers resorted to usual strategies of replanting, deferring planting, substitute planting and growing fodder crops. However, when the drought was prolonged there was a short-fall of grains production and people had to seek employment opportunities on non-farm occupations. As the economy weakened because of the drought, the local labour market collapsed. The cooperative sugar factories were forced to close because most of the sugar-cane crop had been sold as fodder. The demand for labour in brickkilns and rice mills also dropped.

In normal areas the labour from 50 households in the village would migrate. Because of the collapse o the labour market there was a drop in demand for migrant labour.

The 1987 was the worst year for weavers. They could not sell their shawls as the market had collapsed. The demand for the traditional services of babers, genealogists and priests also dropped as their patrons adjusted to the drought conditions. The potter household suffered a decline in demand for pots. Surprisingly, traders and money lenders who normally prosper in drought years also suffered a decrease in volume of trade.

In these conditions, the scarcity relief work played a crucial role in averting large scale starvation. Landless labourers and artisan castes actively participated in the relief work. As the drought became more severe, peasants household from all categories also joined the relief work. Even those castes like shepherds who did not engage in wage labour also joined the relief work. 70% of the small farm household, 80% of the Venkar weaver household and other half of the labour household participated in the relief work. Even the land-rich household joined the relief work. More women than men participated in them. No doubt there were weaknesses in the relief work like corruption in the actual operation of the scheme, but its benefits in providing social security to large number of people outweighed, abuses or leakages of the system. Due to the effective presence of relief work there was no aimless wandering in search of employment opportunities. There was little evidence of family disintegration during the 1985-87 drought, because of the employment offered by the Government relief system. Labour households did not suffer significant trade entitlement failure despite the collapse of the local migrant labour. In fact labour household were able to exchange their labour for more days in 1985-87 drought than in the normal years. The peasant cultivators and tenant farm household suffered both direct and trade entitlement failure because of the prolonged nature of drought. They depleted their stocks and their capital reserves, and many cultivators were in debt. Shepherds suffered both from direct entitlement and trade entitlement failures and were forced to migrate to South Gujarat and during their forced migration they lost their animals, their major endowment. The Venkars were forced to close their weaving operations. The Thakkars did not suffer significant failure. The Brahmins suffered significant entitlement failures.

The Maatisar drought of 1985-87 turned out to be primarily a fodder drought. As a result farmers no longer allowed other villagers to collect grass and weeds from their cultivated fields, or to graze animals on their fields and women began to quarrel over rights to collect cow dung from public places. The Jains as a matter of charity ran camps for sick and dying animals.

The voluntarily organization SEWA played a significant part in lobbying for relief work and in transportation and sale of fodder from South Gujarat to the drought areas, in constructing a cattle trough and in providing subsidised seeds, fertilisers and fuel. There was a significant demand for production loans from institutions. Because of the active help of the relief work only 40% of the total loans taken were for consumption needs.

The suffering of people in 1985-87 drought was much less than that of 1899-1900. This was because in 1985-87 while there was a sharp decline in production, there was no sharp decline in consumption because of the effective presence of relief work and Public Distribution System through which food was made available. As a result food prices did not escalate drastically.

The study has drawn attention to several weaknesses in the relief work undertaken. First, the quantum of relief work is not always adequate to meet the demands during severe droughts. Government funds are limited and finances are not adequate to meet the work capital requirements. Second, the productive component in relief works is not upto the mark. Thirdly even before the crisis hits, there is always the demand for seasonal public works on a regular basis.

The significant long term effect of the drought is the adverse impact on ability of the individual households and traditionally social security system to recover after the drought. The most significant conclusion of the study is that public drought management is isolated from regular development strategies. Both seasonality and drought should be considered as key variables in development policy. Long term approach to drought must replace the crisis management approach.

There should be more emphasis on development in drought management. Rural development programmes must be resource-specific in relation to arid or semi-arid areas. Development has so far focussed on high potential areas and have neglected dry areas. The drought management approach has been developed in isolation from ongoing development strategy or chronic subsistence needs. Village economy remains vulnerable to drought despite growth and development. Drought need to be analysed not only as short-term isolated phenomenon but as long-term repeatitive phenomenon which together with season fluctuations affect rural livelihood options.

26

Some Economic Issues in the Rural Energy: Environment Conflict

ural Energy Scene at Present

Nearly 70% of the total population of India still lives in rural areas hough the rural area gets a share of 20% of energy available. Nearly 80% of he total energy consumption by the rural people consists of noncommercial nergy sources. Of these firewood, agricultural waste, etc. constitute 65% f the energy consumption in rural areas. Another 15% is accounted for by uman and animal power. Commercial energy constitutes 20%. Share of ommercial energy constitutes 23% in agriculture (fertiliser 14%, electricity % and diesel 3%) 2% in domestic cooking and 100% in domestic lighting erosene 87% and electricity 13%). Most of the transportation in rural dustrial sector solely depends on animate and non-commercial energy urces. 64% of the total energy is used in domestic activity, 22% in riculture and 7% in industry, 4% in lighting and 3% in transport.

The energy consumption in India is low; per capita being about 252 GCE of commercial energy in 1980 as against over 12,000 in USA. It is still uch lower in the rural areas. There is, therefore, the need to augment ailability of energy in rural areas. The traditional sources of fire wood and el is going down because of massive deforestation resulting in environ- ental disaster facing the country. Hence the need for developing alterna- e sources of energy in rural areas, such as solar and wind energy.

Strategy for Providing Rural Energy

The strategy for dealing with the worsening energy crisis was the national rural energy planning exercise stared by the Planning Commission during the 6th Five Year Plan which resulted in the integrated rural energy programme. During the 6th Plan, 26 blocks were taken up in 8 States where block level integrated rural energy projects were set up based on rural energy block plans. A newly created centrally sponsored scheme was started in 7th Plan period to provide staff for IREP at State and block levels for preparing and implementing the projects and also for overall coordination.

The rural energy scene in India is grim. While the per capital energy consumption is very low, even at this low level there is a growing gulp between the demand and supply of energy. Rural people are starved of meeting their bare necessities. Although about 56% of the villages in the country have ben electrified, in reality barely 14% of households could use it despite the fact that the rural electrification is heavily subsidized. In view of this grim reality the rural energy programme has to be based primarily on the exploitation of renewable resources. Taking this into account the 7th Plan has envisaged the following programmes for promoting rural energy:

(1) Augmentation of firewood supply through large-scale afforestation programmes especially on waste lands.

(2) Efficient utilisation of firewood, through large-scale programmes for promoting improved chulhas and improved wood-stoves.

(3) Improved utilisation of cowdung through a large-scale programme for family size and community type biogas plants.

(4) Improved utilisation of agricultural waste through programmes for promoting production of briquettes and pellets from agricultural residues for fuel purposes.

(5) Promotion of alternative energy technologies for substituting non-commercial energy sources wherever possible through programmes of solar cookers, solar heating systems etc.

(6) Promotion and efficient development of commercial energy sources in rural areas wherever they are considered economical including rural electrification, soft coke, efficient utilisation of kerosene and other petroleum products.

On the basis of experience of the pilot IREP programmes in the Sixth Plan in the selected states, the programme is being activised in all the states and union terriroties during the Seventh Plan and the institutional mechanism is being developed in all the States/U Ts for planning and implementing integrated projects in selected blocks in every State at the State, district and block levels.

The institutional mechanism at the State level consists of State cells. The cells are manned by professional economists and engineers and other supporting staff. The cell is created in a nodal department of the State as the Planning Department for coordinating and directing the programme in the state. The District and Block cells are set up under the DRDA/District Magistrate and the Block Development Officer to plan and implement IREP at the block level. Implementation consists of demonstration programmes on various energy technologies, extension through involvement of voluntary organisations and non-Governmental organisations and participation of local institutions including banks, R&D institutions, industries, etc.

IREP programmes aims at an optimum mix of different energy programmes for meeting energy needs for subsistence and production activities in the rural areas over the planning horizon upto the year 2000 A.D.

Thus as a part of the integrated planning process rural energy sector is linked with energy and economic sector on the one side and grass root implementation with planning at the block, district, state and national levels, on the other through introduction of computer planning models and implementation of rural energy programmes The following is a statement of major on-going programmes for meeting rural energy needs in India:

Name of the Programme	*Achievements upto the end of 6th Plan*	*Target for 7th Plan*	*Remarks*
(1)	(2)	(3)	(4)
1) Rural Electrification:			
a) Village Electrification	3,68,840 (villages)	1,18,101	64% of the village electrification was achieved by the end of Sixth Plan period 84.5% by the end of the Seventh Plan period.
b) Pump-set energisation	57,05,405 (pumps)	23,99,678	47.5% of the total potential pumpsets were energised by the end of the Sixth Plan and it will be raised to the level of 67.5% of the total potential available in the country.
2) Social forestry	4,60,00,000 Hectares (National Remote Sensing during 80-82)	50,00,000	National Waste Land Development Board has been set up to undertake massive planting of trees, primarily for fuel-wood and pastures at the rate of 5 million hectare every year to help to bridge the gap.
3) Biogas	3,86,000	6,00,000	Biogas programme included family size as well as

Name of the Programme	Achievements upto the end of 6th Plan	Target for 7th Plan	Remarks
			community and institutional plants. A complete programme was taken up since the Sixth Plan. Biogas is a cheap and efficient fuel and its feed stock is a renewable source. The manure products of biogas plants i.e better both qualitatively and quantitatively than farm yard manures. The programme is rapidly picking up in the rural areas and has resulted in the saving of valuable forest wealth.
(4) Improved Chulhas	8,12,000	5,00,000	The programme was started during the Sixth Plan. It has been enthusiastically accepted by the rural population and would be enlarged during the Seventh Plan. It fulfills the aim of preserving forest, environmental benefits like pollution control, relief from health hazards and improvement in the quality of life of rural people.
(5) Setting up of Solar Thermal System	2,000	R & D field demonstration and extension	Solar thermal programmes consist of extension programme for solar cookers, solar water heating, timber kilns, solar distillation driers, steam generators and field demonstration and testing for refrigerators, a cold storage, air conditioning, power generating decentralised systems, solar pond, passive buildings etc. Intensive RD is being carried out for efficiency cost reduction of the solar thermal devices.
(6) Solar Photovoltaics	A wide ranging programme of R&D in the area of SPVs was initiated in the Sixth Plan with a view to reducing costs and improving production technology, solar pumps for drinking water supply and irrigation and photovoltaic street-lighting in villages were installed for		Power generation system of 10 to 100 KW capacity will be promoted (a) RD focus on development of amorphous silicon cells; (b) Extension programme for solar street lighting, solar pumps for irrigation and drinking water; (c) Field demonstration including electrification of remote villages, water pumping, solar system and power generation of 10 KW to 100 KW systems are promoted under the programme.

Name of the Programme	*Achievements upto the end of 6th Plan*	*Target for 7th Plan*	*Remarks*
	demonstration and extension programme under NASPED		
(7) Biomass	...	...	New schemes for large scale energy plantation of fast growing species, biomass based wood gasifiers engines for irrigation and drinking water solid fuel through conversion of agricultural waste into pellets and briquettes and production of liquid for transportation from biomass such as ethanol and methanol are promoted under this scheme.
(8) Kerosene	...	...	Kerosene is supplied through Fair Price Shops/Depots in the villages. Kerosene is used for lighting and cooking purpose in the rural areas. 18% of rural household still depend on kerosene for lighting. A programme or improved kerosene stoves has been taken up in the Seventh Plan period.

3. Need for Coordination at the National Level:

The above programme have been fragmented into different Ministries at he Centre as shown below:

(1)	Rural Electrification	...	Ministry of Energy Rural Electrification Corpn.
(2)	Forest and Social Forestry	...	Ministry of Environment and Forests and National Wasteland Development Board
(3)	Bio-gas/Biomass	...	Department of Non-conventional Energy
(4)	Improved chul'has		
(5)	Solar Energy		
(6)	Wind Energy		
(7)	Kerosene	...	Ministry of Petroleum & Natural Gas
(8)	Mobilisation of voluntary agencies	...	Ministry of Rural Development CAPART

(9)	Integrated Rural Energy Programme	...	Planning Commission
(10)	Bullock Cart Modernisation	...	Ministry of Rural Development.

It is necessary to set up some coordinating mechansim at the Centre to bring together the various activities related to promotion of rural energisation in the country. The Council for Additional Source of Energy (CASE) in the Department of non-Conventional Energy provides the possibility for such a mechanism.

27

Need to Revive Rural Industries

One of the important features of Indian economy is its lopsided structure with agriculture constituting the preponderant sector in providing employment opportunities. Seventyfive per-cent of the people were engaged in agriculture at the beginning of planning and even today this holds good. This mean that the non-farm employment opportunities have not grown sufficiently to make any significant change in the occupational structure.

A chronic feature of the pattern of employment in agriculture is that it is either seasonal or only few hours of the day or at a level of productivity which is too low. This kind of employment is otherwise known as disguised unemployment.

This feature of our economy accounts for its backwardness and was the result of colonial domination.

Before India came under the colonial domination, Indian villages had self-sufficient economy. There were traditional industries which provided goods and services to the rural community, many a time on a barter basis. These were the industries in which the traditional artisans like carpenter, mason, cobbler, blacksmith, etc. were engaged. In addition, there was the widespread spinning and weaving industry. Besides, handicrafts provided high level of employment opportunities. Exquisite products of handicrafts found a market in the urban centres. There was thus a balanced economy where both agriculture and industry flourished.

The advent of British rule broke this balance. The music of the Charkha and the handloom which was there in every village ceased and the products of the British textile industries started flooding the Indian market. The British also did every thing to give a setback of traditional industry. The story of the manner in which the thriving Dacca muslin industry was killed by the Britishers by chopping off hands of the weavers is all too well known and symbolises the discouraging environment in which the village industries and handicrafts rapidly declined. Professor D.R. Gadgil's "Industrial Evolution of India" documents the story of the decline of village industries and handicrafts during the colonial regime. Growing monetisation put an end the barter system of which the cottage industry was an integral part. The expansion of the market economy led to growing penetration of the products of modern industry in the rural areas and the cottage industries wilted under the onslaught. Mahatma Gandhi made a heroic effort to revive village and cottage industries. It was he who discovered the Charkha and made its popularisation a part of the constructive programme which in turn was a part of the struggle for Swaraj. Mahatma Gandhi promoted Charkha not because he was an obscurantist but because he thought that it was the only the means of providing gainful employment opportunities to the vast manpower in rural areas which was chronically unemployed or under-employed. It is his inspiration which led to the formulation of the programmes for the development of Khadi and village industries as a part of our five year plans, inspite of the fact that simultaneously we decided to move in a big way with the establishment of modern and heavy industries based on advanced technology and use of machinery. A Gandhian like late Shri Vaikunth Mehta was at the helm of affairs of Khadi and Village Industries Commission. The Commission had its counterpart in the shape of khadi and village industries boards in various States.

Inspite of the organisation of the Khadi and Village Industries Commission and its various schemes and programmes, it was not possible to halt the decline of khadi and village industries at least in the relative sense.

Despite the progress in our five year plans, the position has not very much improved today. The lopsided employment structure continues. Seventy per cent of the population continues to depend upon agriculture and the employment potential of modern industries is still very limited. The disguised unemployment persists and so does mass poverty.

The revival of village industries is, therefore, still one of the means of providing gainful employment opportunities and wherewithals of life to the masses of people in the countryside. The subject had, therefore, once again received attention at the hands of the National Committee on Backward Areas which issued a special report on village and cottage industries. In analysing the present status of our economy, it has pointed out that because of various inherent limitations to the growth of the organised industry sector and insufficient potentialities of agricultural development and the migration of rural people to urban areas where opportunities are already limited, the role of village and cottage industries is significant.

The principal recommendations of the Committee to revive cottage and village industries are on well known lines, namely:

(i) Making available raw materials at reasonable prices :

(ii) Upgradation of technology;

(iii) Promotion of market for the products of khadi and village industries;

(iv) Supply of credit at reasonable rates of interest; and

(v) Organisational support.

The Committee has recommended that the efforts should be directed towards upgradation of technology so that it is possible to overcome one feature of these industries namely, drudgery without adequate return. The technology has to be upgraded so that artisans move out of the poverty trap and are able to raise their productivity and earning capacity. It is necessary to introduce modernisation of the techniques and improve the skills of artisans. In doing this, mechanisation should not be a taboo. Even Mahatma Gandhi was not opposed to machinery per se. The technology to be introduced is often referred to as "appropriate technology" by whose application the existing artisans and their skills are not only retained but upgraded. The Committee has made a case for introduction of "intermediate technology" on a crash basis but this is not possible without greater research effort and a larger programme of training for artisans and field level officers to propagate more productive technology. The Committee has also recommended a composite training centre in every district where the artisans should be trained in intermediate technology. The Committee has said that once training and equipment are passed on to the artisans, they become a self-employed units with much higher level of productivity and are able to go above the poverty line. This optimism of the Committee would be justified provided there is a back-up for the supply of raw materials and the sale of finished products.

For the supply of raw material, the Committee has, recommended the establishment of State Rural Industries Development Corporation and district supply and marketing society which should be given the responsibility for procurement of raw material. It has also recommended that the system of supply of raw material already existing in industries like khadi and handloom should be continued and streamlined till the proposed new organisation comes into being. As regards marketing of products, the Committee has recommended that the organisational set-up for the supply of raw material should also undertake the functions of marketing. The private retail shops could be fully brought in the chain of distribution. The Committee hopes that if appropriate marketing strategy is evolved, it would be possible to sell the products of village industries in new and distant markets in the country and even abroad.

As regards the organisational side, the Committee has recommended a group approach. Technical support to the artisans should be provided at a group centre which should cover all artisans in the area connected with specific rural industry. It has recommended a Directorate of Rural Industry in every state with its own technical hierarchy. At the district level, it has recommended a nucleus such as one provided by the district industry centre. While the Committee expects the Khadi and Village Industry Commission to go on with its programme, it has recommended that the State Government should play a leading role in directing, monitoring and coordinating various aspects relating to development of rural industry in the State as a whole.

The Committee has not brought out the role of cooperative organisations. This may be because industrial and weaving cooperatives have not been of much success. The Damry Study Group had made several recommendations for the strengthening of industrial cooperatives. There is no doubt that the best form of group approach such as the one commended by the National Committee on Development of Backward Areas is the cooperative approach but the Committee does not seem to have confidence in the cooperatives. That is why perhaps it has recommended an alternative structure. However, it is somewhat naive to expect that other organisations would succeed where cooperatives have failed. This has happened in the field of agricultural finance also. The Farmers Service Societies have not been more efficient than the primary cooperative societies. The commercial banks have not shown better recoveries than the cooperatives. The regional rural banks failed. It would be a mistake to introduce new organizations without examining why the erstwhile organizations have failed. Bringing new organisations into existence does not by itself solve old problems.

Every group approach requires a long process of education of the members of the group and instilling in them a sense of confidence. It also requires sound leadership and dedicated workers. Where these are not available, a mere creation of wide network of organisations will not succeed. It it true that dedicated workers are difficult to find but that is where a start has to be made in the field of village industries.

Apart from traditional village and cottage industries and handicrafts, a big avenue for the promotion of rural industrialisation has been opened up in the field of agro-industries. The scope of agro-industrialisation is two-fold. Firstly, industries to cater to the requirements of agriculture and secondly, industries for the processing of agriculture produce. There is a vast scope for the development of rural industries to manufacture modern tools and equipment required for progressive agriculture. For areas under irrigation, farmers need tools for levelling and reshaping of land like bunds-formers, buckcrapers, etc. The need for seed and fertiliser drills is also very great. The scope for seed processing, soil testing and fertiliser mixing is also considerable. These enterprises require skilled workers and managers. The scope for agro-processing is even greater. The successful examples of agro-processing are cooperative sugar industries in Maharashtra and dairy processing in Gujarat. But there is a vast scope for replication of similar process in other States. Cooperative sugar industry has promoted rural entrepreneurship in Maharashtra. But in a State like U.P. cooperative industry has not made headway. Similarly, while under 'Operation Flood', dairy industry on co-operative basis is established in several States, the other states have yet to reach the standard of cooperative dairying of Gujarat. As regards processing of other commodities like fruit, vegetable, potato, onion, oilseeds, cotton, etc, the potential has hardly been touched. In the absence of fruit processing preservation facilities, it is estimated that 25 per cent of the total fruit production goes waste. If we succeed in dotting the rural areas with agro-processing enterprises, we would have taken big strides in total transformation of the rural economy. What we have to do is to link up the process of agricultural development with the process of industrial development in rural areas. What is needed is a steadfast, continuous and organised effort to work out strategies, identify and plan projects, and execute them successfully. In this effort, administration, institutions and the rural people at large have to work together.

28

Rural Development and Concept of Growth Centres

The concept of "growth centres" has considerable significance in relation to development in India in general and Maharashtra in particular.

Dual-Economy

In the year 1951, India embarked up on a process of planned economic development. Like other developing countries, India too was characterised by a "dual economy". While the three metropolitan centres namely Bombay, Calcutta and Madras and the national capital Delhi as well as other prominent cities like Bangalore, Hyderabad, Ahmedabad and Pune were highly developed with concentrated modern facilities and prerequisites of a developed economy, the vast hinterland of 500,000 villages including most of the district and tashil head quarters towns were steeped in economic backwardness. In this vast hinterland of rural areas, there was an over-whelming dependence on agriculture as a means of livelihood. Of trade, commerce, industry, business and modern institutions like banks, and facilities for civilised existence like potable drinking water, health and educational facilities, electricity, transport and communication, there was very little. It was quite inadequate for what in modern times has come to be considered essential for a civilised life. The level of living was low because of low level of earning in a system of subsistence agriculture. Agriculture was "a way of life" rather than a commercial proposition. It was "a gamble in rain". Quite a large part of India and more specially in Maharashtra came under the rain shadow area and was, therefore, drought-prone. One of the essential goals of planned economic development had, therefore, to be removing the glaring disparities between the prominent city centres and the vast hinterland of rural areas.

Rural-Urban Disparity

It is a mark of a developed country that there are no such glaring disparities between the standards of living in urban areas as compared to the rural areas. Indeed as development goes apace, the country gets increasingly urbanised. For example, in England which became the first country to be the "workshop of the world" following the Industrial Revolution of 1760-1820, the process of urbanisation has gone to such an extent that 75% of the population lives in urban areas and only 25% in the rural areas which is just the opposite of the proportion that exists in India even today. Bulk of the income there is derived from the tertiary section i.e. from the service sector, rather than from the primary sector i.e. agriculture and allied activities. An invariable concomitant of development is the diversification of the economy, increasing preponderance of trade, commerce, industry and services and increasing urbanisation. At the same time, in the wake of development the impulses of development reach far and wide and the standard of living in rural areas is not inferior compared with that in urban areas. Removal of disparities between urban and rural areas follows. One can almost say that country is developed where there is no disparity between urban and rural areas. This process of homogenisation of the economy i.e parity of development of rural and urban areas, is the hall mark of a developed economy.

Removal of Disparity as the Goal of Planning and Development

Before Independence Mahatma Gandhi was never tired of saying that India lived in villages and therefore rural development had to be at the centre of any scheme of developmental efforts in free India. The first important report to be published in India after Independence in relation to rural areas was the Rural Credit Survey Report brought out by the Reserve Bank of India in the year 1951. That report stated that most of India was rural India and most rural India was agricultural India. The implication was that rural and agricultural development should receive priority in the scheme of economic and social development of the country.

Sectoral vs. Spatial Planning

However, our plans for economic development, right from the inception, have been sectoral rather than spatial. The plan programmes deal with various sectors like agriculture, industry, transport, education, health, etc. rather than different areas and regions of the country. The main preoccupation of the plans has been with the rate of growth and the size of investment rather than with the pattern of distribution in terms of distribution of income between different sections of the society or different areas or regions of the country. The consequence of such a sectoral approach to development and preoccupation with rate of growth and size of investment was the perpetuation of inequality of income both amongst different sections of the society and different regions of the country.

Since the spatial dimensions of development in our planning process have been neglected the remedial action for rectifying regional imbalances has not been forthcoming. This is despite the fact that decentralised development had been an article of faith in our country.

Planning from Below

Mahatma Gandhi wanted the village planning to be the core and the starting process of planning. Even the plans talked of "Planning from below". During the course of the second five year plan, an attempt was made to prepare plans from below. In pursuit of this exercise village and district plans were prepared which were further to be integrated at State and national level but this never materialised and India's plans continued to be prepared in Yojana Bhavan rather than in the villages. Planning from below remained only a slogan rather then an operational procedure. The concept of decentralised planning was never operationalised though district plans have been prepared over years and district planning boards have been established. District planning in the real sense must be in terms of mobilisation of local manpower resources for the fulfilment of the local needs. On the other hand, the district plans as we have tend to be district-wise break-up of central and state plan schemes. This is a mockery of decentralised planning. The Planning Commission's report on the approach to district planning is available but the methodology suggested therein has seldom been followed.

Approach to Rural Development

It is in the context of our general approach to development planning outlined above that we have to consider the approach to rural development. In India, rural development has been considered as a sector of development. In every five year plan document, there are chapters on rural development.

Community Development and Extension Service

The earliest programme of rural development in India was that of community development and national extension service. The first five year plan stated that community development was the method and national extension service the agency through which the five year plans sought to bring about rural transformation. The community development programme divided the entire country, in 5000 community development blocks, each block consisting of about 100 village communities. Each block was expected to be a centre of planning and development. An integrated development plan was to be prepared in every block on the basis of a survey of local resources and the felt needs of the people. The block development administration consisted of a Block Development Officer, assisted by a team of eight extension officers and ten village level workers each incharge of 10 villages thus covering the requirement of the 100 village communities in every block. From 1952 onwards till 1962, over a period of a decade, the whole process of establishment of community blocks in the country was completed. The block agency also served as an extension agency and was expected to provide supplies, services and technical know-how to the people of the rural areas.

Panchayati Raj

In the process of evaluation of the community development programme by the Balwantrai Mehta study team in 1956, it was realised that it was not possible to kindle the spark of self-reliance in community development unless the block development administration was made responsible to the elected representatives of the people in rural areas. As a sequel to the recommendations of the Balwantrai Mehta study team a three tier system of Panchayati Raj institutions was set up in rural areas throughout the country. There were variations of the system in different parts of the country. The set up in Maharashtra was on the basis of the recommendations of Vasantrao Naik Committee . It was one of the most advanced in the country intended to make decentralisation of powers and development in the rural areas "real and substantial". The entire work of planning and development of local level was to be transferred to the Panchayati Raj institutions with the Zilla Parishad at the district level taking a lead in decentralised development. Unfortunately, in the State of Maharashtra and in other parts of the country, there was increasing weakening of the Panchayati Raj institutions and many schemes of development and the whole process of local planning was taken up outside the purview of the Panchyati Raj institution.

Cooperation

While community development and Panchayati Raj were concerned with the general and social process of development, the more specifically economic aspects in relation to individual families were entrusted to the cooperative institutions. On the basis of the Rural Credit Survey report 1951, a net-work of rural cooperative credit institutions were established consisting of Primary Agriculture cooperative at the village level and the district central banks as the central financing institutions. They were expected to provide short term and medium term credit for agricultural operations. For investment in land, separate institutions called Land Development Banks were established. The Reserve Bank of India with its affiliate Agricultural and Rural Development Corporation and now NABARD reimbursed and supported agriculture lendings by the cooperatives.

Green Revolution Strategy

This approach to rural development worked out in the initial years after independence in terms of community development and cooperative and Panchayati Raj institutions and was found inadequate in meeting the food requirements of the country. The food security system became extremely precarious. The country was left to live from hand to mouth. It is in this context that the new agricultural strategy was adopted in the year 1967. The strategy was based on a selective approach as against the generalised approach of community development. It was also based on the application of science and technology to a culture. An opportunity was provided by the development of hybrid and high yielding variety of seeds. Given the input of water and chemical fertilizers the new hybrid and HYV seeds were capable of bringing about a manifold increase in agricultural production. The application of the technology came to bc known as the green revolution. However the results of the green revolution were partial. The green revolution was concentrated in Punjab. Haryana and Western U.P. and was also confined mainly to wheat and paddy but did not cover such vital crops as pulses and oil seeds.

Another shortcoming of the green revolution was the perpetuation of inequalities. While the green revolution technology was neutral to scale, it required inputs and resources which the large and middle size rather than the small and marginal farmers could muster. Another source of disparity was the distinction between those areas where irrigation was available and others were it was not.

Anti-Poverty Programmes

Steps were therefore taken to introduce in the seventies special anti-poverty schemes such as the small farmers and rural small farmers development agency schemes and national rural employment schemes. For desert and drought prone areas special programmes were introduced.

Social and Economic Overheads

Plan programmes have also been established for the extension of social and economic over-heads to rural areas. Institutions of education including those in higher education, even in professional fields such as engineering and medicine colleges are coming up in rural areas. Health facilities are made available in rural areas through primary health centres. The presence of modern media namely the ratio, and telecommunication T.V. facilities are bringing about a major change in the rural areas. The T.V. has triggered off the revolution of rising expectations and consequent ever - increasing insurgence of the rural market not only for traditional items but for durable consumer goods.

As a result of strident demands of political parties and voters in rural areas, the Government and the planners have been compelled to provide atleast 50% of the plan funds for rural development.

Disparities Continue — Need for Alternative Development Models

However the results of the process of rural development in terms of removing the disparities in our economic system, are not entirely satisfactory. The disparities continue.

There is a social dimension to these disparities. The landless people and those below the poverty line belong to the socially underprivileged sections of the society such as mostly the Scheduled Castes and Scheduled Tribes. They have been left outside the main stream of development. The sense of deprivation amongst those people and aggressively selfish attitudes and unjust claims of some vested interests has given rise to rural violence with the growing attacks on the Scheduled Castes and the Scheduled Tribes from the stronger and more affluent sections of the rural society. The search for homogeneous society and economy, therefore, continues. It is in this context that alternative models and approaches of rural development in particular and development in general deserve attention. One such alternative is the regional approach to development.

Regional Approach to Development

While community development was sometimes termed as an exercise in area development, the scheme was not based on a regional approach. The regional approach to rural development requires the identification of regions in the country based on homogeneous agro-climatic and socio-economic conditions and development of programmes which are appropriate to these regions. These regions may be identified as hilly areas, desert areas or drought prone areas. For each of these areas special schemes have to be devised. Often, stereo-type general schemes on an all India basis are not appropriate to the diversified requirement of different regions of the country. An attempt was initiated in the 7th five year plan for the identification of regions and region specific schemes and programmes for various regions and but necessary reorientation of development planning has not yet taken place.

Talking of Maharashtra, the approach is still based on administrative rather than on geo-climatic conditions. Thus Maharashtra is divided into Bombay conurbation, Konkan and Western Maharashtra of the erstwhile Bombay province, Marathwada which was a part of the old State of Hyderabad and Vidharba which was part of old Central Province. The Konkan area is undeveloped in terms of availability of infrastructural facilities. The tribal pockets in Vidharba, Nagpur area require different programmes as compared to the other areas. Irrigated areas have to be distinguished from drought prone areas. Thus the process of identification of regions and formulation of development plans for different regions has to take place the country in general and Maharashtra in particular.

In Maharashtra there is a great gap between Bombay urban area and urban and industrial areas developing round Pune, Nasik and to some extent Aurangabad cities as compared to the rest of the States. Attention has been drawn to the different levels of economic development in different parts of Maharashtra as may be seen from the following table :

Net Domestic Product from (i) Agricultural and Allied Activities and (ii) Registered Manufacturing for Selected Districts in Maharashtra 1978-79.

District	*Agriculture and allied activities*		*Registered Manufacturing*	
	Per Capita Value Rs.	*Index**	*Per capita added Rs.*	*Index**
Aurangabad	579.79	111.57	53.44	28.09
Beed	603.43	116.16	2.57	1.35
Nanded	526.94	101.44	32.52	17.09
Osmanabad	696.76	134.13	11.64	6.12
Parbhani	646.31	124.42	3.61	1.90
Greater Bombay	135.68	–	1632.13	–
Thana	193.3	37.23	1442.01	757.92
Pune	477.43	91.91	555.71	292.08
Maharashtra (including Greater Bombay)	519.47		190.26	

*Maharashtra, excluding Greater Bombay = 100

Source : Report of the Fact Finding Committee on Regional Imbalances in Maharashtra, p. 46

In terms of employment opportunities and income generation, Greater Bombay, Thane region and Pune region is head and shoulder over the rest of Maharashtra.

One approach to deal with the disparities is to plan for dispersal of economic development. In the natural process of development of an economy, it tends to get concentrated on city centres. Already developed areas provide infrastructural facilities and the advantage of external economy which make them attractive centres for location of new economic enterprises. The social costs of such concentration in terms of congestion and pressure on common facilities such as transport and housing is not borne by the private enterprise. It becomes a liability of the State and the society at large. As a result of this process, there is sharp deterioration in the quality of life in cities like Bombay and Pune, in terms of growth of slums, traffic congestion and environmental deterioration. These cities are choking and unless more effective steps are taken to disperse the entire process of development, it is bound to prove counter productive. The process of development which leads to apoplexy at the centre and anaemia at the periphery may prove to be self-destructive.

Growth Centres

It is in this context that the concept of "growth centres" dispersed indifferent part of the State and of the country becomes relevant. The process of development that has taken place in the last four decades has no doubt thrown up many growth centres in irrigated areas such as central places where agricultural produce is marketed or where sugar factories are located. The latter in large number in Maharashtra, have shown excellent examples of integrated socio-economic development in areas hitherto known as backward. Similar development has taken place round cooperative dairies in Gujarat. Similar growth centres can be set up in relation to other types of intensive development. For example horticultural development holds great promise specially in hitherto drought prone areas like Solapur as well as infrastructurally backward areas like Konkan. Growth centres can be planned in relation to such development. These growth centres may be located in District or Block Headquarters or elsewhere. Agglomeration of common facilities in these growth centres may greatly support such dispersed process of development.

Regional approach to development, spatial planning, dispersal of economic development and location of a hierarchy of growth centres in hitherto backward areas provide an alternative to the sectoral and inequitable model of development adopted by us in the past. In Maharashtra, at the time of its formation, a constitutional provision was made for equitable development of all regions. Promotion of hierarchy of growth centres in backward areas should be one way of realising this objective.

Such a model should think of "rurbanisation urbanisation" rather than rural and urban development as separate, watertight compartments. While Bombay, Pune and Nasik may be apex growth centres they should not stand in splendid isolation. Development activities may be hived off from these overburdened city centres and transferred to new clusters of growth centres. Such deliberate approach may not only be socially desirable but may well be viable even on the ground of hardheaded economic cost-benefit analysis - if only we reckon the social costs of overcrowded city centres.

Part - VI

CASE STUDIES OF RURAL DEVELOPMENT

29

Saga of Ralegansiddhi

Ralegansiddhi 75 km. from Pune in Parner Tahsil of Ahmednagar district has come to be known all over the country as a model village. It lies in a drought prone area. It is blessed with scanty annual rainfall of 10" to 12". In this village reconstruction programme Shri Hazare, gave the highest priority to the work of conservation of water through systematic water shed management on all lands - private, common as well as government land through a series of check dams and bunds. The intention is to conserve every drop of water. The result has been dramatic. The underground level of water has gone up. This has faciliated sinking of community wells. Water from these wells supplied at a moderate rate has enabled the villagers to grow two or three crops every year. The crops include growing fruits and vegetables which are now even exported to Dubai! The village has strictly eschewed growing of sugarcane which is so water-intensive that large quantities of water are inevitably consumed by only a few farmers leaving a large majority high and dry.

The conservation of moisture on hill slopes and stoppage of indiscriminate grazing has rapidly covered the barren hills with abundant grass which is now available for feeding goats and sheep.

What has been achieved in this village is in sharp contrast to what is happening in most parts of the country, where thanks to availability of electricity, water is intensively drawn upon through electric pumps and bore wells and extravagantly used for water intensive crops. Water is not conserved and hence the water table has gone down rapidly thus threatening the very basis of nature's life supporting system.

Water conservation has to go hand in hand with soil conservation. More than two lakh trees have been planted by villagers which has prevented denudation of soils on hill slopes apart from providing a variety of products like fruits, cattle-feed and fuel.

The same approach of conserving and using nature's gifts as the basis of rural development is seen in promotion of community bio-gas plants, some 35 in numbers using both animal and human excreta, and harnessing. One of the bio-gas plants is a joint effort of as many as 42 families. These together with solar and wind energy are used for lighting and cooking.

These water, soil and energy conservation projects are built through community action. It is this feeling of working for the community that has inspired the villagers to help the Harijan families in the village in getting rid of the buden of an old accumulated loan of Rs. 50,000. With the support of the entire village, the Harijan families improved the productivity of their land, increased their earnings and repaid their loans. Another community project is the construction of a large hostel building worth Rs. 12 lakhs with only a Rs. 5 lakh grant from Government. The rest was provided by Shramdan by the villagers.

There is a moral dimension to development work in this village. Politics is strictly eschewed. There is no crime and no drinking. The villagers have shunned court litigation. There is no extravagent expenditure on marriages. All marriages are group marriages. Villagers shun cheap entertainment of Hindi films on the TV. The moral aspect is particularly emphasized in upbringing of children. The educational process is such as to emphasise moral values. Early morning children get up to the tunes of devotional music. In ex-army person organises drill which instils discipline. Not a single word of abuse comes from the mouth of these children. If they find any article, they will promptly return. The future of the village is safe in the hands of these children imbued with moral values.

The whole basis of the development work in this village is self-reliance. This is not achieved by coercion but by creation of social awareness, and the realisation that purpose of life is to work for others and not for oneself. This is the philosophy of life deeply rooted in Indian cultural and tradition.

Anna Hazare who has provided leadership to the transformation of this village, feels that the transformation brought about in Ralegansiddhi over a period of 14 years can be multiplied. Already work on similar lines has been taken up in 80 surrounding villages. It can be taken up in other parts of the country as well.

What makes the development process of Ralegansiddhi a model for rural India are its outstanding basic features. First, the development is self-sustaining because it is based on conservation and enchancement of natural resources and not their exploitation and denudation. Second, it is based on self-reliance. The village has accepted no gifts or subsidies. Third, it is imbued with deep philosophy of life based on mutual help and cooperation and not self-indulgence and selfish pursuit of material possessions.

Many offices from Central and State Government keep on visiting the village. These visits would be worthwhile if they would lead to a complete overhaul of the rural development schemes now in operation viz the Integrated Rural Development Programme (IRDP) and the Employment schemes including Jawahar Rozgar Yojana. The IRDP is based on loans and grants to individual families and not group and community action, without which individual families in villages below the poverty line will not be able to cross it. The emphasis of the scheme is only on fulfilling targets regarding spending money, distributing loans and subsidies. No wonder Prime Minister Rajiv Gandhi bemoaned that 85% of the money on the scheme leaked out. Same is the fate of the rural employment scheme. Inspite of Rs. 21,000 crores spent in Maharashtra, since 1972, it has hardly left any permanent impact and has little to show by way of building up community assets. Secondly, the programme are not a part of micro planning for the village as a whole related to development of its natural resources. Moreover, the government schemes totally neglect the moral aspects. Unless all these aspects are taken care of, government schemes will continue to suffer from the blemishes of the past leading to waste of resources without achieving the desired results.

The transformation brought about in Ralegansiddhi can be replicated in other villages in other parts of the country given proper leadership. But would such a leadership be forthcoming? That is the million rupee question!

30

Saemaul Undong: South Korean Version of Integrated Community Development

South Korean programme of rural community development known as "Saemaul Undong" has been quoted as a success story in development literature. The word Saemaul Undong literally means a movement to make a new village or a new community. The movement was initiated in the year 1971. In more than a decade of its existence it has brought about significant changes physically and socially in the rural communities.

The movement owes its original inspiration to the late President Park. South Korea set itself on the path of economic development, modernisation, industrialisation and urbanisation starting with its First Five-Year Plan initiated in the year 1960. There followed a rapid process of socio-economic transformation. From being predominently a rural society, South Korea started emerging as a predominently urban society. The pace of such rapid transformation can be appreciated from the fact that while in the year 1962, 70% of the people were living in the rural areas and 30% in the urban areas, the proportion was reversed in 1982 when 70% of the people were in the urban areas and only 30% of the people in rural areas. The migration of a large labour force from rural to urban areas, which was an inevitable concommitant of such transformation, created the real danger that the rural areas would be denuded of active manpower and would be reduced to a state of listlessness. It is to counter such a possibility that the programme of Saemaul Undong was initiated.

Saemaul Undong movement — a movement for better living, had philosophical base. Its watchwords were diligence, self-help and cooperation. They represented the new spirit which was expected to dispel the lethargy and poverty in which the rural society in Korea had sunk through centuries and which, it was feared, would become even worse in the wake of rapid urbanisation. Saemaul Undong has worked wonders. It had ushered in a new age and a new society. It has elevated the quality of rural life and resuscitated the rural communities.

The programme went through several stages. The stage for laying of the ground work was from 1971 to 1973, of self-help development from 1974 to 1976 and of completion of self-support projects from 1977 to 1981. In the early stages of Saemaul Undong, easy projects were undertaken for increasing production and incomes. They included the expansion of farm roads, straightening of foot paths on the rice fields, land consolidation and improvement of irrigation facilities. At the same time efforts were made switch from individual farming to a cooperative system through the operation of community tree nurseries, raising of community fruit bearing trees, joint livestock raising, joint fish farming, joint insecticides spraying, joint management of farm implement and machinery and joint purchase of farming materials and daily necessities.

Gradually attention was also paid to environmental improvement. Environmental conditions were improved by replacing thatch and making shift fences with more permanent ones and modernising toilets and stalls. Communication facilities such as telephones were expanded. Community piped water system was installed and rural road network improved. Community facilities were created including community warehouses, community stores, village halls and community bath houses. Projects were also undertaken to tidy up roadsides and for better landscaping.

Following the phase for the laying of groundwork, steps were taken for self-help development through projects aimed at laying solid infrastructure for production and for increasing income. The period from 1977 to 1981 was a stage for the completion of self-support projects and expansion of non-farm income sources.

Through these development programmes, 34871 villages in South Korea have been developed into rural communities with a standard of living which compares favourable with that in the urban areas.

The successful implementation of the projects has given birth to new needs. For example, rural electrification has led to distribution of television sets and other means of cultural media in rural areas. The small projects which, in the beginning, benefit individual families and village communities have given way to "great sphere" projects which cover broader units like market areas, irrigation zones, and other broader neighbourly cooperative units.

The Saemaul Undong can be classified into four categories:

(1) Infrastructure projects for more production like development of irrigation systems, consolidation of farm lands, construction of farm roads, and bridges and pavement of community roads.

(2) Income increasing projects such as horticulture and cash crop cultivation, common tree nurseries afforestation, development of tourism, development of fisheries, form mechanism and establishment of factories.

(3) The projects for the improvement of the distribution structure include projects for the construction of common compost, community stores and common selling market.

(4) Finally, projects of welfare facilities such as the construction of community halls, communities libraries, preservation and management of cultural assets, expansion of piped water system, prevention of epidemics and improvement of public health.

Saemaul Undong is a movement where the people and the government work together. The Saemaul projects are approved by concensus among villagers at village assembly and are implemented with their total participation. At the village level, the village development committee composed of about 15 members is in -charge of decision-making of the projects which have to be final approved by the village assembly. The projects are expected to redound to the common benefit of the village and not to a particular private interest. The income gained from the projects with people's total participation is equitably returned to the participants. After the Saemaul projects are prepared by the villagers, they are sent for approval to Saemaul central council. On approval of the projects by the Saemaul central council they enter into the stage of implementation. Outstanding leadership of Saemaul leaders and residents' positi ve participation are key to the success of these projects. Organisation of residents is important for the successful accomplishment of these projects. The government's support of Saemaul projects is available in terms of administrative guidance, technical guidance and financial support.

Each village has two Saemaul leaders — one male and one female. The leaders are expected to have a spirit of self-sacrifice in the interest of the development of the community. They must possess skills required for persuading their fellowmen. They must also be able to concentrate on their role of effective mobilisation and human and material resources for successful completion of the projects. When the projects are completed, they are openly evaluated before the villagers.

Women are playing an important role in the Saemaul Undong projects. Traditionally, the women were supposed to look after only the health and home and do only the household jobs. They have now organised themselves into Saemaul womens' clubs participating in the Saemaul projects.

Saemaul Undong movement in rural areas is so successful that it was felt that the same technique could be applied to other spheres of national development. Thus, now, there is urban Saemaul Undong, factory Saemaul Undong, school Saemaul Undong and even olympic Saemaul Undong. The urban Saemaul Undong Movement aims at sound development of cities. It is a movement for the urban people to practice self-help, self-support and cooperation. The urban people tend to be highly individualistic. Urban Saemaul Undon teaches them the importance of community relationships and social integration. The factory Saemaul Undong emphasises the development of a Korean style labour management cooperative system based on the Saemaul ideals. It fosters proper attitude between labour and management by means of improved human relations and labour - management cooperation. The school Saemaul Undong has aimed at instilling Saemaul spirit into students and residents. The Saemaul education includes localised subjects based on the need for regional development in the curricula. It promotes extra-curricular activities to foster the Saemaul spirit of diligence, self-help and cooperation. It introduces adult education under the auspices of the schools and enunciates voluntary service to neighbouring communities. It promotes also science and technology. Schools also become centres of the cultural activities of the society. Finally the olympic Saemaul Undong is preparing the Korean society to welcome their youthful guests coming for Asian Games of 1986 and Olympics of 1990 by enhancing public ettiquette and order and improvement of scenic surroundings.

India's programme of community development and cooperation initiated in the early fifties were also based on the principles of self-help and mutual help. Unfortunately, both did not come up to the expectations. The community development approach for rural area has been given up while the urban community development has seldom been given a serious trial. We could very well draw lessons from the methods and techniques adopted by the Saemaul Undong Movement of South Korea.

31

Village Planning: An Experiment

Planning at the village level is the base of the planning at the State and Central level. The real substance of the plan lie in such innumerable little projects that are to be implemented in rural areas.

Planning at the village level has been attempted only sporadically in the past and such plans even when prepared have neither been followed up nor linked effectively with planning at the higher levels. In her address to the National Development Council on the occasion of the discussion on the Fifth Plan draft, Smt. Indira Gandhi, Prime Minister emphasised that the real substance of the Plan did not lie in some grandiose projects but in the innumerable little projects that had to be implemented in the rural areas. But who will prepare such plans; and who will implement them? Where is the Planning Commission in the village to do this task? These questions constantly cropped up in my mind ever since I assumed charge as first Administrator of the Malaprabha and Ghataprabha Projects responsible for formulating and implementing an integrated command area development programme for the region.

Soon after I took charge, I worked out detailed programmes of all aspects of command area development including construction of water conveyance system, water management, land levelling, drainage, crop planning, supply of agricultural inputs and credit, provision of infrastructure facilities, horticulture, dairy development, pisciculture, marketing processing and planning of growth centres. But soon I realised that planning these programmes at the project level is not enough. That could only be the starting point. The formulation of project programmes must be followed by preparation of plans for intensive irrigation development in the villages based on group and co-operative action.

Response

During my tours I started throwing up this idea in village meetings in the hope that I would get some response. Leaders of one important village by name Munoli evinced interest in this matter. I asked them to collect data regarding dairy and other enterprises that could be taken up in that village and to prepare some sort of village development plan and then discuss the plan at the village meeting. The date was fixed for the meeting. I requested the officers of the various development departments to join the meeting. There was a gathering of more than 500 villagers and a large number of officers representing various departments were also present at the meeting. Also present were the newly elected President and the Vice-President of the District Central Co-operative Bank. Three young leaders of the village were incharge of the meeting. One of them, a double graduate in commerce and law is the Chairman of the village co-operative society. Another with a school leaving certificate is the Chairman of the local dairy society. The third is engaged in some commercial activity. They combined in them youthful enthusiasm, educational attainment and constructive attitude.

Planning for the all-round development of Munoli village as it emerged at the meeting is portrayed below :

Munoli is a medium size village in Soundatti Taluka in Belgaum district in North Karnataka. The total population of the village is 8,767. It is situated on the bank of the Malaprabha river and by the side of a State highway. It is at a distance of 12 miles from Soundatti, the Taluka headquarters and 50 miles from the district headquarters, Belgaum. Its nearest railway station is Dharwar at a distance of 32 miles. Though the average rainfall in the village is only 16 to 17 inches it is located in the midst of green nature with a good number of banana, coconut and papaya plantations, thanks to well irrigation of about 275 acres.

Development Plan

However, new opportunities are opening up for the development of Munoli village since it is situated in the command area of the Malaprabha left bank canal. About 2,000 acres of the village would soon receive irrigation under the blocks 1-5 of the canal. Further, Munoli would be the growth centre for a larger irrigated area demarcated by a radius of about 10 miles around the village. About 43,453 acres around Munoli are expected to receive water from blocks 1-10 under the canal in the next two or three years. I, therefore, suggested to the villagers to prepare a development plan not only for the irrigated area within the village limits but for the total area. The first component of the development plan of the village will have, therefore, to concentrate on the development of the irrigation potential.

The area coming under irrigation will have to be surveyed and plans for the levelling of the land will have to be prepared. The land will have to be levelled either with the help of bullock drawn implements or by the use of tractors. Bullock drawn implements like buck-scraper, bund-former and fleet could be manufactured by the local artisans who could be trained to prepare these new implements. Thus agriculture will stimulate industrial activity and provide employment for the artisans, who in turn will provide tools for irrigated agriculture.

A detailed crop plan should form part of the village development plan. The Joint Director for Agriculture and the Deputy Administrator of the Project explained in detail how irrigation development and crop planning have to be attempted. The officer incharge of Intensive Cattle Development scheme then unfolded the plan for dairy development. There is already a milk co-operative in the village assisted by the project authorities. About 15 young farmers from the village have been trained in dairy development. The existing milk co-operative has now to be strengthened so as to cater to Munoli village and surrounding 12 villages with a cattle population of 1,305 breedable cows and 1,687 breedable buffaloes.

Milk Production

The membership of the existing milk co-operative will have to be increased by registering new members. A new artificial insemination centre has recently been opened to which semen will be supplied from the Central Semen Bank at Dharwar. The rural veterinary dispensary would treat cattle diseases. The milk society will be linked with the dairy at Belgaum or Dharwar. The society will be assisted to procure milk from its members and make daily cash payments. A calf rearing centre may be set up for rearing cross-bred heifers. The submerged marginal lands can be utilised for cultivation of grass when the water level is reduced during summer months. A fodder development programme would be taken up by helping farmers to grow fodder maize. By the end of 1979-80, about 4,000 litres of milk could be marketed per day at Rs. 1 per litre. Thus the annual production will increase by 14.5 lakhs of rupees providing supplementary or full employment to hundreds of people.

Dairy development will also be accompanied by sheep development. A sheep and wool development schemes will be started in the town as a part of which a wool extension centre will be established at the village. This will make cross-bred rams available to the shepherds. Sheep dosing and vaccination work will be taken up by the staff of the centre. A centre will be set up in the area of sheep shearing, collection and grading of wool and for marketing. The wool processing unit in the project area will utilise all the wool and the wool produced will get remunerative prices.

Horticulture

The village has already a tradition for fruit growing. 500 acres will be taken up for banana plantation under a scheme of the Banana Corporation. Flower cultivation would also be encouraged. Crysanthamum, mari-gold and jasmine can be successfully cultivated in the area.

There is also scope for a number of other cottage industries and food industries in the area. There are 150 weavers, 20 wool weavers, 50 carpenters and blacksmiths, and 50 oil ghanis in the village. A number of industries like bakery, fruit-preserving and dehydration of bananas can also be set up. Forty to fifty powerlooms can also function. Soapmaking based on neem seeds can be started. There are 1,500 tamarind trees and starch out of tamarind seeds and tamarind juice can be manufactured.

The Belgaum District Industrial Co-operative Bank and the Belgaum District Central Co-operative Bank can provide the finance for this agro-industrial development. The Rural Industrial Project has been extended to Belgaum district and assistance can be secured under the project.

The Malaprabha area has been selected for development of regulated markets as a part of World Bank aided State project. At Munoli will be located a sub-market attached to the main market at Soundatti. The market would provide a package of services and facilities like market yards, auction platforms, godowns, market roads, etc. It can attract marketable surplus from surrounding irrigated area.

Spatial Plan

But a development plan is not just a sectoral Plan. It will also be a spatial plan. A Development plan for the village is necessary to check the haphazard growth of the village. This spatial development plan will take into account the various schemes envisaged for Munoli. The employment that would be generated will be assessed and the total population to be accommodated in a decade will be estimated. Village extension schemes will be proposed to accommodate the increased population and to provide the necessary socio-economic facilities. For about three hours all these various programmes were explained and discussed at the village meeting.

I suggested that the village should immediately set up their 'Planning Commission' —a development plan committee in which the local institutions like village panchayats, large size co-operative society, dairy society etc., would be represented. The members of the committee might work out, with the help and guidance of the officers, the various chapters of the plan. I am now awaiting the finalisation of the village development plan by the village planning committee. What has happened in village Munoli must happen in every village, particularly in growth centre villages. This alone could impart realism and significance to national planning.

32

Rural Development and Local Organisation in Asia

Developing countries are predominently rural in character and hence rural development constitutes the most important sector of development in all the developing countries of the world. During the past twenty five years, Asia has become an active laboratory of experiments designed to promote rural development. By now, the developing countries have accumulated a great deal of experience in introducing new development programmes, building up institutions for rural development, recruiting and training personnel, and developing and refashioning the administrative structure and organisation for rural development. There have been cases of failure as well as success and much can be learnt from the accumulated experience of the developing countries in the sphere of rural development. It is to have a picture of the comparative efforts in the field of rural development and local organisation in Asia that the rural development cell of the Cornell University undertook a project to bring out case studies in the field of rural development and local organisation in various countries from the far–least to the north-east encompassing a great diversity of countries with different cultural conditions and political and ideological orientation. The Asian region includes South Asia, East Asia South East Asia and West Asia.

*This is the first in the series of case studies related to the countries in the South Asia region namely India, Pakistan, Bangla Desh and Sri Lanka. They focus attention on one question, namely, how important are local institutions in raising agricultural productivity and improving the well-being of the poor people.

---

* The Book Rural Development & Local Organisation in Asia by Norman T. Uphoff Macmillan India Ltd. New Delhi.

Attempts at rural development have aimed at not only raising the economic and agricultural productivity per acre and worker but also at providing distributive justice to the weaker sections of the rural society namely small holders, tenants, landless labourers who represent the majority of the rural people. Programmes of Rural Development require expanding public services which enhance the welfare and security of the rural people and broaden the base of opportunities for their participation. Rural development agencies have to have linkages with other administrative and institutional structures which provide services and allocate resources. Often, the strength of the local administration and institutions is not adequate for the task of rural development and there is an "organisational gap" within most developing countries. Without proper organisation neither technology nor resources can be used properly to accomplish the development task.

The three Indian case studies relate to the States of Andhra Pradesh, Punjab and Rajasthan.

The state of Andhra Pradesh has accorded a high priority to agriculture; however a substantial percentage of resources meant for agriculture is allocated to major irrigation projects with increasing emphasis on cash crops.

One of the defects of irrigation planning is the fact that while millions of rupees are spent on the construction of projects, sufficient attention is not given to and funds provided for utilisation of the irrigation potential.

A large number of holdings are small and they are at a disadvantage in getting access to amenities provided by development agencies. The supply of agricultural inputs has not been handled satisfactorily. Adequate and timely supply of seeds is hampered in the absence of effective coordination amongst the agencies connected with the production and distribution of improved seeds. The procedures for the supply of seeds are outmoded. As regards supply of fertilisers, the farmers have become fertiliser minded but due to inadequacy of supply of shortcomings in the organisation for the supply of fertilisers, the time schedule of the supply to farmers is affected. The supply of credit is arranged through the cooperatives and though there has been an impressive increase in the disbursement of loan, the traditional lending agencies in the shape of money-lenders are still the major sources of credit to the farmers. The farmers need for credit has increased due to introduction of modern technology. The weaker sections of the society find it particularly difficult to obtain the necessary credit. Only the middle size and large farmers have prospered. The small farmers and tenants are at a disadvantage. The red-tape of the cooperative development kills the enthusiasm of the members. The time taken in approving loan frustrates the agriculturists.

The panchayati raj institutions were introduced on the recommendation of the Balwantrai Mehta Committee who gave its report in 1956 but agriculture did not receive much attention at the panchayat level. However, new leadership has arisen in rural areas due to the panchayati raj institutions, and the basis of rural leadership nas widened. Rural leadership consists of farmers themselves who better understand the problem of agriculture than the civil servants. These panchayati raj leaders constitute a strong agricultural lobby, and are also capable of communicating new ideas and programmes. However, the new leadership does not represent the interests of the weaker sections, suffers from lack of integrity and fritters away energies for political aggrandizement. There is much scope for better coordination between departments of government and the elected panchayati raj institutions.

The VLWs are the symbols of development. However, they are used for all kinds of work. They lack technical competence which needs to be improved. The rules and complicated procedures inhibit administrative initiative. The field units have little discretion. The panchayati raj officials whose main job is to impart technical knowledge to the farmers fritter away their time in attending to a mass of paper work which has increased enormously, though not much use is made of the periodical reports from the subordinate offices. One of the maladies of the panchayati raj is the frequent transfers of officials. Though the rules say that the officer should be kept at a post for five years, these rules are not followed.

The finances of the panchayati raj bodies are limited and inelastic and this makes them heavily dependent on government and stiffles their initiative. As a result of paucity of finances and its adverse impact on the pace of development, the image of panchayati raj bodies as agencies of development has suffered. The autonomy of the panchayati raj institutions is limited because it is subject to control of various types by the state government. There is no planning from below. Targets are fixed by the state government and handed down to the panchayati raj bodies.

The overall conclusion of the author is that the administrative approach to rural development is inadequate. Bureaucratic agencies are not sufficient bodies to promote political development and social justice and hence non-bureaucratic institutions like cooperatives, farmer's associations or panchayats ought to be developed. They can provide the needed thrust and dynamism for rural development.

Punjab is considered to be a success story in the field of agricultural development. There has been a substantial and continuous increase in the production of most major crops except in the case of maize and gram. However, the panchayati raj institutions have not made much contribution to agricultural development. At the village level, panchayati raj institutions have aroused little enthusiasm in popular participation and there is visible apathy on the part of the villages towards the deliberations and programmes, if any, of the panchayati raj institutions. They have not been able to develop the confidence of the people. The level of education of panchayat members is not adequate to enable them to shoulder the extensive development responsibilities envisaged for them in the charter of panchayati raj. The panchayati raj institutions have made little impact on the economic fabric of the villages and have not broken any new ground in terms of social change. The author concludes that whatever rural development has taken place in Punjab, has been irrespective of panchayats. The co-operative institutions in the Punjab cover 85% of the rural households. 75% of the total fertilisers in Punjab was distributed through the cooperatives and the remaining 25% through private agencies. However the basic philosophy of cooperatives has not been imbibed by most societies and they have been used by the politicians to increase their hold. The image and perception of the local government institutions and cooperatives is not high because these institutions are utilised for political ends. To be effective, these institutions have to function on the strength of technological skill and business acumen. The author concludes that rural development in Punjab has taken place, irrespective of the village panchayats and the cooperatives. To be effective, these institutions should have trained extension personnel. There is also need for coordination amongst various institutions at the local level.

The Rajasthan study is connected with the distribution of electricity, a scarce commodity. The development plan is rationally formulated by the national and state planners. However, at the point of implementation an irrational factor is introduced in the form of panchayat politicians and cooperative leaders. It is for the administrator to sort out local pressure to influence the direction of local development. Political and economic goals often conflict. The time horizons of politicians are usually short. Politicians seek benefits for their constituencies whereas economic efficiency generally requires that the resources be concentrated in areas where they bring in the highest returns. If political responsiveness is not to harm economic efficiency, there is to be what the author has called controlled decentralisation.

After the reorganised Rajasthan came into existence, for the first several years the first task in the field of electrification was of putting the existing operations on a commercial basis. It is only after the Third Five Year Plan that the Rajasthan State Electricity Board was in a position to define in terms other than those of rationalization and consolidation. In view of the limited resources, it was decided that electricity should be given only to those villages with population over 5,000. In 1963 the Rajasthan Electricity Board decided that electrification of villages with population of over 5,000 is complete, and development of agriculture should form the new priority. Positive steps were taken to increase the number of agricultural connections, and rather than the size of the village, emphasis was placed on agricultural potential as the criterion for selecting villages for electrification. A decision was taken at the instance of the Planning Commission and the Union Ministry for Irrigation and Power, that the schemes for rural electrification should be originated at the district level. Increased attention was paid to electrification of villages under the existing lines since this would help more efficient use of existing resources for increased agricultural production. While the Centre and the State laid down general policies the local leaders like zila parishads used their position to help their constituencies by creating a demand for electricity in accordance with the prescribed criteria. The author terms this as controlled decentralisation. There may be many advantages in decentralisation in the decisions regarding location of villages for electric installation. First, the local officials had more knowledge about villages than the Rajasthan Electricity State Board engineers. The cost of obtaining information decreased with decentralisation. Secondly, decentralisation decision-making process can re-enforce productive criteria. Controlled decentralization where criteria are laid down above but proposals consistent with the criteria are sent from below retains the best features of centralisation and decentralisation. Controlled decentralisation promotes both economic and political efficiency.

In Pakistan, in the early years slow moving farm sector growing at the rate of 1.3% annually was responsible for the nation's stagnation. With the advent of Ayub Khan regime in 1958 the national economy began to revive and the annual growth rate rose to 5.5% which was sustained upto the mid sixties. Rapid improvement in private investment in spite of the poor performance in the public sector played a catalytic role in this transformation. Large public spending on development of infra-structure and new farm technology of the mid sixties made investment in industrial, agricultural and commercial sectors very attractive. The Mexi-Pak variety of wheat and Irri-Pak variety of rice and rapid increase in the number of private tubewells (from 1000 in 1953-54 to 16200 in 1963) contributed to the Green Revolution. Pakistan became one of the few underdeveloped countries where the increase in agricultural production significantly exceeded the growth of population.

Because of the poor performance of the public sector in the distribution of fertilisers, pesticides, and seeds, the government sought the services of private sector consisting of urban base commercial and industrial entrepreneurs. They reached distribution points in the rural areas. The private sector also played an important role in furthering the growth of the rural sector by marketing farm surpluses. The private sector also emerged as a major source of cash and in-kind credit for the Green Revolution. It also played an extensive role in manufacturing tube-well engines and related components. Small towns became centres of engines and pump manufacture. The private sector also manufactured other farm implements like spraying and pest equipment harvestors. As compared with the private agencies, the cooperatives were riddled by misappropriation of public funds.

The basic democracies were introduced in Pakistan by Ayub Khan regime in 1959 which established elected councils at four levels. At the grass root level were the Union Councils, for 3 to 4 villages with a population of 8,000 to 14,000. Above this level, councils were established at the tehsil and district level. Above the district were the divisional councils for purposes of coordination. The higher level local governments consisted of indirect elected representatives and government officials in equal numbers. The village Chairman of the Village Council was the bigger land owner. Thus, the informal hierarchy of power in the rural society was formalised by the democracy. The local councils were not autonomous local government agencies but adjuncts to planning and administration. The basic democracies were dependent entirely on the flow of provincial funds. The councils had very limited power and few resources of their own. The Basic Democracies therefore, operated simply as a distributive mechanism for projects which could fit within the patterns established at higher levels. The tax-raising performance of the Union Councils was unimpressive.

During the Ayub era, the "basic democracy" structure made hardly any substantial contribution to the development process which was determined by centralised planning machinery and entrenched bureaucracy. The District Councils accomplished little. Political influence remained limited to securing ad hoc personal favour. The Union Council was not involved in the distribution of canal irrigation water.

The institutional credit was made available from four sources namely: (i) taccavi loans, (ii) cooperative loans, (iii) Agricultural Development Bank, and (iv) private banks. The Agricultural Development Bank was oriented towards the large farm. There was no relationship between the lending institutions and the supply of input of the marketing structure. Several sources of credit have never been integrated. Thus, the institutional structure of Pakistan has been extremely weak. Neither basic democracies nor the cooperatives have proved viable. The local institutions had little success in facilitating public action at the local level. The local government and market served to strengthen the rural elite at the expense of the rural poor.

The Bangla Desh situation (as in other States) vindicates Gunnar Myrdal's observation that "Efforts to create machinery for self-government, cooperation, and popular participation without changing the basic social and economic structure are essentially attempts to bypass the equality issue." Due to high growth of population, there has been a rapid growth in the labour force. At the same time, the proportion of population in agriculture has increased as non-agricultural sector could not provide enough jobs. The country has to import 2 to 4 million tons of grain per year. Thus, the situation in Bangla Desh was very difficult. 28.6% of the households had less than one-quarter of an acre. Almost one-third of the rural families had no cultivable land. One of the most remarkable rural development programmes in Bangla Desh was instituted by the Academy of Rural Development in Comilla. It operated during the late fifties and sixties and included rural public works, power, irrigation and cooperative credit organisations. The following four principles were emphasized in the Comilla experiment :

(i) farmers must begin by forming village cooperatives;
(ii) mobilisation of rural savings and provision of credit are inseparable;
(iii) inputs have to be provided if the farmers were to implement new technologies and
(iv) training is necessary to provide the knowledge required to use credit and the new physical inputs to the best advantage.

Thus the Comilla approach was conceived a holistic endeavour to transform rural life. The Comilla experiments suffered from the massive and seemingly unremovable subsidies. 25% of the cost of fertilisers was subsidized and insecticides were subsidized at 100% and the rich tended to take most benefit of the subsidies. The subsidies also encouraged waste of resources. Another defect in the programme was deterioration in the administrative supervision. The members of cooperatives would take loan funds from one society and form a new one to get more loans and thereby avoid the problem of paying back dues to the first society. Moreover, the Inspector cadre itself became corrupt. The cooperatives were taken over by the local elite. Thus, the societies became an instrument for re-enforcing distributional status quo in both economic and political sense.

In the mid seventies the Rangunia model was developed as an alternative to the Comilla model. The Rangunia approach put a strong emphasis on self-help and local initiative and control exercised from below, as against the excessive bureaucratic domination in the Comilla programme. However, more autonomy may not result necessarily in more egalitarianism. There is every reason to expect that the local elites who run the Rangunia programme would use it in their own interest.

As an extension of the Development Programme the Thana Irrigation Programme was introduced in 1967-68. Under this programme, groups were set-up for lifting water for irrigation. However, these groups were organised by a few men of substance who enrolled as non-participating or non-existent members for the purpose of securing the benefit of the new government programme for themselves. They had absolutely no incentive for using the water carefully.

The Rural Works Programme was expanded to cover the entire province. It concentrated on the construction of water control embankments. However, this programme designed to mobilize the entire countryside acquired the character of government sponsored programme, from the above. It was left in the hands of a favoured class of villagers who used it for their personal advancement. The miniscule elite consisting of 40,000 basic democrats were given discretion over the large funds meant for the programme. The conclusion from the Basic Democracy experiment in Bangla Desh is that the administrative machinery is not simply there to supervise effectively a programme in which significant decision-making must take place at the village level.

By the usual measure of economic development, Sri Lanka's economy has not made rapid progress. The Marga Institute Report in 1977 speaks of economic stagnation. The sector most stagnant was the estate sector which suffered from decline in management and reduced investment. On the other hand, Sri Lanka had advanced Social Welfare Programme including free health service, subsidized food distribution and free education with are the three pillars of the government's welfare policy. These measures reduced the maternal mortality and the birth rate. The public distribution system through cooperatives served the entire rural population. Rural literacy is 84%. However, spread of education has created the problem of educated unemployment. The peasant sector is predominently small sector. The average size of holding dropped from 3.3 acres in 1946 to 2.2 acres now. However, agricultural sector showed dynamism specially in paddy, through the adoption of high yielding seed and fertiliser use.

Sri Lanka has experimented with a large number of rural development institutions. The first amongst them are the Rural Development Societies. By the middle of 1960s, 9,000 Rural Development Societies were registered. The second organisation was the multi-purpose cooperative societies at the village level, supplying consumer goods, agricultural inputs and buying agricultural produce. 5800 such societies were reorganised in 1971-72 into 372 large multi-purpose cooperative societies, but in the process their participatory character was lost. The third organisation was Cultivation Committee under the Paddy Lands Act of 1958. The Cultivation Committee covered a single paddy track "Yaya". A fourth type of rural institution was the Agricultural Production Committees established under the Agricultural Land Law of 1973. 494 APCs covered the whole island by 1977.

No wonder that all this proliferation led to overlapping functions of rural organisation, the competition between APC and MPCS was compounded by that between the two national banks serving the rural areas, namely the Bank of Cylone and the Peoples Bank. Different ministries wanted to have their own channel of communication and access to the rural power resulting in confusion and waste.

The problem was worsened by the politicisation of these rural organisations. A feature of rural development was the attempt at decentralisation of planning and implementation introduced at the district level in 1975 through political authorities. These were committees of MPs.

The village councils are old traditional institutions in Sri Lanka. But in their new form the British regime reestablished them in 1871. They covered 40 sq. miles and 20,000 persons. Thus, the jurisdiction was much larger than the village. The tasks of the village councils were ostensibly numerous but in practice limited. There were structural problems arising out of overlapping of functions between the village councils and other administrative area of local organisations. The village councils' contribution to agricultural and rural development has not been very positive. The leadership of rural development societies often came from the better educated and more prosperous members. The principal feature of rural institutions in Lanka is multiplicity or organisations and unproductive competition amongst them along with continuing bureaucratic dominance towards most of them. As a result of politicisation the office-bearers of these organisations serve the interest of the MPs and the political parties rather than those of the people.

The general conclusion emerging out of these case studies is not very favourable to the role of the rural local organisations in promoting agricultural and rural development. However, one reason why they have not succeeded is that they have not been given a fair trial. They can make a significant contribution and need to be given a reasonable chance to do so.

Index